Village Development Planning

Prof. (Dr.) H.R. Yadav

LOGOS PRESS
New Delhi-110 002

This study was supported by NRDMS,
Department of Science & Technology,
Government of India, New Delhi

© H.R. Yadav

ISBN-13: 978-81-7268-187-6
ISBN-10: 81-7268-187-9

First Published 2009

Printed and Published by
LOGOS PRESS
Building No. 4788-90, Street No. 23, Ansari Road, Darya Ganj
New Delhi-110 002 (India)
Phone : 23272187
Email : mail@logospressindia.com
Website : www.logospressindia.com

कपिल सिब्बल
KAPIL SIBAL

सत्यमेव जयते

विज्ञान और प्रौद्योगिकी तथा पृथ्वी विज्ञान मंत्री
भारत सरकार, नई दिल्ली
MINISTRY OF SCIENCE & TECHNOLOGY
AND EARTH SCIENCES
GOVERNMENT OF INDIA
NEW DELHI

FOREWORD

India being a vast country having diverse agro-ecological regions, planning process for better management and optimal utilization of available resources always has been the challenge. There is thus an urgent need to evolve a planning strategy applicable at different levels including village as lowest unit of planning.

I am happy to note that the book on "Village Planning" written by Dr. H.R. Yadav, Director, IWARD, Sultanpur, U.P. has addressed wide range of issues which are very important for local Area Development Planning. In the present context, when efforts are being made to allocate resources at Panchayat level, the methodology described in this book would be of immense help to the planners. The author has relied upon Remote Sensing and Geographical information System techniques to aid in the planning process. The case study of Pratapgarh District given in the book is instructive.

I hope the book on "Village Planning" will serve as a useful guide for planners while implementing development schemes. It will also be useful for academic researchers equally to understand the micro level planning process in India.

(KAPIL SIBAL)

ACKNOWLEDGEMENT

Department of Science & Technology, Govt. of India sanctioned a project for the establishment of Natural Resources Data Management System (NRDMS) database at Pratapgarh District, UP in which socio-economic component was intrusted to the Institute of Wastelands Reclamation & Rural Development, Payagipur, Sultanpur (U.P.). Through this study, an attempt has been made to document the outcome of the study in the book form forwhich the appreciable assistance and guidance of Dr. T. Ramasami, Secretary, Dept. of Science & Technology and Dr. (Brig.) R. Shiva Kumar, Advisor & Head, NRDMS Division and Dr. Bhoop Singh, Director, NRDMS, Dept. of Science & Technology, Govt. of India deserves heartiest thanks. Author is also greatful to Dr. B.D. Acharya, Advisor & Head, Earth Sciences Division, Dept. of Science & Technology, Govt. of India & Sri S.K. Ojha the then Minister of Science & Technology, Govt. of U.P. & Sri Rajendra Pratap Singh, local M.L.A. for their cooperation and help.

Needless to mention the cooperation and guidance received from Sri R.S. Verma, I.A.S. District Megistrate, Pratapgarh and Sri M.L. Paswan, P.C.S., Chief Development Officer, Pratapgarh District and Block Development Officer, Mangaura Block and other officials of the District Rural Development Agency, Pratapgarh and they all deserves special thanks for their support.

The guidance and support received from Dr. A.N. Singh, Director, Remote Sensing Applications Centre, U.P., Lucknow is greatly acknowledged. I am also greateful Mr. Dinesh Kr. Tiwari & other staff members of the IWARD for their support. The tedious typing of the huge data, menuscript and mapping etc. have been very carefully arranged by Mr. Ratnesh Kr. Singh who deserves special thanks. I thank to those who directly or indicretly supported for the completion of the book.

Last but not the least, I am indebted to my beloved wife Reeta and son Sahit without their support writing and completion of the book would not have been possible.

Prof. (Dr.) H.R. Yadav

CONTENTS

CHAPTER I

VILLAGE DEVELOPMENT PLANNING – A CASE STUDY OF PRATAPGARH DISTRICT

I. INTRODUCTION :

1. Planning :

Planning is an organised process by which the people achieves its developmental goals or planning is a means to achieve development. But when the intentions and objectives of development are distorted, then planning also becomes a distorted exercise.[1]

The planning is a systematic procedure which objects at the implementation of several specific aims. Therefore it is necessary to :

(i) Specify quantified targets;

(ii) Specify potential variants of reaching such targets i.e. variants of utilization of various resources;

(iii) Find out the resources available reaching such targets;

(iv) Revide the targets if some of the resources are hot fully utilized or prove insufficient for reaching the targets;

(v) find out which variant is optimal (in the sense of allowing the 'best set' of targets to be reached with the available resources);

(vi) organise the instruments which will ensure operational implementation of the variant finally chosen;

(vii) organise the instruments which will ensure operational implementation of the variant finally chosen;

(viii) supervise the process of implementation in order to find out eventual discrepancies and to set in motion adaptive achivities.[2]

Presently in India planning is done without willing consent of the local people, in some cases planers interpret people's need and aspirations for developing a plan for the people, lastly planning is the task of the people in which planners can provide backup support to achieve their planning goals. The government is stressing for the involvement of people in development i.e. developmental planning from within.

Thus the planners will have to provide developmental planning, scientific technical backup support to the grass root village level people's representatives, villagers and officials involved in village development & planning. The planners should not only be a technocrat to provide projections but they should assist villagers as a social scientist who can easily understand the basic grass root level need of the village people so that the need of the people is planned and developmental activities are carried out as per the need of the people, with the involvement of the village people and for the village people and the development is achieved as per planned target.

---

1. Misra, R.P. " Regional Planning" 1992, Concept publishing Company, New Delhi.
2. St. Ouffer S.A. "Intervening opportunities : A. Theory relating Mobility and Distance American Sociological Review, Vol. 5, Dec. 1940 P.P. 845, 67 and W. Isard, Location and Space Economy, op. cit, P.P. 64-65, footnote 13.

2. DEVELOPMENT :

"Development is after all a multifaceted phenomenon, it can neither be understood, nor promoted unless it is seen from interdisciplinary and holistic perspectives. Moreover development is basically a human enterprise and therefore it requires the combined efforts of all systems of knowledge, be they physical, biological, social human to comprehend and articulate it. It is more so with respect to planned development. Planning must draw upon all relevant disciplines including physics on the one extreme and linguistics on the other."[3]

Development is one which is pursued with genuine concern for human values. Development means the evolution of people in which the people acquires better perception and best control over it's natural and human resources. In the process of development growth alone does not ensure development.

The development must ensure the betterment & welfare of all the local people. Thus, the feelgood of development has to been not only from national, state, district but also from Block and village level perspectives. The present development processes is neither true, nor good, nor beautiful but it does not mean that every thing is wrong. Really the development lies in the development of Science & Technology and it's application by the common people. The progress of the people in the socio-economic front has made more destructive than constructive approach of development for all the people.

3. DEVELOPMENT PLANNING :

In India there is quest for evolving a model for planning. Macro level resource planning is adopted in India. The approach of macro-level planning in India did not yield the desired results due to inequities amongst people and disparities between regions. The environmental conditions continued to degrade leading to severe stress on land and water resources. Around late 70s, sustainable and integrated development of the area has been ensured. In this regard conceptual changes in the planning practice was adopted in the micro or local level process of planning.

Objectives of the decentralized planning are :

- Increase the productivity of land.
- Increase scope for employment with focus on asset generation.
- Poverty alleviation.
- Providing minimum amenities and infrastructure facilities.

Institutional changes were brought to implement this strategy through the 73rd and 74th Constitutional Amendment Acts (1992 & 1993). The State Governments were empowered from the institutions of locals self governance right from the village level upto the district level and within the municipal jurisdiction i.e. Panchayats and Nagar Palikas in the context of rural and urban development respectively. The Eleventh and Twelfths Schedules of the constitution while specifying the sectors for the Panchayats and Nagar Palikas, have also defined the role for the multi-level institutions of governance in planning and implementing the integrated developmental schemes. The

---

3. Mishra, R.P. (ed) "Changing Deceptions of Development problems" Singapore, Maruzem, Asia, 1983.

State Governments have accordingly constituted such local level bodies with definite mandates to collect revenues, draw up and implement integrated development programmes. It needs capacity building at institutions of local self governance to prepare and implement local-specific integrated development schemes by assessing and utilizing the available natural and human resources.

Formulation and implementation of developmental programmes in urban and rural areas is an information intensive work. Natural and Human resources data management system which are existing at grass root level (village-wise), Block and District level are not properly arranged but such available information needs to be integrated for development planning. The conventional methods of data collection, collation, storage are not amenable for quick updation, retrieval and holistic analysis and several problems which are existing in the conventional system are as follows:

(a) Incompatible and non-standard data sets inhibiting integration.
(b) In efficient inter-sectoral data flow.
(c) Lack of information on quality, completeness and lineage of data.

Integrated approach to planning process requires a detailed knowledge of the interrelations and interdependencies between various sectors to resolve often-conflicting demands. This lead to a requirement for appropriate data management and analysing tools and techniques and large matrix of sectoral indicators data, in a digital format, on natural resources, demography, socio-economic and invites for specific scientific & technological interactions in –

(i) Need based data creations.
(ii) Development and improvement in data handling and analysis tools.
(iii) Efficient distribution of data and information to the user institutions and developmental planning implementing agencies.[4]

Inview of the above requirements and the developments in the areas of Information and communication Technology (ICT) and geo-Spatial Data Management and Analysis Techniques like- Remote Sensing and Geographical Information System (GIS), Certain initiatives had been taken at the national level to create awareness on the usefulness of these technologies amongst planners and decision makers. Natural Resources Data Management System (NRDMS) Programme of Department of Science & Technology was one such pioneering efforts, the others being :-

(a) National (Natural) Resources Information System (NRIS) of the Department of Space.
(b) Integrated Mission for Sustainable Development (IMSD) programme of Department of Space.
(c) Geographical Information System (GIS/NIC) and District Information System (DIS/NIC) of the National Informatics Centre.

4. NATURAL RESOURCES DATA MANAGEMENT SYSTEM (NRDMS)

There is longest known tradition of systematically collecting spatial data through various organisations at national level in India. Different line Departments are engaged for collection of non-spatial data in a strong traditional system. Hanumanth Rao

4. Natural Resources Data Management System – vision document published by Dept. of Science & Technology M/o Science & Technology, Govt. of India, Sept. 2003.

Committee (1984) has emphasized on management of the spatial data for efficient local level planning.

In view of the above requirements, Department of Science & Technology, Government of India during 1982 started a programme on Natural Resources Data Management System (NRDMS). Natural Resources Data Management System is a multi-disciplinary and multi-institutional Research & Development programme with vision to provide appropriate scientific and technological inputs for operational zing the concept of decentralized planning. The main objective was to develop scientific data base approach to support the local level planning. At the end of the first decade of the programme, 73rd & 74th constitutional amendments came in to being and with the entry of computers at District level and Geographic Information System (GIS) in India during late 1980's the goals of NRDMS programme were evolved to develop spatial data management technologies for integrated rural development planning and its demonstration in the local level decision making. In the context of Natural Resources Data Management System, any natural resource, which is important for local area development, is relevant for study. NRDMS has been supporting several academic and R & D institutions through grant-in-aid projects.

NRDMS has always been focusing on technological and institutional capacity building in a multi-level frame work, so that the people utilizing the local resources. In this regard NRDMS develops and provides tools and techniques for assessing local level natural resources endowment their utilization, potential and generating alternative scenarios for development. NRDMS operates through District Data Base Centers as its hubs. 45 pilot District Centers are located in Karnataka, Andhra Pradesh, Orissa, West Bengal, Bihar, Uttar Pradesh, Uttarachal, Haryana, Gujrat and North East Region.

Inspite of the national efforts, spanning two decades large segment of end-users are yet to explore the full potential of the system and use it in most of their planning activities due to lack of technical organisational and institutional capacity. To reduce the impediments in the wide spread use of the technologies and make it an effective tool in the process of local level integrated planning, NRDMS is focusing its research on simplifying the methods and techniques of data collection, organisation and analysis, devise suitable strategies to transfer the techniques for adoption by the end user in their planning activities.

Considering the recent trends in the development of spatial data technologies, the emerging changes in the system of governance planning, policies, institutionalization of National Spatial Data Infrastructure (NSDI) meet the aspirations of the users and in support of the overall transformation in the concept of information sharing, the need felt for refocusing the R & D thrusts of the programme.

(a) The Spatial Data Management and Analysis Technologies.

(b) Advanced Technology Applications in large scale spatial data gathering.

(c) Land & Water Management.

(d) Technology transfer and capacity building.

4.1 Vision :

Enabling people, communities and Institutions of self-governance, with Spatial Data Technologies, for informed participation in Decision making for Integrated Development of local areas.

4.2 Goals :

To strengthen the S & T inputs for integrated resource management through development of appropriate tools and techniques in data collection, organisation and analysis.

Technical capacity building at various levels of administration for enabling the adoption of the technologies developed in integrated development planning.

4.3 Objectives :

(a) Demonstrate and promote the use of Spatial Data Technologies for micro level planning under diverse terrain conditions –
- Provide software support for data management, modeling and operation research.
- Promote R & D in spatial data technology.
- Technology Transfer & Capacity Building of potential users.
- Forge linkages with users at different levels.

(b) Provide Science & Technological inputs for framing policies related to Spatial Data Technologies.

(c) Develop & Demonstrate pilot scale spatial infrastructure and provide research support to National Spatial Data Infrastructure.

(d) Documentation and dissemination.

In order to implement atleast some of the activities to realise the vision of NRDMS, support from a large segment of scientists, and entrepreneurs are required. NRDMS is expected to stimulate the imagination of the research community to relate specific problems in their areas of interest and evolve suitable research proposal to pursue line of investigation to arrive at meaningful solutions to the problems as well as in advancing the existing knowledge in certain spheres of activity thereby aiding the overall development of the country.

5. DEVELOPMENT OF NATURAL RESOURCES DATA MANAGEMENT SYSTEM (NRDMS) FOR PRATAPGARH DISTRICT :

In order to implement at least some of the Natural Resources Data Management System (NRDMS) activities NRDMS Division of Department of Science & Technology, Government of India, supported a large segment of Scientists, Non-Government organisation (NGO's) and entrepreneurs. Development of NRDMS data base is expected to stimulate the imagination of the research community to relate specific problems in their area of interest. NRDMS activities also aimed to evolve suitable research proposal to pursue the line of investigation to arrive at meaningful solutions to the problems. NRDMS activity is also expected to advance the existing knowledge of National and Human Resources Data Management System in certain spheres of activity thereby aiding the overall formulation of planning process and development of micro-level area.

In view of the above Natural Resources Data Management System (NRDMS) Division, of Department of Science & Technology, Government of India, supported a project entitled Development of Natural Resources Data Management System for Pratapgarh District, U.P." jointly Remote Sensing Applications Centre, Uttar Pradesh, Lucknow and Institute of Wastelands Reclamation and Rural Development, Sultanpur, Uttar Pradesh.

Development of Natural Resources Data Management System was assigned to Remote Sensing Applications Centre, U.P.. Detailed socio-economic parameters data base development of Pratapgarh District, Uttar Pradesh was assigned to Institute of Wastelands Reclamation and Rural Development, Sultanpur, Uttar Pradesh.

The main objectives of the Development of Natural Resources Data Management System (NRDMS) for Pratapgarh District, U.P. are as follows :-

- Development of Natural Resources Data Management System (NRDMS) for Pratapgarh District.
- Collection of socio-economic data for Pratapgarh district at Block level.
- Collection of Socio-Economic data at village level for Mangraura block in Pratapgarh district.
- Participation of personnel from various line Departments, actual users and Panchayat representatives.
- Development of Action Plan based on available socio-economic data.
- Collection of data for various rural developmental programmes.
- Development of need base action plan as per need of the local people.

Development Planning at block level for Pratapgarh district and village level in Mangraura block of Pratapgarh district, adopting Natural Resources Data Management System (NRDMS) has been developed, through Natural and Human resources as depicted below-

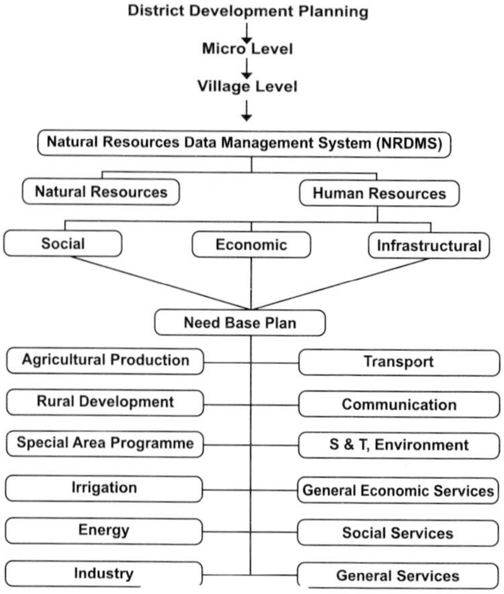

The human resources major sectoral indicators are socio-economic and infrastructure. The agricultural production, rural development, special area programme, Irrigation, Energy, Industry, Transport, Communication, Science & Technology, Environment, Economic-social & general services are the major sectoral indictors. The collection & collation of socio-economic & infrastructural data has been ensured at block level for Pratapgarh district and village level for Mangraura block.

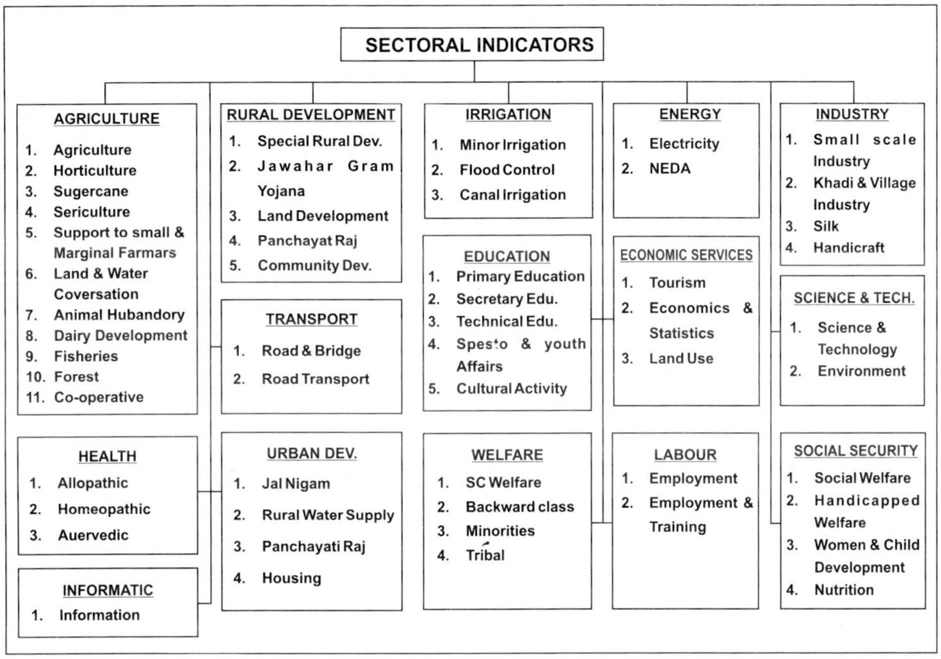

Various sectoral indicators related to social-economic and infrastructural indicators are mentioned in detail in the depicted chart. The selected indicators are also related to the various implementing agencies working at District, Block level and village level. The selected programme implementing agencies are also responsible for the collection of data as per their official requirement and also the implementation of various developmental programmes supported by Government of India, State Government and other agencies.

Programme implementation process need base action plan and collection of available information/ data has been ensured as per the sectoral indicators data and programme implementation agencies at village. Block and District level line departments. It is evident that three tier Panchayati Raj Institutions i.e. Village, Block, District and local M.L.A., M.L.C., M.P. & other representatives including District, State & Central Govt. financial supports are made available to the local programe implementing agencies. The financial flow for various rural development programes in the Pratapgarh District is depicted in the flow chart.

Natural Resources Data Management System (NRDMS) data base for planning and development has been divided into different themes mainly available socio-economic, infrastructural data base, progress of rural developmental programmes and need base action plan for Pratapgarh District at Block level and also for Mangraura Block at village level in Pratapgarh district.

FINANCIAL FLOW

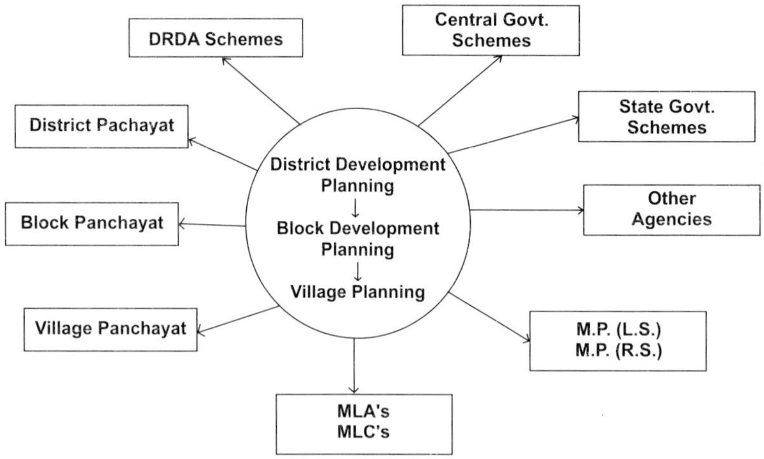

Existing sources of data at village, block & district level in Pratapgarh district are mainly Khasara/ Khatauni of Revenue Department, Economic Register of Block Development Office, statistical Hand Book of District statistical/ Economic officer and Primary Census Hand Book of Census Department.

Collection of ground truth level data has been ensured through involving Peoples Representative i.e. Pradhan of the concerned village, Lekhpal/Patwari of concerned Revenue village, Panchayat Secretary of the village and Primary village survey i.e. door to door survey for data collection. Collected data has been collated, tabulated and analysed for development planning at village level for Mangraura Block and Block level for Pratapgarh district.

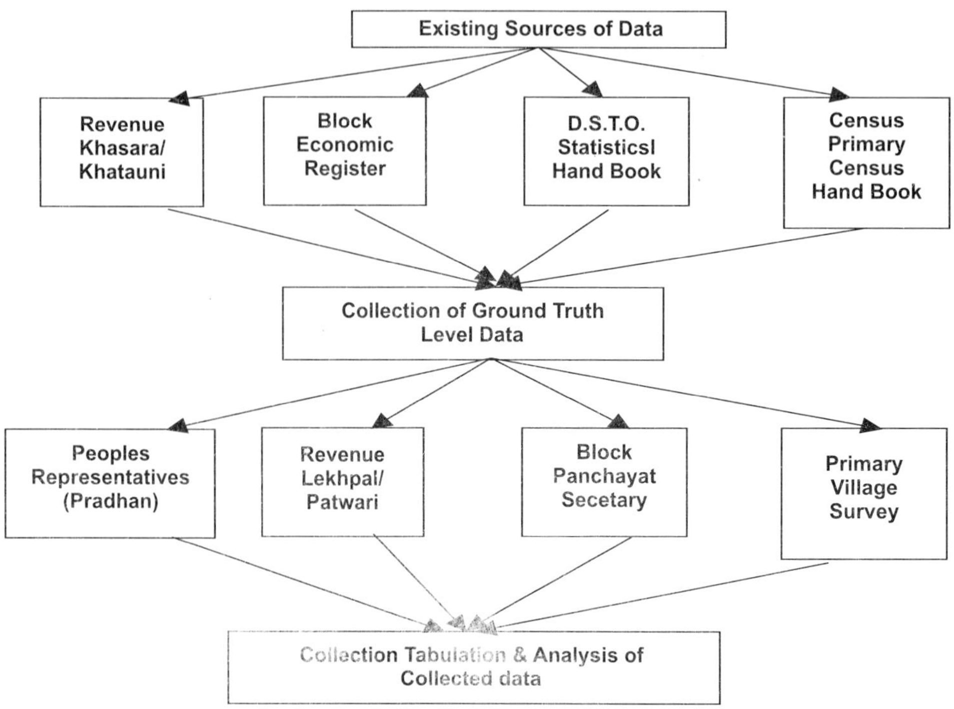

Micro-level data collection (village level) for existing socio-economic-infrastructure, various developmental programme and need base action plan has been done through involving Peoples Representatives, Block Development/ Village Development officials and involved Field Investigators for collection of Data at village and Block level in Pratapgarh district.

In view of the above block level & village level development planning in Mangraura block in Pratapgarh district has been done geographic location of Pratapgarh District and Mangraura block and its administrative set up has been analysed based on the available information through District Administration of Pratapgarh District.

6. DISTRICT PRATAPGARH :

6.1 Geographic Location :

Pratapgarh district lies between 25034' to 26011' north and 81019' to 82027' east. It stretches about 115 km. from west to east and 40 km north to south extending over an area 063717 esq. with a total population 2210700 persons (1991). North of Pratapgarh, Sultanpur district, East Jaunpur, South-Allahabad & Kaushambi west Fatehpur and north-west Raebarelli districts located (Map. 1)

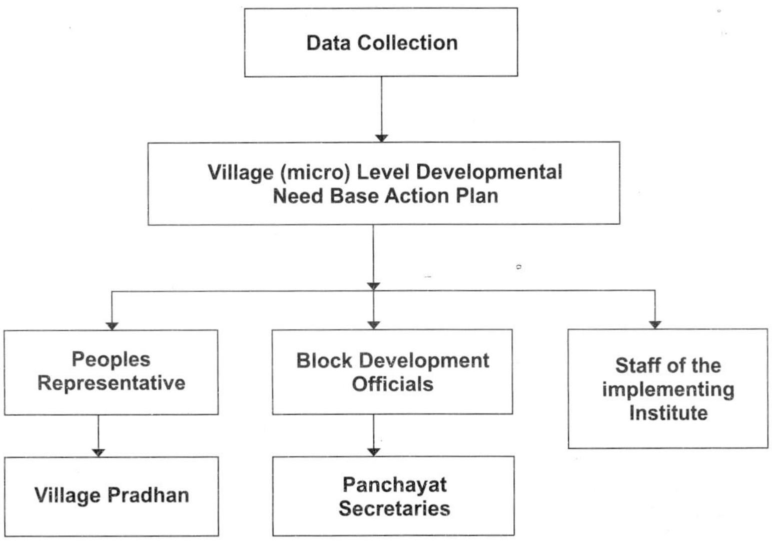

Administratively, Pratapgarh District comprised of 5 tehsils namely Pratapgarh Sadar, Lalganj, Kunda, Patti and Raniganj tehsils. There are 17 blocks in Pratapgarh district namely – Pratapgarh Sadar, Sandwa Chandrika, Mandhata, Patti, Mangraura, Aspur Devsara, Gaura, Shivgarh, Baba Belkharnath Dham, Lalganj, Sangipur, Lakshmanpur, Rampur Sangramgarh, Kunda, Kalakankar, Babaganj, Bihar blocks. Approximately 80% of the total population is dependent on agricultural activity.

Map-1

Source : National Atlas & Thematic Mapping Organisation, Dept. of Science & Technology

District headquarter of Pratapgarh is located at the distance of 173 km. East from Uttar Pradesh State capital of Lucknow. Location of Uttar Pradesh in India and location of Pratapgarh district in Uttar Pradesh and general information regarding location of tehsils and blocks of Pratapgarh district are depicted in the location Map-2.

Map-2

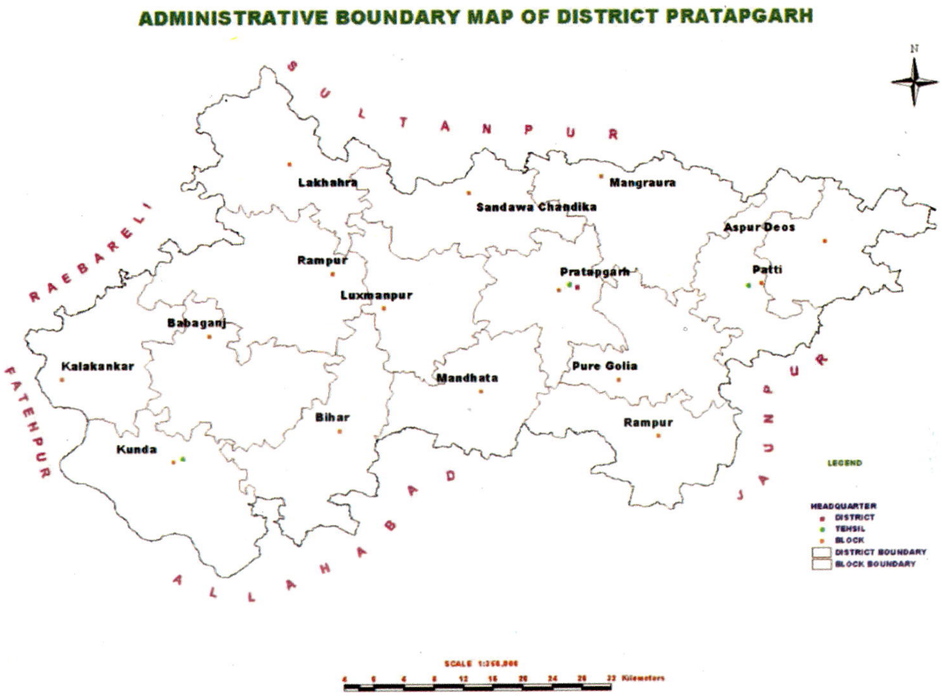

6.2 Mangraura Block :

There are 171 village Nyaya Panchayat in Pratapgarh district and 1105 number of villages. There are total 2219 number of villages including 38 non-habited villages in Pratapgarh district. There is one Nagar Palika Parishad and 6 Nagar Panchayat in Pratapgarh district.

Out of 17 blocks of Pratapgarh Mangraura block is very backward than other blocks of the district due to excessive saline land and waterlogged land and poor agricultural productivity and very poor living standard of life because of socio-economic backwardness.

Due to very backwardness of Mangraura block of Pratapgarh district, Mangraura block has been selected for micro-level / village level developmental planning. There are 209 inhabited revenue villages in Mangraura block and 62 village Panchayats in Mangraura block. These 62 village Panchayats are selected for door to door village survey including socio-economic infrastructure data, rural developmental programmes and need base plan at village level. Detailed location of Mangraura block including location of 62 village Panchayats and its boundaries are depicted in the Map-3 of Mangraura block of Pratapgarh district.

Map-3

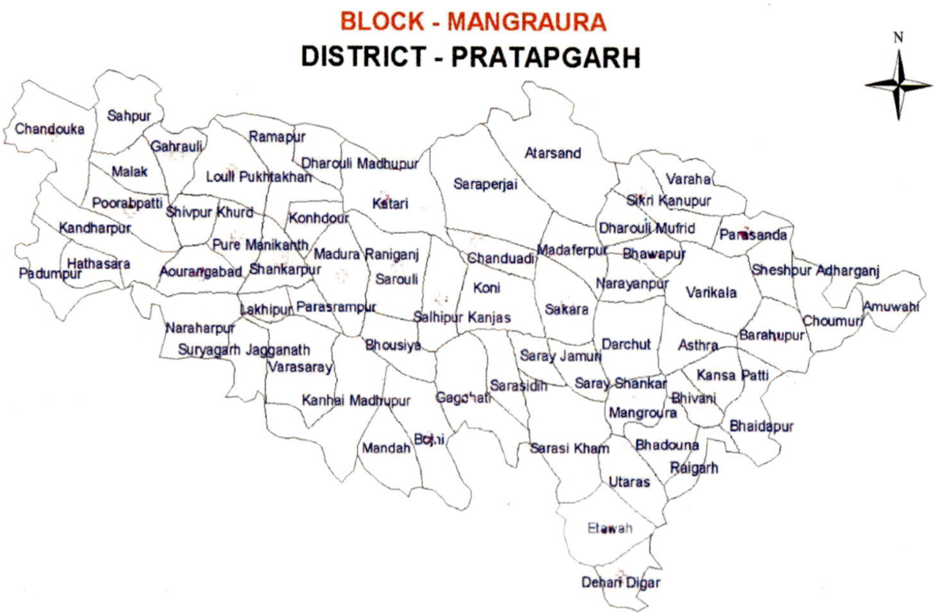

6.3 Religious Importance :

Pratapgarh district is religiously very important because of Belha Devi Temple, Chandikan Devi Temple in Sandwa Chandrika block, Chauhar Jan Devi Temple in Shivgarh block Jwala Devi Temple in Kalakankar block, Ghuisarnath Temple in Sangipur block, Shanidev Temple in Sadar block, Belkhar nath Temple in Belkharnath Dham block, Bhaya Haran Nath Temple in Mandhata block, Hodeshwarnath Temple in Kunda block are most imporatant religious places in Pratapgarh district.

6.4 Historical Importance :

Historically it is found that the Chinese traveller Hieun Tsiang visited the tehsil Kunda during seventh century A.D., since then the Buddhist monasteries are found in Pratapgarh district. Manikpur in the district had been a noted place for its historic past. The district was under the rule of Rajputs, Muslims, Hindus and British. The district took a courageous stand against the British rule during the first war of independence.

Historically and culturally most important Pratapgarh district has been irrigated by the water of Gomati, Sai and Holi Ganga River. Politically awarded era of Audh Region had been the playing ground of Lord Rama.

There is Ajgara Temple at the bank of Nahush Tank in which the statue of Ajgar and Dharmraj yudhisther is available. There is Pandav (Padvasi) village where Pandavas passed hidden time during Mahabharat period.

Buddhist Dharmpal established Buddha Bihar in Bihar village, where Chinese traveller Hieun Tsiang stayed. During Mahabharata period Miss Hidimba got married with powerful Bhim and its memory is still lying in village Handaur.

Historically important place Manikpur is located at the bank of Holy River Ganga. King of Kannnauj Jaichand's brother Manikchand established the Estate during 12th Century. Emperor of Delhi Jalaluddin's Nephew & daughter-in-law Alluddin khilji was appointed as administrator of Manikpur. Jalaluddin came to Manikpur to congratulate Alauddin but he cut the head of Jalaluddin in village Khemsara and announced himself emperor of Delhi.

Thus Manikpur had privilege of being capital of the country like calcutta, Delhi and Ajgara. One Mughal Emperor Aurangjeb came to Manikpur and celebrated Id festival at Manikpur.

District Pratapgarh had been ruled by Bharshiv about 400 years ago and its capital was Panchosiddh near Mohanganj Bharshiv left Mankipur being defeated by Kshatriya. Patti was ruled by Bajgoti Kashtriya, Kunda was ruled by Visen banshi king and Sadar Pargana of Sadar Tehsil was ruled by Somvanshi and Atheha was ruled by Kanpuriyno.

Kalakankar estate has important contribution in the freedom struggle of India. Lal Pratap Sing died while struggling with Britishers near chanda during 1857 in the first freedom struggle. Raja Ram Pal Singh was the founder of the congress. Mahamana Malviya was made editor of 'Hindustan' Ist Hindi daily news at remote rural area of Kalakankar. Historical address of Mahatma Gandhi was addressed at Kalakankar. King Awadhesh Singh burnt foreign cloths in the presence of Gandhi ji at Kalakankar.

District Pratapgarh was divided into 5 parts. South of Arwal-Rajgarh, in the north Sultanpur district, in the east Kadipur Khajurani, Prithviganj, Sipaham Leri and in the west kund area had been located. Vishnuahi was the IInd estate of Kunda. Arual was the IIIrd estate, Atheha was the 4th Estate of Kanpur iyno and Pura Patti was teh 5th estate.

Pratapgarh was one district among 12 districts of Audh Region and it was ruled by Talu Kendars. There were 52 Talukadars for 33 Talukar's. Jhinguri Singh leaded on behalf of the farmers against exploitation of Talukedars. Acting Deputy Commissioner arrested 32 farmers alongwith Baba on 28 August 1920 and sentensed them in Pratapgarh Jail in the fake theft case and refused for bail. Pandit Nehru and Gaurishankar came on 29 August for investigation and on 11 September 5000 farmers came to see Baba in the court. The farmers protested infront of the Jail. Pandit Mata Badal Pandey, Parmashwari Dayal went to Baba and requested farmers to displace and lastly officers acquitted Baba.

6.5 Important Historical Places :

6.5.1 Rocky Ka Tila :

Rocky Ka Tila is located 6 miles away from Sangipur in the Sangipur block of Pratapgarh district. Length of Tila is 2 miles and width 1 mile and 30 feet height.

Kaningham and funeror archaeologist from Europe accepted the importance of Rocky Ka Tila and once upon a time Tila was densely populated area. Southern part of Tila is being leveled from agricultural activity and people achieved valuable goods from southern Tila. Tila was populated city of great district of Kaushal during Buddhist period.

6.5.2 Ajgara :

Ajgara is located near Raniganj having 15km distance from Pratapgarh city then the great district of Kaushal in the west on Varanasi-Lucknow National highway. Presently Nahush Tank is only 5-6 Bigha Nahush was related to Ajgara yoni due to which the place is named as Ajgara and local Mela is being organised in the month of Bhadon on Panchami.

6.5.3 Sun's statue :

Sun's statue was achieved while digging for building construction in west of Pratapgarh city. Sun's statue has beautiful Mani & handi craft and painted for decoration.

6.5.4 Handaur :

Handaur village is historically important place about 24 km. away in the west from Pratapgarh district Headquarter on the Varanasi-Lucknow National Highway. On the name of Hidimbasus, the place is known as Handier. There is 1 km. spreaded tila, in which most part of it is being used for housing and agricultural activity. Safe central part of tila is 100 m. high from general surface. It is being said that it was a fort of king Hidimba which destroyed. There is statue of queen Hindwi which was achieved while cultivating the field by a villager.

6.5.5 Dih Hardo :

Archaeologically important Dih Hardo Tila is 1 km. away from Naubasta market in the south-west on Pratapgarh Kunda Road having 20 km. distance from Pratapgarh district headquarter. Some land is being used for agricultural work from ancient period. Most part of Tila is still left barren. Total land of Pratapgarh district is most fortunate because many important places belongs from ancient to stone period.

6.5.6 Sandwa Khas Tila :

Village Sandwa khas is located 3 km. away from Sarai Anadev market about 15km. distance in the west on Pratapgarh-Kunda Road from Pratapgarh district headquarter. Archeological survey done in the Sandwa Khas provides that half km. spreaded Tila is being used for housing and agricultural activities even then some part of the Tila is still lying barren & vaccant. In the east of the village there is ancient temple of chaturbhuji devi and there is also a statue of Lord Vishnu. It is estimated that these statues belongs to the gupta era.

6.5.7 Shani Dev Temple :

Shani Dev Temple is located on the bank of Bakulahi river in Kushfara village at the distance of 18 km. from Pratapgarh city in the west corner of Sadar Block. Lav Kush was born in this village that is why on the name of kush, the village is named as Kushfara. It is said that in an area of 50 acres there is Sitakund in which at the 10 feet depth there is black soil which burns like wood on the east of the river there is high Tila which is knownon the name of Mahavir. It is said that it had been the Ashram of Balmiki. There is Shani Dev Temple in the south of the Tila. Shani Dev is being worshipped usually. In this scientific era of 20th century more than 10000 devotees visits to worship Shanidev on every Saturday. Some of the historians estimated that the statue is 1100 year old.

6.5.8 Gode :

Archaeologically very important place in the village Gode is located about 9 km. away in the north from Pratapgarh district headquarter on the Faizabad-Allahabad National Highway village is named as Gode in the government records. There is ancient temple in the centre of village which was constructed during the gupta period. There are more than two dozen statues of Devis & Devatas at the centre of the temple, specially the statue of Ganesh Ji having 18 hands is most important. There are written records on the stone in the east wall side of the temple and it is written in the Sanskrit language. The clear reading of the stone is not yet possible but it is assumed that it had been written during the Gupta period. Another writing in the temple is related to an ancient well which is located is front of the temple.

6.5.9 Kahala Shaheed :

In the Gaura block of Raniganj Tehsil at the distance of 32 km. from district headquarter of Pratapgarh, on the Lucknow-Pratapgarh-Varanasi way at the distance of 190 km; on the Gazi ki Bagh-Mubarkpur road about the distance of 6 km. village-Kahala is located. In the freedom struggle on 16 Feb. 1931 freedom fighter Sri Kalika Prasad, village-Kahala, Ram Das-village Nath Ka Purwa, Mathura Prasad from village Kaulapur did sacrificed their lives. In their memory Late Smd. Indira Gandhi former Prime Minister of INdia laid foundation stone on 16 Feb. 1973. This place is being developed as tourist place having 11 meter height stone in the memory of sacrificed freedom strugglers by the government.

6.5.10 Ghuisarnath :

Historical Ghuisar Nath temple is 40 km away from Pratapgarh city in the tehsil Lalganj Ajhara's block. Sangipur at the 8 km. distance on Lalganj-Sangipur road on the bank of Sai river. On the era of every Shivratri a very big local Mela used to be organized in the historical temple in which devotees comes from far away villages National unity festival used to be organised since 1996 on the holy day of Shivaratri, in which large number of people belonging to all section of society participate in this festival. Famous artists used to present their programmes on this holy occassion.

The archaeology remains of a Buddist monastery is found in the Pratapgarh Mankpur the ancient town stands by the Ganga is full of ruins of residences built during the reign of Akbar. A ruined brick fort exists in Ranki. In Yahiapur stands the temple of Belkhar nath Besides Dahiawan and Daudpur are noted for bloodshed during the mutiny. A building of great antiquity exists here which was teh residence of Raja Pratap Bahadur Singh.

7. VILLAGE DEVELOPMENT PLANNING :

Planning is an organised process by which people achieves its developmental goals or planning is a means to achieve development. Development means the evolution of people in which people acquires better perception and best control over its natural and human resources. Macro-level planning adopted in India, while micro-level planning did not yield the desired results. Natural Resources Data Management

System (NRDMS) programme has been initiated by Department of Science & Technology, Govt. of India during 1982, focusssing on technological and institutional capacity building, so that the people can plan their own development through utilizing the local available resources. Micro-level/ village development planning for Pratapgarh District at block level and at village level in Mangraura block for human & natural resources have been surveyed and analysed adopting various sectoral indicators.

Geographically Pratapgarh district lies in the Allahabad Division of Uttar Pradesh, Pratapgarh district comprises of 5 tehsils, 17 blocks and 2219 villages Mangraura block is one of the backward block of the district Pratapgarh. There are 62 village Panchayats in Mangraura block. There 62 village Panchayats have been taken for micro-level village development planning. Pratapgarh district is religiously and historically very important and the people of the district sacrificed their life in the freedom struggle.

Natural resources of the Pratapgarh district has been analysed in the IInd chapter of the study because Pratapgarh district is endowed with the natural resources. Most of the land of the district is affected by the saline soils and ravines of Sai river, comparatively good quality soil for agricultural activity is less, even then approximately 90% people of the District are dependent on agricultural activity. Natural resources of the district plays an important role in its economic development.

Human resources of the district Pratapgarh has been explained in the IIIrd chapter of the study socio-economic sectoral indicators have been adopted to study the development planning at village level in Mangraura block and block level in Pratapgarh district. Various sub-indicators related to economic data have been collected through secondary data and primary survey at village level has been discussed in the IV chapter.

Infrastructural resources of the Pratapgarh district has been explained in the V chapter of the study. Various infrastructural indicators data have been collected through secondary data and door to door survey/ primary survey have been ensured at village level and to study the need of the people for better village development planning.

Various Rural Development Programmes being implemented in Pratapgarh District have been described in the VI chapter of the study. Attempt is made to study various rural developmental programmes at block level in Pratapgarh district and various rural developmental programmes including 20 point programmes and their implementation have been surveyed at village level to desire the need base action plan for finalizing the village development planning.

Development planning at block level in Pratapgarh and village level in Mangraura block have been analysed in the VIIth chapter of the study. The district development Planning i.e. Zila Yojana have been explained at Block level in

Pratapgarh district and village Development Planning. i.e. Gram Yojana as per need of the villagers and as per available human and natural resources have been discussed in the study which will be a mile stone in the overall planning of village – block-district level planning.

District & village Development Planning based on the natural & human and infrastructural resources, various rural developmental programmes and need base action planning have been analysed in the VIIIth chapter of the study. The importance and need of the district-block-village developmental planning at village level in Mangraura block and block level for Pratapgarh district have been explained in detailed in this study.

8. CONCLUSION :

Development Planning is a means of the evolution of the people in which people acquires better perception and best control over its natural and human resources. Natural Resources Data Management System (NRDMS) have been adopted as a tool for collection & collation of socio-economic data base including natural resources adopting Geographic Information System (GIS) for district-block-village level development planning. Geographically Pratapgarh district is endowed with natural and human resources. It has religious and historical importance.

Socio-economic data among the human resources and its various sub-indicators data have been collected & collated at block level and village level. Similarly infrastructural data at village level for Mangraura block and block level for Pratapgarh district have been analysed for formulation of need base development planning.

Various rural developmental programmes being implemented at block level in Pratapgarh district and village level for Mangraura block have been collected for analysing need of the people and to develop need base planning at village level in Mangraura block and block level in Pratapgarh district.

Need of the people and requirement of the people for common minimum programmes have been studied and as per requirement of the people need base action developmental planning have been developed for village level in Mangraura block and for block level in Pratapgarh district.

Development planning as per need of the people at micro level i.e. village level in Mangraura block and block level in Pratapgarh district will have an important role in an integrated development of the village & block level development and it will have good impact among the people, no doubt the development planning adopting Natural Resources Data Management System (NRDMS) programme for collection & collation of data and its analysis at village level in Mangaruara block and block level in Pratapgarh district will be a mile stone in the integrated development of village – block Mangraura , district-Pratapgarh.

CHAPTER II

NATURAL RESOURCES

1. INTRODUCTION :

Available natural resources has special contribution in the economic development of any area underground water, forest cover, mines and soil etc. are the main important component of the natural resources. Pratapgarh district is endowed with natural resources. In some part of the district natural resources has been boon for the economic development like the sediments of river Ganga and Sai river are very fertile for agricultural activity while waterlogged land and saline soil have lead for increase in barren and wastelands causing non fertility of land which has been the main reason for the backwardness of district Pratapgarh.

In view of the positive and negative aspects of the available natural resources of the Pratapgarh district, it is most important task to study and analyse the available natural resources which have been playing an important role in the socio-economic and infrastructural development of the district and the available natural resources of Mangraura block are also responsible for the development of the block and natural resources available in the villages will play major role in the formulation of planning programme for micro/ village development. In view of the above an attempt is made to analyse in detail the available natural resources, which has been an asset for integrated development but also creating hinderance for development of the district.

2. PHYSIOGRAPHY :

The district Pratapgarh can be divided into two physiographic divisions:

(a) Midland 100-150 meters and (b) Low land – below 100 meters

The district Pratapgarh is mainly drained by Sai river which flows from west to east. The Ganga and Gomati river from the south west and the north-eastern land of the district respectively. The general slope of the district is towards the east. The whole district is covered by unconsolidated sedimentary rock formation and alluvium. The alluvial plain is formed by the Ganges system. Alluvium soil of Kunda, Babaganj, Kalakankar, Bihar, Rampur khas block located in the south of the Sai river is fertile and most useful for agricultural productivity. General fertility status of the soil have been observed in such land located on the river banks.

3. RELIEF AND SLOPE :

Relief of the Pratapgarh district is divided in two parts i.e. midland – 100 to 150 meters and low land – below 100 meter. Midland and low land relief of the Pratapgarh district is shown in the Map 4. The slope of the land is less than 10 meters per kilometers, which is shown in the relief and slope map of the Pratapgarh district and the general slope of the district is towards east. The relief of the district is marked by generally a level plain which shows influence of rivers and streams. The flat terrain at some places shows gentle undulations but in the vicinity of rivers and streams, the land is extremely dissected with the consequent development of ravines. The drainage pattern indicates the general slope of the area. The average altitude is 100 meter above the mean sea level, and the land slopes gently from north-west to south-east. In the western half of the district Pratapgarh the land generally slopes from west to east.

Map-4

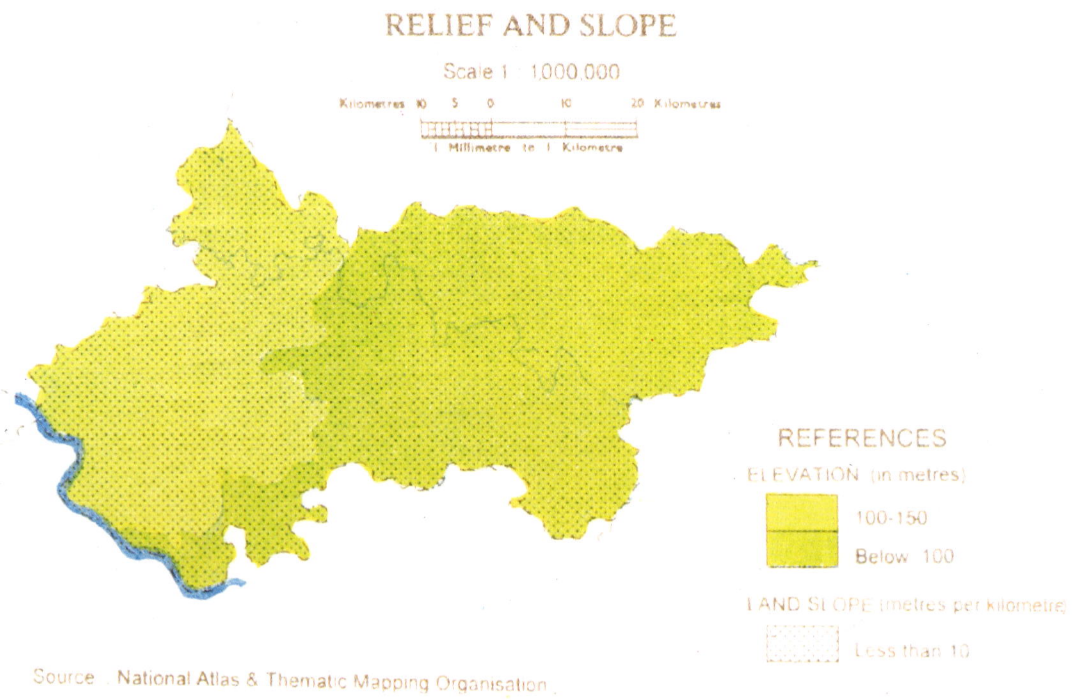

Source : National Atlas & Thematic Mapping Organisation, Dept. of Science & Technology

4. ROCKS AND MINERALS :

The whole district of Pratapgarh is covered by unconsolidated sedimentary rock formations and alluvium. Rocks and minerals of Pratapgarh district is depicted in the Map-5. It is noted that Pratapgarh district has no exploitable minerals except sands exploited alongwith the river banks of Ganga and Sai river. The alluvial plain is formed by the Ganges river system. No important mineral are found in the Pratapgarh district Kanakar is available in saline land which is used for construction of road and saline soil is used for washing the clothes.

Map - 5

ROCKS AND MINERALS

Scale 1 : 1,000,000

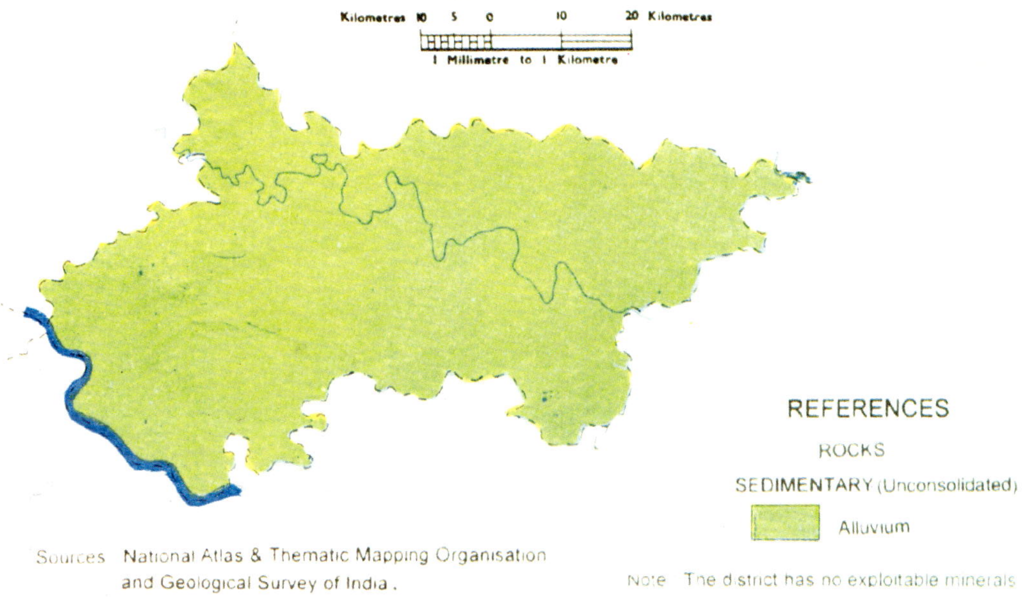

Source : National Atlas & Thematic Mapping Organisation, Dept. of Science & Technology

5. DRAINAGE :

The largest among the rivers flowing through the district is Ganga river near the south-western border of the distrtict Pratapgarh. From Kalakankar to Gotauni, the river flows close under the old bank which in places, as at the Manikpur Fort, rises to a great height above the stream.

Sai river is the other important river whose banks are in many places high and generally well defined. The banks of Sai river are broken at certain places due to ravenous and comprise of light textured soil. Naiya cham raura, Loni and Bakulahi rivers are some of the important tributaries of Sai river. The northern tributaries of Sai river generally flow from north to south, but those on the right bank are more meandering and generally flow eastward and finally join the Sai river in the north.

The district Pratapgarh is conspicuously marked by a series of old meanders of a former drainage channel, which are periodically inundated causing extensive waterlogging. In view of the highly contoured patterns of these 'Jhils' the drainage in the area is chaotic. These Jhils are usually narrow & deep and appear to be a antiquation of the similar features scene in the neighbouring district.

6. Climate :

The climate of district Pratapgarh used to be more not during summer season and vary cold during winter season and general rainfall is recorded during the rainy season. The detailed observations of climatic conditions of the Pratapgarh district including temperature and rainfall is depicted in the Map-6.

Map – 6

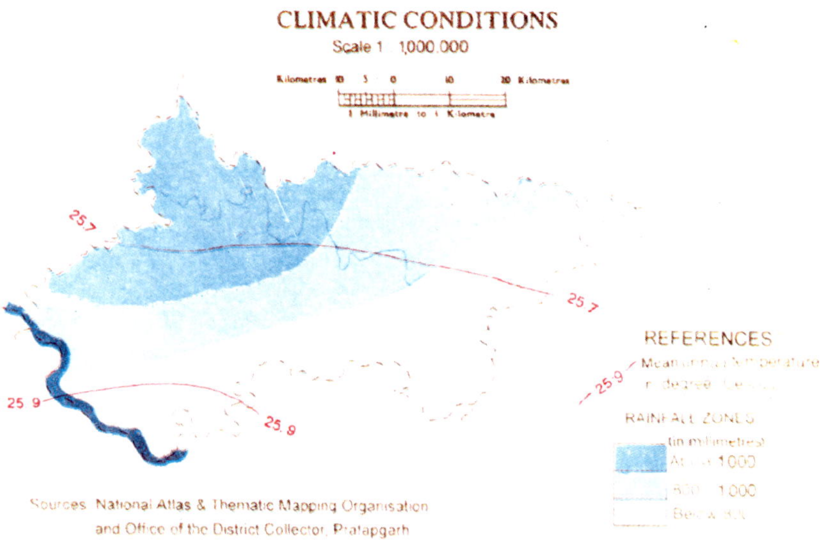

Source : National Atlas & Thematic Mapping Organisation, Dept. of Science & Technology

6.1 Temperature :

District Pratapgarh has a maximum and minimum temperature of 480C and 60C respectively. There is no metearological laboratory in the Pratapgarh district for recording temperature. The description is based on the records of the observatory in the neighbouring district, having similar climatic conditions. January is the coldest month, when the minimum temperature some time falls to about 20 to 60C. Temperature begins to rise rapidly in March, May and early June are the hottest months, when the maximum temperature occasionally reaches 480C. The mean annual maximum and minimum temperatures are 32.10C and 16.920C respectively. The mean annual temperature varies between 27.70C to 25.90C from south to north respectively as shown in the Map-6.

6.2 Rainfall :

The average annual rainfall of district Pratapgarh is 1000 mm. of which Pratapgarh Sadar Tehsil gets the minimum share followed by Patti and Kunda Tehsils. Almost 90% of the annual rainfall is received during the monsoon months viz., from June to September north-west part of the district shares more than 1000 mm. rainfall as depicted in the Map-6. Central part from north to west side receives 800 to 1000 mm annual rainfall while Patti, Raniganj and southern part of Kunda Tehsil of the south-east part of Pratapgarh district share below800 mm. annual rainfall. Thus rainfall in Pratapgarh district below 800 mm to above 1000 mm. as depicted in the Map-6.

7. SOILS :

Whole Pratapgarh district is covered by unconsolidated sedimentary rock formations and alluvium. The alluvial plain is formed by Ganges system. The soil associations in different geomorphic regions of the Pratapgarh district are older alluvial saline and saline-alkaline and younger alluvial soil as depicted in Map-7. The soils are affected by salt and can be categorised in three groups.

(a) 20 to 50 percent

(b) 50 to 85 percent

(c) more than 85 percent salt affected are as which is shown in the Map-8.

In Pratapgarh district nearly 61 percent of the total area is under cultivation followed by 5% forest land, 6% wasteland, 17 % fallow land and 11% other uses of land.

Spatial characteristics of wastelands in Pratapgarh district is analysed in three parts viz., saline soils, waterlogged and Ravine land.

Map-7

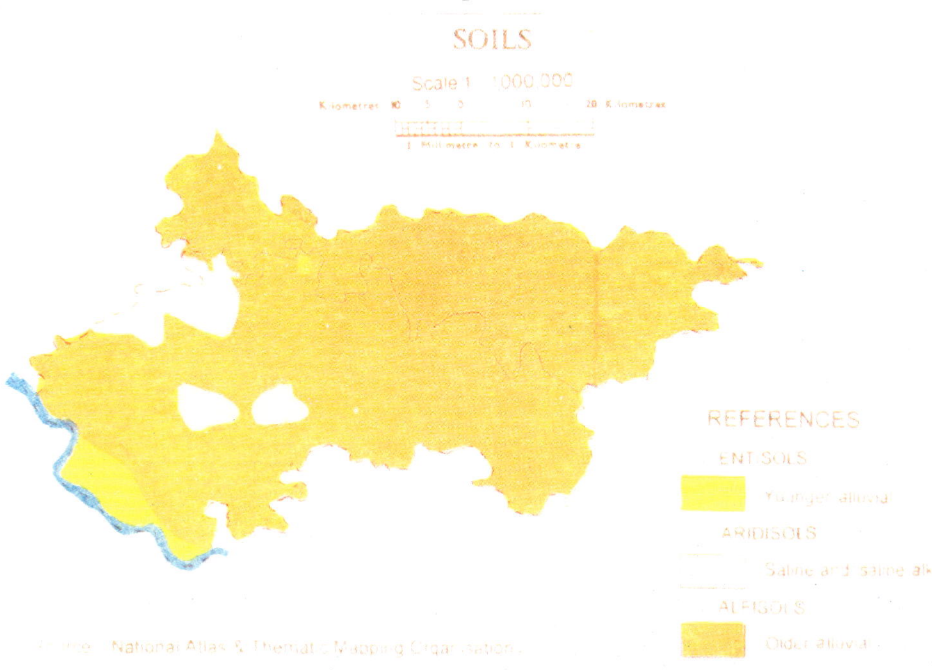

Source : National Atlas & Thematic Mapping Organisation, Dept. of Science & Technology

7.1 Saline Land :

Salinity occurs in 52477 ha area, accounting for 82.55% of the total wastelands in Pratapgarh district. Saline land is major wasteland category occurring extensively in Kunda, Sadar Pratapgarh and Patti Tehsils. The occurrence of salt affected wastelands is less extensive to the north of Sai river than in the south as shown in the Map-8. In the northern half of the Pratapgarh district the salt occurrence is markedly less than the southern. Saline wastelands are mostly lying barren and are characterized by a salt incrustation of varying thickness, ranging from a few mm to as much as 4 cm. Saline category of wasteland includes such areas where cultivation has been tried during some years but could not prove successful. Thus leaving the remnants of field bunds and a thin incrustation of salt with grasses on the surface. Saline land is conspicuously seen between Sai and Ganga rivers in Kunda and in the neighborhood Patti tehsil very large tract of saline land extends from village Kong and Atarsand in the north and south and east part of the district. The problem of saline land is equally servers in south Patti tehsil but Sadar Tehsil is less affected by saline land. Generally most of the saline land have a subsurface layer of 'Kankar' nodules at varying depths. In some areas saline land has been compounded by soils erosion, as seen alongwith the small streams like Loni river in tehsil Kunda.

Map-8

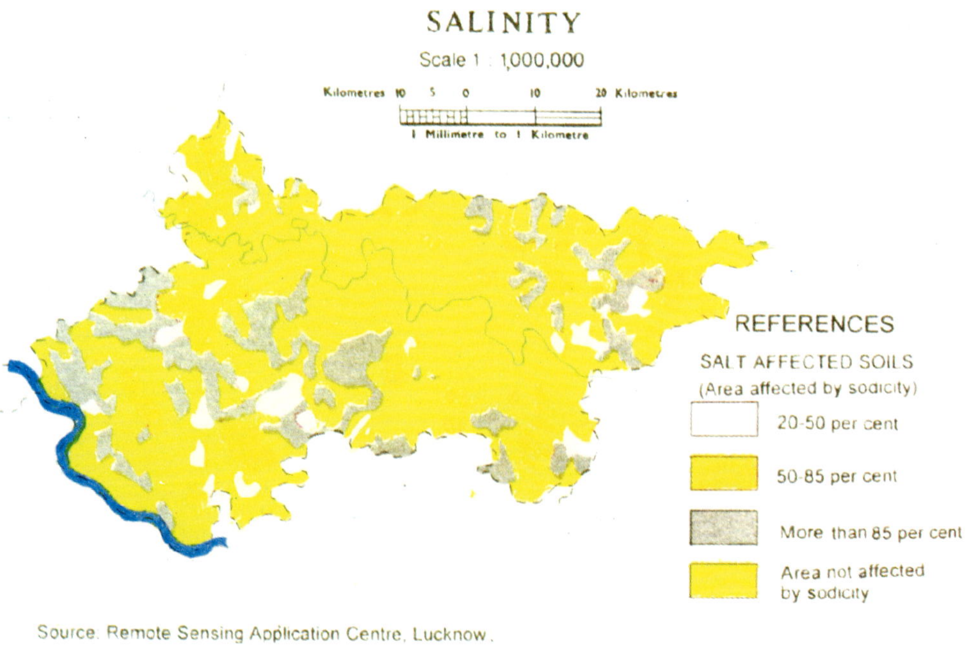

Source : National Atlas & Thematic Mapping Organisation, Dept. of Science & Technology

7.2 Waterlogged land :

Waterlogged had occurrence in 7111 ha, accounting for 11.18% of the total wastelands in Pratapgarh district. Waterlogged land is the IInd important category of wasteland in Pratapgarh District. Waterlogged land has assumed alarming proportion in the vicinity of Baikulahi river in Kunda tehsil and in south Patti tehsil. Large area of waterlogged land are inunded in and around Umran Tal and Chanwa Tal in the south of

Patti tehsil. The waterlogged areas in the vicinity of these 'Tals' and along the Daikulahi river are due to extension in the appeared of surface water. The natural drainage appears to be sluggish in south Pratapgarh district as evidenced by numerous waterbodies in Kunda and Patti tehsil. The tall grasses are grown around the waterlogged land.

7.3 Ravine Land :

Ravine land occurs in 3985 ha area accounting for 6.27% of the total area under wastelands in Pratapgarh district.1 Ravine land is least extensive and it is largely confined along the banks of Sail, Baikulahi and Ganga rivers. Ravines are shallow to deep in the area, with a vegetative cover of scattered tree of Babool, grasses comprising mainly of Munj. In the west of Pratapgarh town, the ravines are deep but since these have broad valley bottom occassional rainfed cultivation is done in the scattered patches of ravine land.

8. IRRIGATION AND HYDROLOGY :

There is about 1090mqm. water in Pratapgarh district as per available data, out of which approximately 44% water is being utilized. Ground water aquifers with primary inter granular porosity from 10-25 have been observed in the north of Sai river mainly in Sangipur block of Pratapgarh district, while rest of Pratapgarh district shareas 25-40 aquifers with primary intergranular porosity as seen in the Map-9.

Map-9

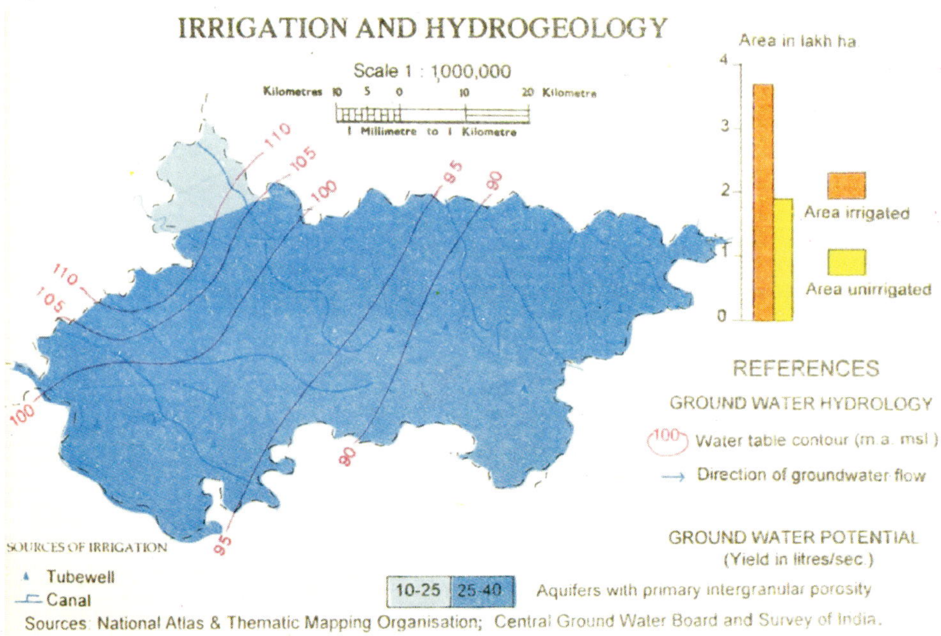

1. Mapping of wastelands from satellite imagery – Pratapgarh district, U.P. 1988, published by Remote Sensing Applications Centre, U.P., Lucknow

Source : National Atlas & Thematic Mapping Organisation, Dept. of Science & Technology

Ground water hydrology, water table contour varies from 110 m.a.msl. in north west part of Pratapgarh district to 90 m.a.msl. water table contour in south east part of the district – Direction of ground water flow is from north west to south-east of the Pratapgarh district. Irrigated area in Pratapgarh district is 3.75 lakh ha while unirrigated area is 2.91 lakh ha as shown in the Map-10. Irrigation source in Pratapgarh district are canal and tubewell. The details of irrigation and hydrological water potential.

9. FOREST AND VEGETATION :

Pratapgarh district lacks forest and vegetation, as per the available data there is approximately 568 ha forest land in Pratapgarh district. In the Pratapgarh district from Gotani to down streams there is rich Khadar tract of varying width which is relatively low lying and covered partly with Jhau and Tamarisk jungles. The more elevated parts of the river banks are bare of covered with coarse grass, while the ravine/ gully beds get inundated during monsoon and cultivated there after for the rabi harvest. According to the forest statistical data there is only 5% forest land of the total area of the District Pratapgarh and 6% area of the total land of the district are wastelands.

Dhak/Palash is the dominant tree in the plain land. Alongwith the Sai river Babool mixed with other traces occur in the north part of Pratapgarh district. Pipal, Bargad, Pakar, Amaltas, Kachnar and Bakain are the other common trees in Pratapgarh district.

The orchards and groves comprises mainly of Mango, Aonla, Mahua, Tamarind, Jamun, Ber and others have been planted as per needs of the local people. Aonla & Ber plantation is very popular in the northern part of Pratapgarh district specially in Patti tehsil. Horticulture Dept. of Uttar Pradesh has earmarked Pratapgarh district as Aonla plantation belt for which special package support has been also made available of the District Administration and State Government of Uttar Pradesh various fruits & vegetables preservation & processing units have been established in the north part of the Pratapgarh district specially at Chilbila & Kohndaur area. The excessive production of Aonla is also exported. Thus Pratapgarh district is not only popular but famous for Aonla plantation and production in the state of Uttar Pradesh. In view of the above most of the farmers have done the Aonla plantation in their field and anole is being marketed through Pratapgarh Mandi. Thus forest and vegetable cover, which is low in terms of area, have an important share in the per capita income of Pratapgarh district. Generally tall grasses grow around waterlogged land in Pratapgarh district.

Ravine land are shallow to deep in the area with a vegetative cover of scattered trees of Babool and grasses mainly munj. Salt tolerant grasses like Karnal grass, Rhodesgrass, Bermuda grass, paragrass, Doob etc. are the grass species are being grown successfully along with trees or individually on some of the saline lands.

In the ravine land prosopis Juliflora and Acacia nilotica have been planted. The ravine bottom has been utilized for syzygium cumini, Haplophragma adenophylum Dalbegia sissoo and cassia siamea plants have been planted. The gentle slope of the ravine land have been utilized for cassia articulate, Acacia nilotica etc. plantation steeper slopes have been utilized for plantation of Ellipsis binate and Saccharin munja.

10. CONCLUSION :

Thus Pratapgarh district is endowed with natural resources. Available natural resources have positive and negative impact in the overall economic development of Pratapgarh district. Natural resources available in Mangraura block and Pratapgarh district plays an important role in the socio-economic infrastructural development. Therefore natural resources may be considered as major indicator in the formulation of village and block development planning of Pratapgarh district.

Physiography of the Pratapgarh district is divided into midland (100-150 m) and low land (below 100 mt). Main river of the Pratapgarh district is the Sai river which flows from west to east. The Ganga and Gomati river from the south-west and north-eastern land of the district. Pratapgarh is covered by unconsolidated sedimentary rock formation and alluvium. Alluvial plain is formed by the Ganges system.

Relief of the district is divided as midland (100-150 mt contour) and low land (below 100 mt) general slope of the Pratapgarh district is towards east. The relief of the district is marked by a level plain which shows influence of rivers and streams. The flat terrain at some places shows gentle undulations but in the vicinity of rivers and streams, the land is extremely dissected with the consequent development of ravines. Generally in the western part of the district the land slopes from west to east.

Pratapgarh district is covered by unconsolidated sedimentary rock formation and alluvium. Pratapgarh district has no exploitable minerals. Kankar pan is available in the saline land.

The largest amongst the rivers flowing through the district is Ganga river near the south-western border of the Pratapgarh district from Kalakankar to Gotani. Sai river is the another important river whose banks are in many places high and generally well defined. The banks of Sai river are broken at certain places due to ravenous and comprise of light textures soil. Naiya, Chamraura, Loni and Bakulahi rivers are some of the important tributaries of Sai river. The northern tributaries of Sai river generally flow from north to south but those on the right bank are more meandering and generally flow eastward and finally join the Sai river in the north.

Climatic conditions of the Pratapgarh district are appropriate. Pratapgarh has a maximum and minimum temperature of 480C and 60C respectively. Average annual rainfall of Pratapgarh district is 1000 mm. of which Pratapgarh Sadar tehsil gets the minimum share followed by Patti and Kunda Tehsils. Thus overall rainfall of Pratapgarh district varies below 800 to above 1000 mm.

Pratapgarh district is covered by unconsolidated sedimentary rock formations and alluvium. The soil associations in different geomorphic regions of the Pratapgarh district are older alluvial, saline and saline-alkaline and younger alluvial soil, nearly 61% of the total area is under cultivation. There is saline, waterlogged and Ravine land is Pratapgarh district.

Salinity occurs in 52477 ha area accounting for 82.55% of the total wastelands in Pratapgarh district. The occurrence of salt affected wastelands is less extensive to the north of Sai river than in the south. Saline land is conspicuously seen between Sai and Ganga river in Kunda and in the neighborhood Patti tehsil.

Waterlogged land has occurrence in 7111 ha area accounting for 11.8% of the total wastelands in Pratapgarh district. Waterlogged land has assumed alarming proportion in the vicinity of Baikulahi river in Kunda tehsil and in south Patti tehsil.

Ravine land occurs in 3985 ha area accounting for 6.27% of the total area under wastelands in Pratapgarh district. Ravine land is largely continued along the banks of Sai, Baikulahi and Ganga rivers.

Pratapgarh district has about 1090 m.q.m. water out of which approximately 44% water is being utilized. Ground water hydrology, water table contour varies from 110 m.a.msl. in north west part of the Pratpgarh to 90 m.a.msl. water table contour in south east part of the district.

Approximate irrigated area is 3.75 lakh ha while unirrigated area is 2.91 lakh ha. Pratapgarh district lacks forest and vegetation cover. Jhau, Dhak, Babool are the dominant trees in the plain land. Pipal, Bargad, Pakar, Amaltas and Kachnar etc. are the other common trees in Pratapgarh district. Or-chards and groves specially Mango, Aonla, Ber and other plants have been planted is declared as Aonla belt. Aonla is being marketed within and out of the country.

Thus Pratapgarh district is endowed with natural resources. Available natural resources in the various villages .of Mangraura block and in the other blocks of Pratapgarh district contributes major role in the overall development of the district. Natural resources are one of the major sectoral indicators, which will have an important role in the formulation of village – block- district level development planning. Need base action plan can be formulated considering the available natural resources of the villages and blocks of Pratapgarh district. Thus it is evident that natural resources will have an important role in the formulation of village development planning.

●●●

CHAPTER - III

HUMAN RESOURCES

1. INTRODUCTION :

Planning process and implementation of development programmes is an information intensive task. The management of data as available in the village-block-district level is not properly geared to meet the information needs of integrated development planning. The traditional / conventional system of data collection/ collation, storage are not amenable for quick updation, retrieval and holistic analysis and several problems because of incompatible datasets inefficient inter-sectoral data flow and lack of information on quality of data.

Process of integrated approach to planning requires a detailed knowledge of human resources data and it's interdependencies between various human resources i.e. socio-economic sectoral indicators to resolve often conflicting demands. It requires appropriate data management and analysing sectoral data on human resources, socio-economic data base. Detailed socio-economic data base is being analysed for Pratapgarh district and Mangraura block.

2. SOCIAL-INDICATORS :

Social indicators play on important role not only in the planning process of the district but also the implementation of the development programmes. Peoples involvement in the formation of the planning and participation in the implementation of programmes, will not only ensure successful complementation of the developmental programmes but it will be an asset & tool for maintenance and sustainability of the completed programmes. Therefore an attempt has been made to analyse all suitable indicators related to the social sector of economic development. In view of the above area, household, population, workers, education and other indicators have been analysed through data and developed maps through Geographic Information System.

Various indicators of social sector have been analysed for Pratapgarh district at block level and also for Mangraura block at village level respectively.

3. GEOGRAPHICALAREA :

Geographically district Pratapgarh stretches about 115 km. from west to east and 40 km. north to south extending over an area of 3717 sq.km. Administratively district Pratapgarh comprises of 5 tehsils and 17 blocks, 171 Nyaya Panchayats 2219 total villagers and 1105 village Panchayats. Pratapgarh district has cultural, religious and historical importance. Pratapgarh district took a courageous stand against the British rule during the first war of independence. Geographically Sadar block Pratapgarh and Mandhata block are having highest geographical area in the district, while Belkharnath Dham has lowest geographical area, because Shivgarh block has been divided into two parts i.e. north of the Sai river demarcated as Belkharnath Dham block and south of the Sai river was red marketed as Shivgarh block. Belkharnath Dham block has been named on the religious importance of Belkhar Nath Dham Temple.

There are 62 village Panchayat in Mangraura block, which has been taken as village/ micro level unit study. The other revenue villages of the Village Panchayat has been taken as one Panchayat village. Taking village Panchayat as a unit of the study detailed survey have been carried out to study socio-economic structure of the Mangraura block at village level. In Mangraura block there are only 8 Nayay Panchayat. Village Panchayat Atarsand located in the north of Mangraura block has highest geographical area in the block while Shivpur khurd in the west and Lakhipur village in south-west are having very low geographical area in the Mangraura block. There is considerable variations at village level in Mangraura block and inter district differences, which has to be given due importance in the decentralized planning at village level, block level and district planning to ensure integrated balanced development of the Pratapgarh district.

4. HOUSEHOLDS :

There are 427219 number of houses and 438936 number of households in Pratapgarh district. Kunda block of Pratapgarh district is having highest 36566 number of houses while Patti block is having low 15009 number of houses in the district as seen in the Map-10. Similarly Kunda block is having maximum number 36566 households and Patti block is having lowest number of households as evident from Table-1. Thus it is evident that proportionately number of houses and number of households are distributed densely at block level in Pratapgarh district in comparison to area and other infrastructural resources.

Map –10

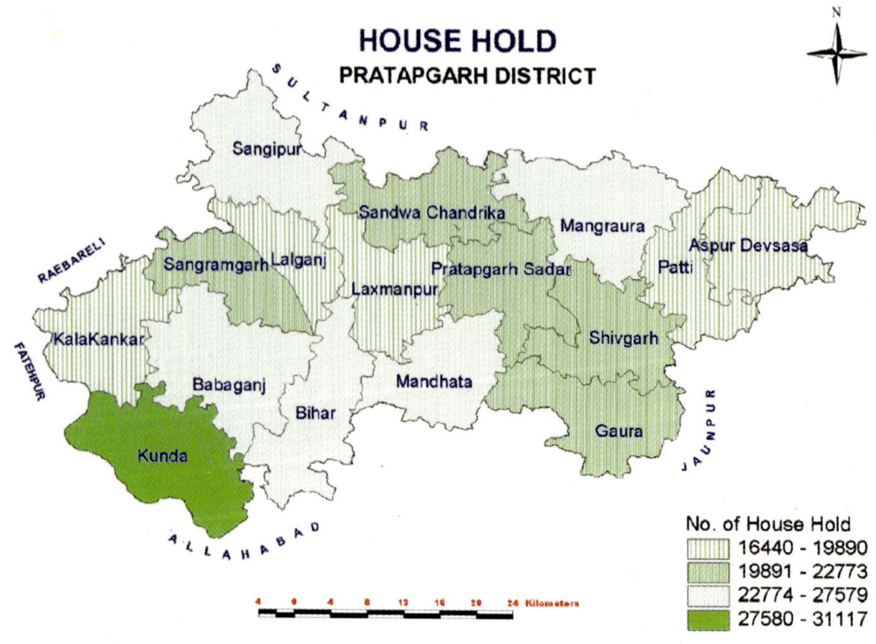

There are 24834 number of houses and 25619 number of households in Mangraura block. Varaha village Panchayat is having very high 1290 number of houses and 1370 number of households in Mangraura block, while lowest number of houses are found in Shivpur khurd village seen in the Table-2 and 167 number of household respectively. Distribution pattern of household is depicted in the Map-11.

Map-11

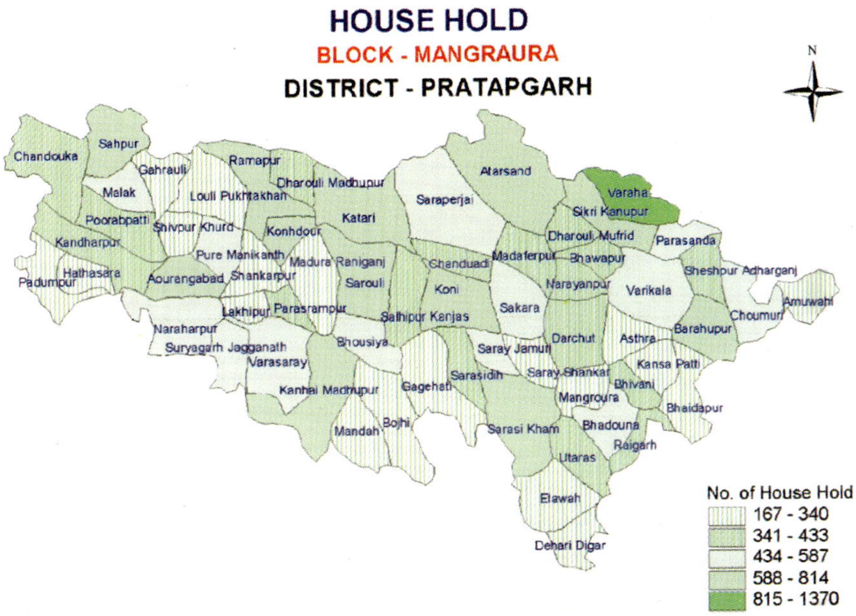

It is observed that number of houses are less than the number of households at block level in Pratapgarh district and also at village level in Mangraura block because in some case the households are divided like brothers or son & father but residing in the same house. Thus the division of household has led to increase in the number of households while number of house have not been increased, therefore the divided households are residing in the same house and termed themselves as separate households due to social structure of the area and to obtain various facilities at village, block and district level.

5. POPULATION :

Total population of Pratapgarh district is 27,31,174 comprising 1368226 female population and 1362948 male population. The literacy ratio is 58-67% of Pratapgarh district. It is clear that Pratapgarh is populated district. Lowest populated block of Pratapgarh district are Patti, Lalganj, Sangramgarh and Kalakankar as seen in the Map-12 and highly populated blocks are Kunda, Bihar, Mandhata and Mangraura due to fertility of the land and other activities including appropriate agricultural farming. Detailed distribution of rural and urban population of Pratapgarh district is shown in the Map-13.

Map-12

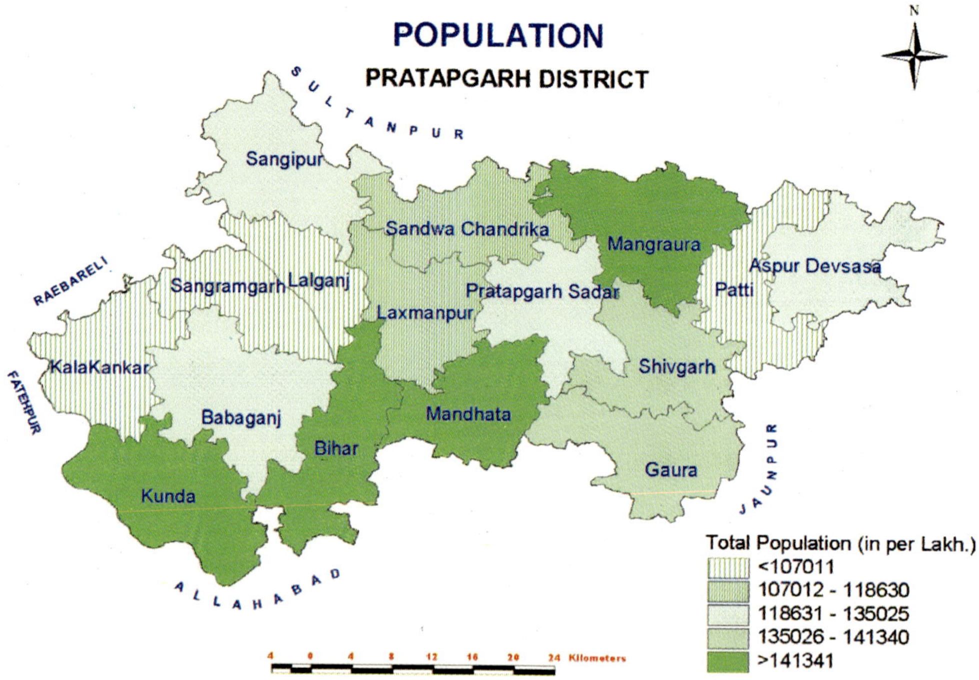

Map-13

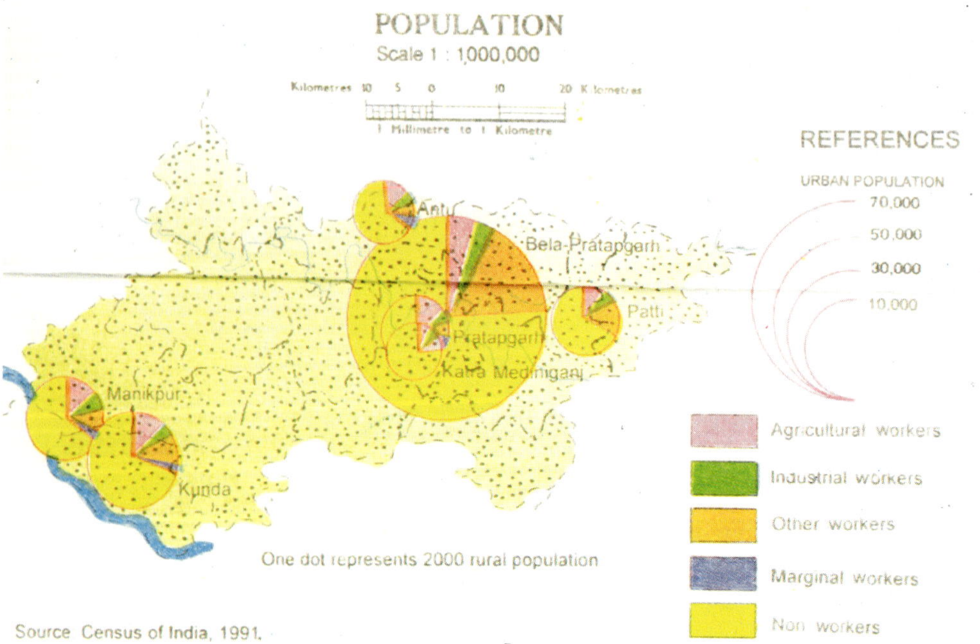

Source : National Atlas & Thematic Mapping Organisation, Dept. of Science & Technology

Highly populated village is Atarsand as per the village Panchayat geographical are and lowest populated villages are Padumpur, Shivpur Khurd, Darouli, Madhupur, Katari, Mandah, Bojhi, Dehrai Digar, Raigarh Kensa Patti, Asthara, Amuwahi villages of Mangraura block which is shown in the Map-14. It is observed that most of the villages of the Mangraura block are having highly populated villages in comparison to the area, number of houses and households, which is one of the reason of the backwardness of the villages.

6. SCHEDULED CASTE :

Bihar block is having highest number of scheduled caste population followed by Kunda, Babaganj and Mangraura blocks as evident from Table-1. Proportionately very low scheduled caste population is found in Patti, Sandwa Chandrika, Laxmanpur and Gaura blocks.

Proportionately scheduled caste population is very high in Varaha village having more than 60% scheduled caste population in Mangraura block as seen in the Map-15, while less than 30% scheduled caste population is found in most of the villages of Mangraura block.

Map-14

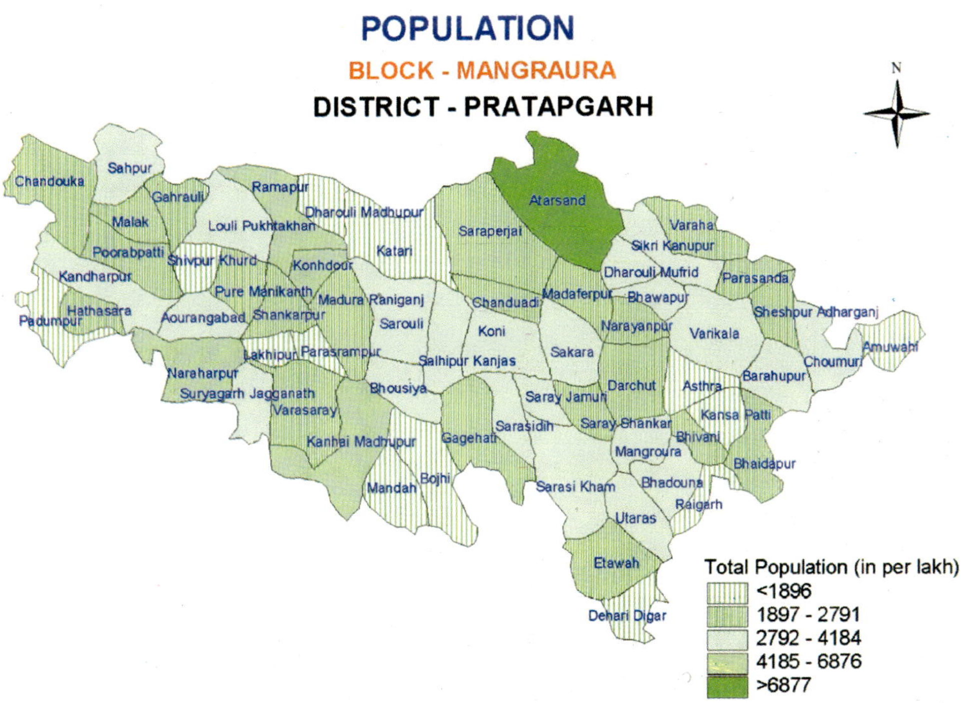

The general caste population is very high in village Kanhai Madhupur and low general caste population is found in village Varaha of the Mangraura block which is evident from Table-2.

Map-15
SCHEDULED CASTE

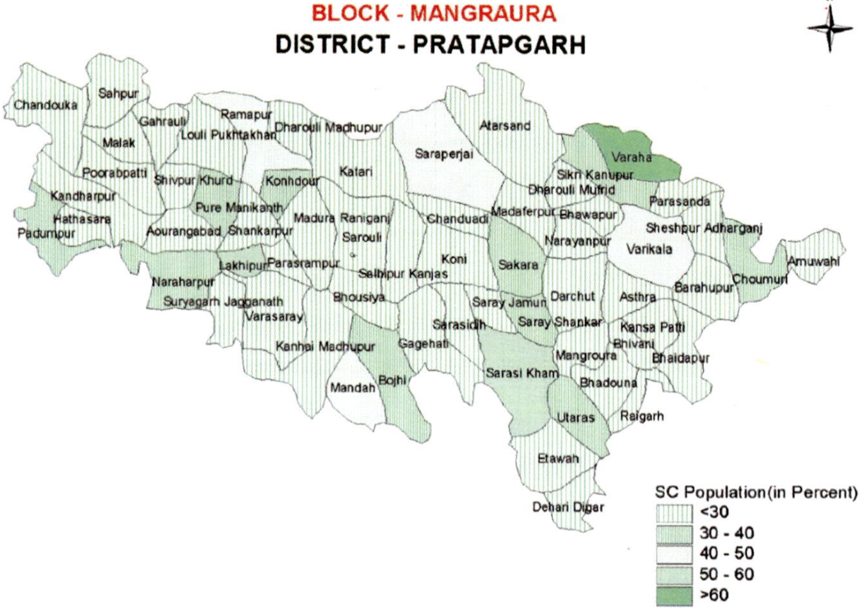

Backward caste population is very high in Atarsand block and very low backward class population is observed in Shivkhurd village of Mangraura block, which is seen in the Table-2. Distribution of other caste population is very low in the various villages of Mangraura block, but the general caste, backward class and scheduled caste population is proportionately distributed in the various villages of Mangraura block. The scheduled caste and backward caste population is comparatively high than the general caste population. It is clear from the available data that the villages of the Mangraura block area socially backward due to maximum distribution of backward and scheduled caste population. Thus social sectoral indicators including Backward class scheduled caste population are one of the major factors responsible for the backwardness of the various villages of the Mangraura block, hence the social factors will be given due importance in the process of formulation of planning for the integrated development of the villages of Mangraura block of Pratapgarh district.

7. WORKERS

Total workers of the Pratapgarh district are 710754. Highest number of total workers are found in Kunda block while lowest number of total workers are observed in Patti block of Pratapgarh district, while total 47405 number of workers are recorded in Mangraura block. Highest number of total workers are seen in village Sarouli and lowest number of total workers are found in village Shivpur Khurd of Mangraura block. Proportionate distribution of workers engaged in different trades are explained, which may be responsible for the development of the district and it may play and important role in the process of planning of the Pratapgarh district. Agricultureal, industrial, marginal, other workers and non-workers distribution as motioned in the Table.

7.1 Farmers :

There are 410199 farmers in the Pratapgarh district. Highest number of farmers are recorded in Gaura block as evident form Table-1 and lowest number of farmers are found in Pratapgarh Sardar block of the district Pratapgarh.

In Mangraura block there are 27555 numbers of farmers. Highest number of farmers are recorded in Varaha village as seen in Table-2. while lowest number of farmers are observed in village Madura Raniganj of the Mangraura block.

7.2 Farm Labours :

In Pratapgarh district, there are 141739 farm labours out of which highest 12117 number of farm labours are seen in Kunda block and lowest 4857 number of farm labours are found in Patti block of the district.

There are 10199 farm labours in Mangraura block out of which highest 413 number of farm labours are found in Kanhai Madhupur village and lowest number of farm labours are found in Kandhar village of Mangraura block.

7.3 Plantation & Animal Husbandry workers :

There are 2254 plantation & husbandry workers in Pratapgarh district. Highest number of plantation & husbandry workers are observed in Pratapgarh Sadar block while lowest number of plantation and husbandry workers are recorded in Sandwa Chandrika block of Pratapgarh district.

Mangraura block is having 185 plantation & husbandry workers are found in Sarouli village as seen in the Map-16 and lowest number of plantation and husbandry workers are seen in village Koni Gahrauli, Poorab Patti, Kandharpur, Atarsand and other villages of the Mangraura block of the district.

Map-16

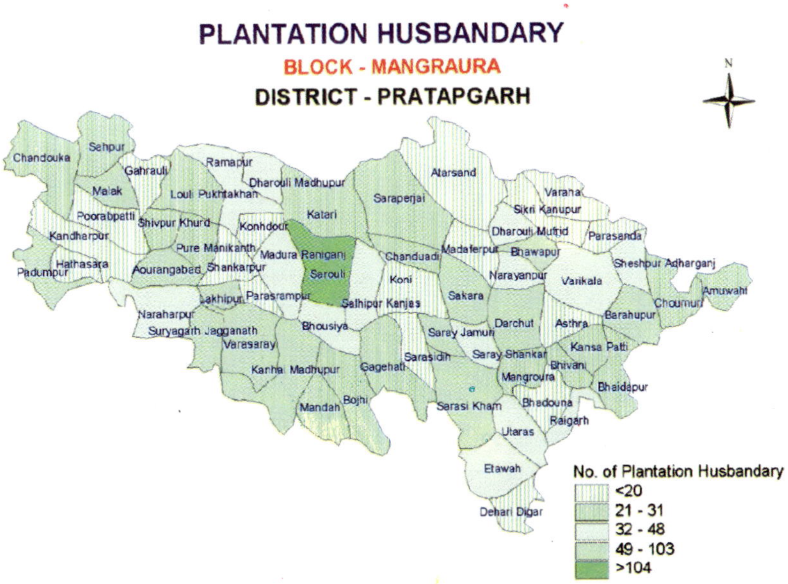

7.4 Family and Non-family workers :

There are 11305 family workers and 12777 non-family workers in Pratapgarh district. Highest number of family workers are found in Shivgarh block while highest number of non-family workers are seen in Mangraura block, while lowest number of family workers are seen in Lalganj block and lowest number of non-family workers are observed in Sangramgarh block of the Pratapgarh district.

There are 783 family workers and 1322 non-family workers are found in Mangraura block out of which highest number of family workers are seen in Shankarpur village and lowest number of family workers are observed in Sarouli & Varikala villages of Mangrura block. Highest number of non-family workers are seen in Dharauli Madapur and lowest number of non-family workers are observed in Varikala and Shivpur khurd village of Mangraura block.

7.5 Construction workers :

Construction workers in Pratapgarh district are 2553 out of which highest number of construction workers are seen in Pratapgarh Sadar block and lowest number of construction workers are recorded in Sangipur and Sangramgarh block of Pratapgarh district.

There are 346 construction workers in Mangraura block out it highest number of construction workers are found in Atarsand, Varha and Shivpur khurd villages while lowest number of construction workers are recorded in Baidapur, Etawah, Utaras, Hathasara, Gajehati, Amuwahi, Madura Raniganj, Salhipur Kanjas villages of the Mangraura block.

7.6 Business workers :

Pratapgarh district has 20441 business workers. Highest number of business workers are seen in Pratapgarh Sadar block and lowest number of business workers are found in Sangramgarh block of the Pratapgarh district.

Mangraura block has 1361 business workers out of which highest number of business workers are seen in Kohndau, Rampur, Kandharpur and Mangraura villages of the block while lowest number of business workers are observed in Bhadauna, Sarasidih, Saray Shankar, Sikari Kanupur villages of the Mangraura block.

7.7 Transportation and communication workers :

There are 766 transportation and communication workers in Pratapgarh district. Highest number of transportation and communication workers are found in Pratapgarh Sadar block while lowest number of transportation and communication workers are recorded in Sangipur and Sangramgarh block of the Pratapgarh district. It is observed that highest number of transportation and communication workers are found in city or urban/ business centers like Pratapgarh city which is the headquarter of the district while low number of transportation and communication workers are recorded in the rural areas where agriculture is the dominant activity.

There are 879 transportation and communication workers in Mangraura block out of which highest number of transportation and communication workers are observed in Shivpur khurd, Varaha, Rampur, Kohndaur, Kandharpur and Dharauli Madapur village of the Mangraura block, while very lowest/ least number of transportation and communication workers are found in Sakara, Koni, Chandauka, Parasanda, Barahupur, Varikala, Amuwahi, Dharauli, Muphrid, Sikari Kanupur, Mandah Varasarai, Suryagarh Jagannath, Pure Manikanth, Poorabpatti, Saray Shankar, Hathasara, Sarasi Kham, Saray Jamuari, Utaras, Bhadauna, Kansa Patti and Raigarh villages of the Mangraura block. Therefore it is observed from the above description that transportation and communication workers are found in urban-unurban or marketing places and local hots and the transportation and communication workers are not found in remote rural areas.

7.8 Other workers :

Pratapgarh district is having 41409 other workers. Other workers are recorded high in Mandhata and Pratapgarh Sadar block while low number of other workers are found in Sangramgarh, Lalganj, Kalakankar block of Pratapgarh district.

There are 2438 number of other workers in Mangraura block out of which highest number of other workers are seen in Sarouli and Rampur villages and very low number of other workers are found in Sekara, Varaha, Puremanikanth village of Mangraura block. Thus the other workers are also found in urban and marketing centers and low in rural areas.

8. EDUCATION :

There are 1881 Junior basic schools & 488 Senior Basic Schools and 195 Senior Secondary Schools in Pratapgarh district. There are 5 degree college and 7 post graduate college in the district. Number of Industrial Training Institute is 3 and one polytechnic institute in Pratapgarh district. The literacy of the Pratapgarh district is 58-67% of the total population. Educationally it appear that the Pratapgarh district is one of the backward district of Uttar Pradesh. Details of educational pattern indicating primary. Junior, Inter and Higher education literates are analysed at block level in Pratapgarh district and at village level in Mangraura block, because level of education plays an important role in the overall socio-economic development of any region.

There are 750950 educated person in Pratapgarh district. Highest number of educated person are seen in Patti block as seen in Map-17 while lowest educated persons are observed in Sangramgarh and Kalakankar blocks of Pratapgarh district. Details of educational pattern at block level including Primary, Junior and Inter level educated persons are depicted in the Map-18. It is clear from the available information that proportionately primary educated persons are very high followed by Junior, Senior Secondary/Inter and lastly higher education. Increase in the primary education is due to adult education and education for all programmes launched by the government. Lowest proportion of higher education is due to the socio-economic backwardness and ignorance including the traditional feeling regarding female child education.

Proportionately the literate persons are recorded very high in Mangraura block in comparison to other block of the Pratapgarh district. Highest literate persons are found in village Atarsand while lowest literate persons are observed in Kansa Patti and Sarai Achal villages of the Mangraura block of Pratapgarh district.

8.1 Primary Education :

There are 454646 primary educated persons in Pratapgarh district out of which highest primary primary educated persons are observed in Mangraura block followed by Aspur Devsara Gaura and Bihar block while very low primary educated persons are recorded in Lalganj block of the district. The variation in the distribution pattern of primary education is depicted through pie diagram in the Map-17. The available information's through district statistical and economic officer of the Pratapgarh district through district statistical Hand book is depicted in the Table-1 makes it clear that those block located in isolation or situated in the remote areas are having low educations pattern but there is significant increase in the primary education due to various programmes launched by the state and government of India including district Administration.

Map-17

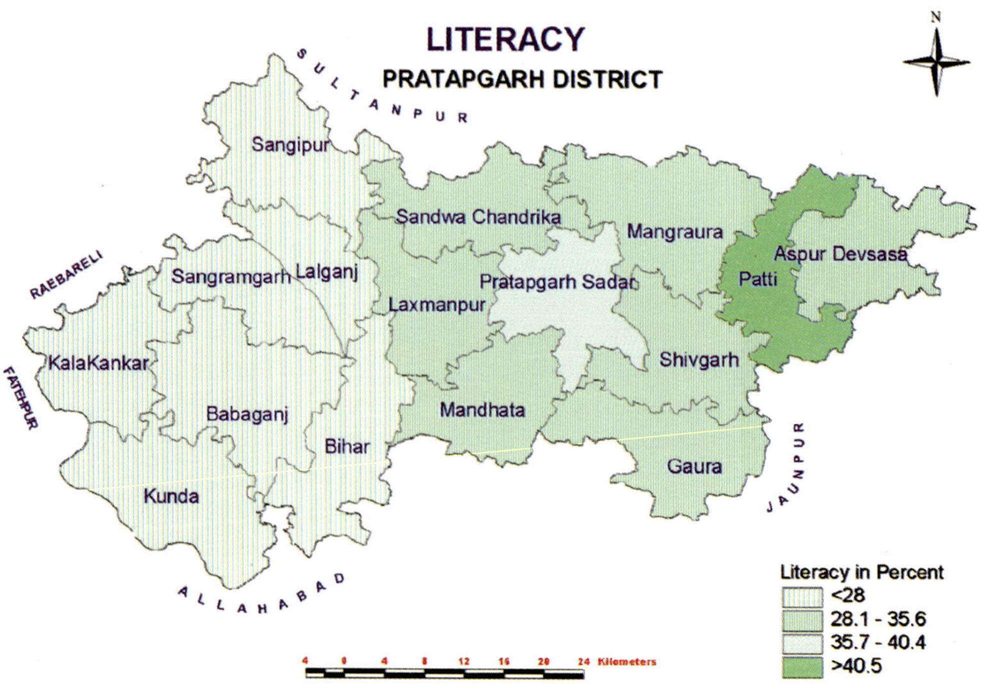

The primary educational pattern is recorded very high in Mangraura block. The highest number of primary educated persons are found in Atarsand village as seen in Table-2 while lowest primary educated persons are seen in Kansa Patti and Sarai Shaker villages of the Mangraura block of district Pratapgarh.

8.2 Junior Education :

It is observed from the available information that there is 117563 junior educated persons in Pratapgarh district out of which highest junior educated persons are found in Sangipur block while lowest Junior educated persons are seen in Sangramgarh block of district Pratapgarh.

There are 6475 junior educated persons in Mangraura block. The highest number of junior educated persons are found in Rampart and Kohndaur villages and lowest number of junior educated persons are observed in Lakhipur and Varaha villages of Mangraura block of Pratapgarh district.

Map-18

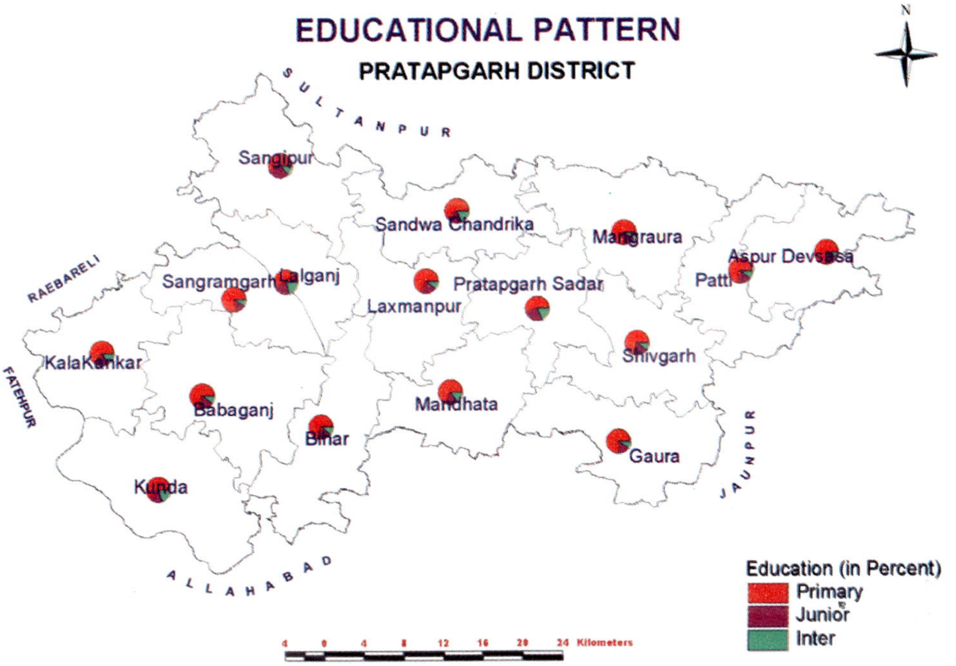

8.3 Intermediate Education :

There are 82848 inter mediate educated person in Pratapgarh district. It is observed that highest inter educated persons are seen in Kunda block while lowest inter educated persons are recorded in Sangarampur block of Pratapgarh district.

It is recorded that there are 3937 intermediate educated persons in Mangraura block of Pratapgarh district, out of which highest intermediate educated persons are observed in Ramapur and Kohndaur villages while lowest intermediate educated persons are found in Barahupur and Etawah villages of Mangraura block of Pratapgarh district.

8.4 Higher Education :

There are 5 degree colleges and 7 post graduate college in the district. It is recorded, as per available data from district statistical Hand Book of Pratapgarh district, that there are 10,332 higher educated persons in district Pratapgarh. Proportionately highest higher educated persons are seen in Pratapgarh Sadar Block, Kunda, Patti blocks and lowest higher educated persons are found as per Devsara and Mandhata blocks of Pratapgarh district.

It is recorded that there are about 2485 higher educated persons in Mangraura block. The highest higher educated persons are found in Rampur and Kohndaur villages while lowest higher educated persons are seen in Amuwahi, Varikala Chaumuri villages of Mangraura block of Pratapgarh district.

8.5 Technical Education :

There are 3 Industrial Training Institutes in Pratapgarh district and one polytechnic district is not having appropriate progress in the technical education due to which the proportionate distribution of technically educated persons are very in significant. As per the population density and requirement the number of technical educational institutions are very less. Administratively no importance has been given to promote the technical education in Pratapgarh district.

In Mangraura block there is no technical institution except few private typing and tailoring small level centers are functioning casually. The level of such technical training for the purpose of employment generation is meaningless. District Employment and Training officials have also established training centre in the block office of Mangraura block in which vocational training programmes are being organised.

In view of the above it may be concluded that Pratapgarh district is backward in technical education but some of interested youths used to obtain technical education out Pratapgarh district, which has caused poor growth in technical education.

9. CONCLUSION :

Human resources play an important role in the planning process and also in the implementation of various developmental programmes. Human resources mainly consists of socio-economic and infrastructural sectors of socio-economic and infrastructural sectors. An attempt has been made to analyse various indicators related to social sector responsible for the planning process and play an important role in the implementation of developmental programmes. The management of social sectors data is not properly geared to meet the information need of integrated development planning. There is traditional system of data collection which are not amenable for quick updation and holistic analysis and there is lack of information on quality of data.

Social indicators data at block level has been collected from the secondary source of information viz., District statistical Hand Book, of district Pratapgarh, while village level data has been collected through primary survey. It has been observed that data at village-block-district level are varying but there is no option left than to rely on such available data.

Since the main objective is to analyse the various social indicators with the view to planning process, therefore available data from various secondary sources of information have been analysed keeping the facts into consideration that these data are varying from one level to another, but the collected data through primary survey at village level is authentic because these data have been collected with the involvement of village level officials of Block Development Office of Mangraura block, Revenue officials, Village Pradhan and other peoples representatives and the collected data have been duly verified by Block Development Officer, Mangraura block of district Pratapgarh.

Geographical area of Pratapgarh district is 3717 sq. km. Administratively district Pratapgarh comprises of 5 tehsils, 17 blocks, 1105 village panchayats. Previously there were only four tehsils Raniganj was made new tehsil and Baba Bhelkhar nath Dham was made new block, few years collected for only 16 blocks as per availability of data and rural developmental programmes and need based plan have been developed for 17 blocks including new Belkharnath Dham block of Pratapgarh district. There are 62 village Panchayats in Mangraura block. Mangraura block has been taken for village level analysis of village development planning.

Proportionate distribution of houses and households are recorded in Pratapgarh district as well as in Mangraura block. Comparatively number of households are more in numbers while houses are less than households because some of the families are divided and have formed separate households but still residing in one house, which has led an increase in the number of households.

Population of the district is 27,31,174 including male and female population. It is clear from the collected information that Pratapgarh district is density populated than the neighbouring district. Scheduled caste population of the district is also significant. It is observed that the scheduled caste population is found more in the remote rural areas. Proportionately scheduled caste population distribution is seen very low in the urban areas including city and marketing centers.

Total workers of Pratapgarh district is 710754, which comprises 410199 number of farmers followed by 141739 number of farm labours. Plantation and Animal husbandry workers family and non-family workers construction workers, business workers, transportation and communication workers and other workers are very low in Pratapgarh district. In other words it may be concluded that farmers and farm labours are significantly distributed not only in Pratapgarh district but also in Mangraura block at village level because most of the population of Pratapgarh district and Mangraura block at villages level people are dependent on agriculture. Thus agriculture is the main occupation in Pratapgarh district. There agricultural activity is the main component of economic development of Pratapgarh district.

Educationally Pratapgarh district has not been developed because there are only 750950 educated persons in the district. As per the population distribution ratio number of Primary, Junior, Intermediate and Higher Educational institutions are very low, similarly the educated persons at different educational level are also very nominal, which is evident from the available data and depicted in the map.

Thus it is observed that the significant distribution of farmers and farm labours, as per the total population makes it clear that agriculture is the dominant occupation in Pratapgarh district and in Mangraura block. Educationally Pratapgarh district is not properly developed. The available data related to social indicators provide an indication that agriculture is the main economic activity which is labour intensive and low productive because of less application of high yielding variety of seeds, fertilizers, highly developed agricultural implements, insecticides-pesticides. Lack of awareness and knowledge for increasing productivity. Poor educational pattern has led to the social backwardness because the district has been ruled by kings, Talukedars, Zamiandars which evident from the historical-cultural-religious-social importance of Pratapgarh district.

In view of the above the social, population, workforce, education patterns etc. and other major social factors are responsible for socio-economic backwardness of the Pratapgarh district because historically Pratapgarh district has been ruled and only certain section of the society could avail an opportunity to develop themselves while poor section of the society i.e. scheduled caste, backward caste and minorities etc. were sufferers and working class and they were not given an opportunity develop them selves. Thus the downtrodden deprived section of the society was bound to work as working class but recently the reservation in the District, Block and village Panchayats have provided an opportunity to such socially backward people to involved them selves in the planning process and participate in the implementation of various developmental programmes. Therefore the process of planning and involvement of such socially backward peoples representatives in the implementation of developmental programmes will be a mile stone in the integrated development of villages of Mangraura block and various blocks of Pratapgarh district.

●●●

Table -1 : Natural Resources Data Management System (NRDMS)
Pratapgarh District
A - Social Information

Sl. No.	*Block*	*Houses*	*House-holds*	*Popu-lation*	*Schedule Caste*	*Farmer*	*Farm Labour*	*Plantation & Husbandary*	*Non-Family workers*
1	*2*	*3*	*4*	*5*	*6*	*7*	*8*	*9*	*11*
1	KalaKankar	18626	22800	128363	30384	22289	6754	132	544
2	Babaganj	23671	28190	159210	47509	24981	10704	137	579
3	Kunda	30030	36566	215486	52566	29632	12117	117	1015
4	Bihar	26677	32275	197000	58851	26233	13548	192	829
5	Sangipur	25060	28919	163781	35129	32607	7550	85	890
6	Lalganj	18788	21176	121952	28520	20738	6967	91	530
7	Laxmanpur	19117	22649	139327	28419	18991	7791	91	697
8	Sandwa Chandrika	20636	23659	142852	27048	21974	6328	47	321
9	Pratapgarh Sadar	21440	25735	169304	30749	17048	9252	259	965
10	Mandhata	24717	28672	187568	37389	26349	8566	106	705
11	Mangraura	24834	25619	109257	34631	27555	10199	185	1322
12	Patti	15993	15009	107911	22336	20191	4857	90	713
13	Aspur Devsasa	18646	22065	156760	34961	24210	6606	114	678
14	Shivgarh	21086	20490	134304	25482	24289	9250	115	827
15	Gaura	22188	22270	146529	28915	36546	7542	199	995
16	Sangramgarh	20055	22975	130314	37623	24786	7403	146	314
17	Bhelkharnath	20816	20106	136704	24201	21780	7305	158	853
	Total	427219	438936	2731174	601043	410199	141739	2254	12777

Table -1 : Contd.....

Sl. No.	Block	Construction Workers	Business Workers	Transportation& Communication	Other worker	Literacy	Primary	Junior	Inter
1	2	12	13	14	15	16	17	18	19
1	KalaKankar	114	1096	220	1491	26777	25714	6679	5856
2	Babaganj	78	1077	294	1988	34799	26389	6934	3846
3	Kunda	80	1283	366	2440	46764	27132	7209	8535
4	Bihar	123	1430	327	2192	43385	32921	7813	4769
5	Sangipur	57	920	180	1540	36358	22226	11204	4769
6	Lalganj	113	998	244	1379	28224	17753	6399	6527
7	Laxmanpur	105	1311	522	1754	37375	22896	6896	3667
8	Sandwa Chandrika	130	1090	344	2138	38603	23347	8055	6783
9	Pratapgarh Sadar	446	1835	1194	2548	54659	21269	8896	6929
10	Mandhata	385	1347	683	2774	49197	29264	5788	5932
11	Mangraura	346	1361	879	2438	50364	33445	6475	3937
12	Patti	104	1029	253	1402	120490	30451	7215	4237
13	Aspur Devsasa	96	1240	404	1716	41493	32548	6730	3631
14	Shivgarh	72	1630	695	2250	49749	26909	6701	4011
15	Gaura	137	1233	617	1755	44076	32374	6600	3750
16	Sangramgarh	57	747	124	1146	24966	25877	3831	2884
17	Bhelkharnath	68	814	317	1458	23781	24131	4138	2785
	Total	2553	20441	7661	41409	750950	454646	117563	82848

Table -2 : Natural Resources Data Management System (NRDMS)
Mangraura Block, Pratapgarh district
Social Indicators

Loc_ code	Village Name	Houses	House Hold	Popu- lation	Scheduled Caste	General Caste	Backward Caste	Others Castes	Farm- ers	Farm_ Lab	Plantation and Hus- bandary
1	2	3	4	5	6	7	8	9	10	11	12
1	Konhdour	557	681	4520	1439	1445	1636	37	122	97	17
2	Ramapur	535	693	4548	2208	310	1505	525	499	200	48
3	Dharouli Madapur	325	400	1573	273	150	900	250	225	130	36
4	Bhawapur	301	422	3109	446	1320	944	399	107	226	51
5	Shankarpur	260	300	2600	566	718	609	707	400	150	20
6	Madura Raniganj	231	316	2149	364	716	1069	0	87	116	37
7	Parasrampur	329	433	1751	389	1073	289	0	145	138	9
8	Lakhipur	140	282	1409	774	173	763	16	126	209	55
9	Atarsand	463	809	12674	1806	1941	6132	2753	681	265	11
10	Madaferpur	357	407	2136	276	117	1676	48	178	125	17
11	Chanduadih	301	358	2791	492	382	1614	297	187	168	21
12	Sakara	463	537	3340	1062	536	1742	0	286	237	56
13	Koni	786	814	3161	385	959	1817	0	126	287	10
14	Sarairajai	455	479	2473	1155	80	1238	0	96	134	23
15	Salhipur Kanjas	315	398	4066	776	1488	1802	0	131	88	40
16	Katari	476	652	1681	216	467	928	70	120	176	29
17	Malak	397	567	2737	755	430	1487	48	256	149	63
18	Padumpur	198	276	1890	687	153	950	100	122	196	51

Table -2 : Contd....

Loc_ code	*Village Name*	*Houses*	*House Hold*	*Popu- lation*	*Scheduled Caste*	*General Caste*	*Backward Caste*	*Others Castes*	*Farm- ers*	*Farm_ Lab*	*Plantation and Hus- bandary*
1	2	3	4	5	6	7	8	9	10	11	12
19	Gahrauli	243	326	2356	254	386	1690	26	290	197	19
20	Sahpur	490	617	3407	588	177	2702	0	273	300	26
21	Kandharpur	381	432	3082	273	273	2012	0	112	49	19
22	Chandouka	282	389	2781	431	716	1424	210	263	189	25
23	Parasanda	357	462	2742	743	1186	813	0	150	203	17
24	Choumuri	292	584	2927	982	1117	726	102	263	198	30
25	Varaha	1290	1370	2500	1980	150	700	120	1200	250	19
26	Barahupur	498	663	4184	1227	1248	1609	100	413	298	62
27	Varikala	431	513	3109	1413	778	989	9	326	182	35
28	Asthra	164	328	1605	367	257	869	85	156	181	16
29	Amuwahi	138	276	1376	362	330	610	74	113	89	24
30	Dharouli Muphrid	309	402	3119	271	725	1897	33	206	307	46
31	Sikri Kanupur	497	632	3612	1233	586	1641	152	289	300	13
32	Sheshpur Adharganj	216	370	2471	487	822	1062	100	116	152	39
33	Kanhai Madupur	623	751	6876	1257	2910	2709	0	326	413	103
34	Bojhi	172	340	1695	568	429	698	134	160	180	22
35	Bhousiya	489	536	3184	590	560	427	498	261	125	35
36	Mandah	173	332	1679	803	367	396	113	132	122	28
37	Varasaray	480	530	2489	617	754	1061	57	253	163	58
38	Gagehati	204	298	2162	240	676	1085	61	148	200	31
39	Sarouli	380	740	4013	615	632	1266	1500	190	250	300
40	Suryagarh Jagannath	256	463	3147	698	1510	939	0	243	156	60
41	Aourangabad	321	630	3084	693	745	1121	525	230	193	53
42	Naraharpur	469	513	5846	1052	2429	1413	52	361	261	39.
43	Pure Manikanth	503	587	2124	797	786	487	54	180	366	24
44	Poorabpatti	267	351	2696	553	363	1780	0	199	152	13
45	Shivpur Khurd	135	167	1350	366	704	180	100	250	180	30
46	Saray Shankar	216	333	2172	777	435	856	104	176	269	33
47	Hathasara	198	246	2581	672	445	1364	100	261	306	13
48	Louli Pukhtakham	291	340	2908	572	320	1507	509	850	120	25
49	Darchut	263	376	2630	635	460	1437	106	163	217	52
50	Narayanpur	242	368	2432	196	1026	1210	0	268	100	39
51	Sarasi Kham	498	723	3536	1038	159	1181	137	323	196	50
52	Mangroura	282	326	2970	647	270	2165	65	226	173	28
53	Saray Jamuari	319	486	3600	632	792	2014	162	203	168	71
54	Utaras	312	401	3521	1231	242	1938	83	197	230	36
55	Sarasidih	231	364	2913	718	466	1729	0	261	198	19
56	Etawah	214	309	2197	595	621	876	105	192	135	36
57	Bhadouna	356	529	3094	566	1106	1422	0	303	166	14
58	Bhivani	304	409	2658	613	583	1454	122	213	157	22
59	Bhaidapur	269	297	2129	423	203	1506	97	195	103	26
60	Kansa Patti	146	267	1537	117	262	1306	47	98	56	31
61	Raigarh	198	396	1832	489	517	703	96	198	102	40
62	Dehari Digar	186	272	1896	465	750	497	.102	189	86	19

Table -2 : Contd....

Loc_ code	*Vill_ Name*	*Farm workers*	*Non-farm workers*	*Construction workers*	*Business workers*	*Transportaton workers*	*Other workers*	*Lite-rates*	*Pri-mary*
1	*2*	*13*	*14*	*15*	*16*	*17*	*18*	*19*	*20*
1	Konhdour	17	44	11	123	7	46	1540	1560
2	Ramapur	135	50	8	125	15	165	1700	900
3	Dharouli Madapur	100	157	11	35	10	122	943	790
4	Bhawapur	13	22	4	13	4	50	60	869
5	Shankarpur	123	152	6	30	2	66	900	640
6	Madura Raniganj	17	37	1	9	3	57	735	490
7	Parasrampur	9	20	4	13	7	29	517	466
8	Lakhipur	3	18	2	11	2	53	576	2900
9	Atarsand	24	29	12	9	6	32	3043	793
10	Madaferpur	11	9	6	50	2	37	833	811
11	Chanduadih	6	17	11	23	1	14	956	809
12	Sakara	10	14	5	17	0	3	940	886
13	Koni	12	31	4	9	0	35	948	590
14	Sarairajai	14	17	3	8	2	54	635	1065
15	Salhipur Kanjas	9	18	1	7	3	57	1126	569
16	Katari	2	13	8	9	2	36	673	665
17	Malak	8	11	7	7	6	31	767	580
18	Padumpur	6	10	5	19	1	53	639	678
19	Gahrauli	13	22	10	6	0	26	797	875
20	Sahpur	3	15	5	18	4	29	960	856
21	Kandharpur	7	21	9	119	7	37	924	580
22	Chandouka	9	17	4	13	0	57	612	780
23	Parasanda	19	24	7	19	0	49	832	790
24	Choumuri	13	22	2	6	1	34	823	600
25	Varaha	50	103	13	15	18	4	700	1130
26	Barahupur	3	8	7	7	0	17	1290	992
27	Varikala	2	6	3	33	0	35	1043	529
28	Asthra	11	17	7	12	1	57	627	496
29	Amuwahi	8	13	1	6	0	25	537	561
30	Dharouli Muphrid	4	19	8	19	0	57	627	1090
31	Sikri Kanupur	6	21	6	4	0	13	1155	692
32	Sheshpur Adharganj	13	24	2	7	1	57	756	2200
33	Kanhai Madupur	18	19	7	8	0	17	2270	560
34	Bojhi	11	20	9	21	1	27	679	1026
35	Bhousiya	7	33	4	8	2	51	1073	523
36	Mandah	4	10	2	3	0	54	655	706
37	Varasaray	3	7	9	14	0	29	796	714
38	Gagehati	9	21	1	19	1	61	863	870
39	Sarouli	2	12	11	35	4	218	960	1047
40	Suryagarh Jagannath	14	31	4	14	0	31	1057	955
41	Aourangabad	6	14	3	31	0	39	1033	2266
42	Naraharpur	5	13	7	9	3	15	2337	578
43	Pure Manikanth	8	36	6	30	0	3	637	492
44	Poorabpatti	13	23	5	11	0	43	585	470
45	Shivpur Khurd	19	7	12	13	7	27	535	395
46	Saray Shankar	3	11	3	4	0	47	487	710
47	Hathasara	4	36	1	13	0	29	780	919
48	Louli Pukhtakham	17	68	9	18	6	12	950	705

Table -2 : Contd....

Loc_ code	*Vill_ Name*	*Farm workers*	*Non-farm workers*	*Construction workers*	*Business workers*	*Transportaton workers*	*Other workers*	*Lite-rates*	*Pri-mary*
1	*2*	*13*	*14*	*15*	*16*	*17*	*18*	*19*	*20*
49	Darchut	13	34	2	21	1	41	789	795
50	Narayanpur	10	28	6	13	1	37	873	1000
51	Sarasi Kham	2	13	3	11	0	27	1040	869
52	Mangroura	13	26	8	125	1	31	987	869
53	Saray Jamuari	9	19	7	7	0	51	890	785
54	Utaras	8	21	1	18	0	17	860	803
55	Sarasidih	11	32	2	4	0	26	963	910
56	Etawah	7	24	1	9	3	42	570	487
57	Bhadouna	13	40	7	3	0	39	905	830
58	Bhivani	6	16	6	14	1	44	837	740
59	Bhaidapur	3	9	1	19	2	38	851	763
60	Kansa Patti	31	14	9	16	0	43	429	346
61	Raigarh	15	25	7	10	0	37	604	550
62	Dehari Digar	9	30	3	24	1	49	639	580

CHAPTER - IV

ECONOMIC RESOURCES

1. INTRODUCTION :

Information Management of Economic sector has been the major programme of the Natural Resources Data Management System (NRDMS). Various indicators of economic sector needs to be integrated for the use of remotely based rural areas. The collection and collation of economic indicators data based in the frame work of spatial information system for optimal management is required for sustainable development. Proper linkage of economic data base within a framework of suitable information system to enable customized retrieval and analysis for specific needs to be managed at grass root level. Economic data base management system is to be visualized in a network based nodes covering village –block and district. Technological innovations is to be popularised to promote existing abilities to do more things to do things better and faster. Never the less not every innovation that looks like productivity – enhancing tool eventually promote that role. Therefore, if not carefully introduced, it may run counter to natural modes of expectations, thereby leading to rejection of the technology. Economic sectors based planning programmes at village level requires routine basis updated data base at village, block and district level so that as per economic growth process of planning can be formulated. The greatest constraint in large-scale economic data capture is the limitation of currently available technologies regarding data collection and updation from grass root level / village level to block level and district level. It requires technology development and training initiatives for development of appropriate indices of economic sector data base. It also requires employment of hyper spectral economic data in applications relating to agriculture, irrigation, land use, land ownership, agricultural implements and other related areas.

It has been realized that economic development and commendable advances made by the nation in diverse field would in reality be incomplete, if they fail to translate into better and dignified life for the majority of peopole who live in rural remote villages. Economic development should be participatory, tapping the local talent and available socio-economic resources in order to be sustainable. Planning process for economic development has been implemented aimed at sustainable development of village people with a focus on enhancing the livelihoods of weaker and vulnerable sections of the society. It has been the commitment of Government to accord foremost priority to integrated rural development for which a number of steps have been initiated to formulate planning programmes at grass root level i.e. Village Panchayat- Block Panchayat- District Panchayat level and make the implementation of planned ongoing programmes and schemes more effective and accelerated through peoples participation and their continued involvement in the implementation of various development programmes, hence ensuring sustainable development of the village, block and district.

In view of the above an attempt has been made to analyse the collected economic sector data base including cultivation, land ownership, source of irrigation, area under agricultural production and commercial crops, agricultural implements, fertilizer application and bio-energy, and animal wealth at village level in Mangraura Block and Block level in district Pratapgarh. It is assumed that above mentioned indicators related to economic sector may play an important role in the overall development of the area, therefore the collected and collated data base related to economic indicators are analysed because these are one of the available resources which plays an important role in the planning process and henceforth in the development of planning and its successful implementation for sustainable development. Thus the various indicators of economic data base has been analysed at village level, in Mangraura Block and Block level in Pratapgarh District, because economic sector data base is one of the major indicator of the natural and human resource data setup.

2. CULTIVATION :

Cultivation is the main occupation of the people in the District. In Pratapgarh district nearly 61% of the total area is under cultivation followed by 5% forest; 6% wastelands and 17% fallow land and 11% other uses of land. It is also observed that approximately 76% of the population of the district Pratapgarh is dependent on agricultural activity which includes farmers and farm labours. District Pratapgarh is dominated by agricultural activity. Thus it can be said that the agriculture is the major economic activity in District Pratapgarh. There are 74958 ha area under cultivation in Pratapgarh district (Table-3). Highest cultivated area is found in Sangipur block, while lowest cultivated area is observed in Pratapgarh Sadar block of district Pratapgarh.

It is recorded that there is 5318 ha cultivated land in Mangraura block proportionately highest cultivated land is observed in Atarsand village, while lowest cultivated land is found in Shivpur khurd village of Mangraura Block.

It has been observed that in some villages new sown area is less but gross sown area is more due to multicropping which has caused on increase in net irrigated area also. In some villages net cultivated area is more and there is low gross cultivated area. Therefore variations in net cultivated area and irrigated area is due to multi-cropping pattern has caused an increase in gross irrigated area as per the fertility status of the land.

3. LAND OWNERSHIP :

Land ownership pattern in Pratapgarh District is different than other neighbouring districts due to kingship, Zamindari and Talukedari traditions. Large number of farmers are owner of less than 2 ha of land, while very nominal land owners are holding highest cultivated area in the Pratapgarh District. It is observed from Table 4 that 96251 number of land holders are owning 68624 ha land between 0.5 to 1.0 ha land. The highest 8080 number of land owners are holding 5346 ha land between 0.5 to 1.0 ha land in Sangipur block owners are holding 2793 ha land in Pratapgarh Sadar Block of the District.

It is recorded that 50075 number of land holders are owning 66657 ha land between 1.0 to 2.0 ha land in Pratapgarh district. The highest 4205 number of land owners between 1.0 to 2.0 ha land area owning only 5595 ha land in Pratapgarh District. Lowest 2199 number of land owners are owning 2929 ha land in Pratapgarh Sadar Block of the district.

Land owners between 2.0 to 4.0 ha land are found very high in Sangipur block in which 1519 land owners are holding 4013 ha of land, while 18089 number of land owners are owning 47891 ha of land in Pratapgarh district between 2.0 to 4.0 ha of land. The lowest 795 number of land holders are owning 2100 ha of land between 2.0 to 4.0 ha of land in Pratapgarh Sadar Block of the District.

Land ownership pattern between 4.0 to 10.0 ha of land in Pratapgarh District as evident from Table-2 makes it clear that 2999 number of land owners are owning 15335 ha of land. It is observed that highest 252 number of land owners are owning 1314 ha of land in Sangipur block while lowest 132 number of land owners are owning 703 ha of land between 4.0 to 10.0 ha of land in Pratapgarh Sadar block of the district.

It is evident from the table-3 that 132 number of land owners are holding 1754 ha of land above 10.0 ha of land owners are highest in Sangipur block where 11 land owners are holding 146 ha of land. It is found that lowest 6 number of land holders are owning 80 ha of land above 10.0 ha of land in Laxmanpur block of the district Pratapgarh.

Land ownership pattern in Mangraura block makes it clear that the land concentration in the block is high because very few number of land holders are owning proportionately very high land area, while lowest area is owned by highest number of land owners in the block. It is recorded that 6826 number of land owners are owning 9513 ha of land between 0.5 to 1.0 ha of land, while 3554 number of land holders are owning 4729 ha of land between 1.0 to 2.0 ha of land in Mangraura block. The land ownership between 2.0 to 4.0 ha of land provides that 1283 number of land holders are holding 3390 ha of land in Mangraura block. It is observed that 213 number of land owners are owning 1134 ha of land between 4.0 to 10.0 ha of land in Mangraura block. It has been observed that 10 number of land holders are holding 133 ha of land above than 10.0 ha of land in Mangraura block of the district Pratapgarh.

It is evident from map 19 that above 10.0 ha number and owned land is recorded very high in Sangipur block and lowest number is found in Laxmanpur block, while 4.0 to 10.0 ha of land owners and land area is recorded very high in Sangipur block and lowest in Pratapgarh Sadar block of the district. The highest number of land owners and land holding is found in Sangipur block and lowest land owners and land holding is found in Pratapgarh Sadar block between 2.0 to 4.0 ha of land in Pratapgarh district Land ownership between 1.0 to 2.0 ha land is recorded very high in Sangipur block and lowest in Pratapgarh Sadar block of the district. Similarly land ownership between 0.5 to 1.0 ha of land is seen very high in Sangipur block and lowest number of land owners and land holding is found in Pratapgarh Sadar block of the district Pratapgarh.

Land concentration in Pratapgarh district is high because very few land holders are owning highest land area, while highest number of land owners are owning very less land. Land concentration is very high in Sangipur block because most of the geographical area of the block is having undulated ravine land and the land fertility is also very poor due to which few land owners are owning maximum land but the less fertile cultivated land is owned by maximum number of land owners in Sangipur block of the District Pratapgarh.

Map-19

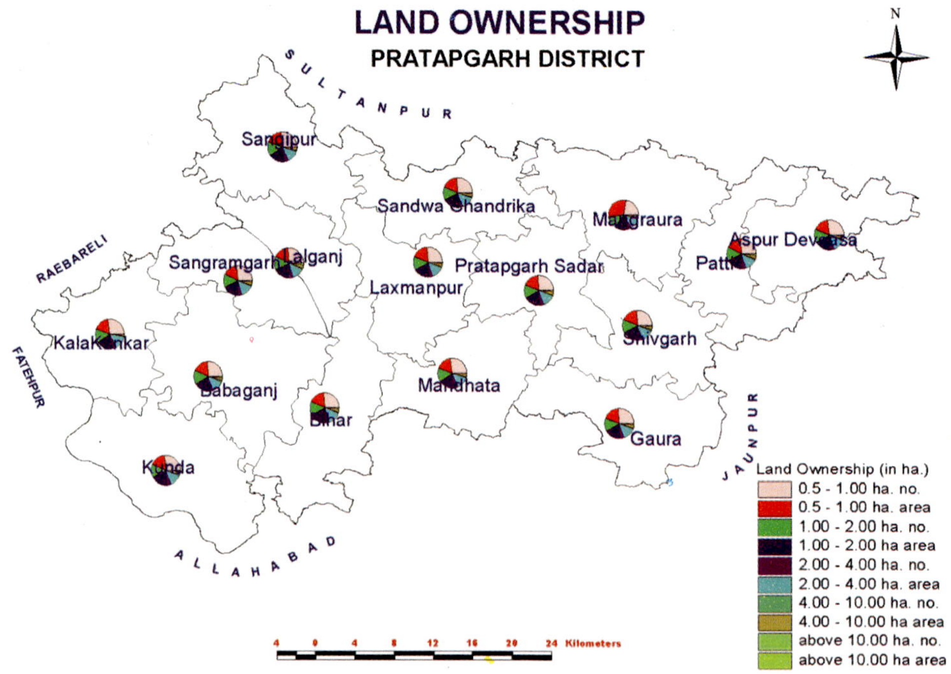

Pratapgarh Sadar block is having low number of land holders who are owning low land because the Pratapgarh city is an urban centre, which has cause high inflation rate of land and the land is divided into different parts very few land owners are owning between 4.0 to 10.0 ha and above 10.0 ha of land due to Zamindari/ Talukedari and kingship system but some of the land owners hold the land due to low fertility status of the soil around the Sai River where the topography of the land is undulated and ravines.

Thus it may be concluded that the historical importance of kingship, Talukedari and Zamindari system has been one of the factors for maximum ownership of land and ravines, saline and low fertility of the land is also owned by very few land holders, but the fertile cultivated land is subdivided within the family members and households which has been one of the reason for maximum number of land holders to own less area of land i.e. between 0.5 to 1.0 ha and 1.0 to 2.0 ha of land is owned by maximum number of land holders in most of the villages, of Mangraura block of the Pratapgarh district.

4. IRRIGATION :

Gross irrigated area of Pratapgarh district is 175825 ha out of which highest irrigated area is found in Mangraura block (Table-3) and low irrigated area is seen in Pratapgarh Sadar block of the district. About 60% of the net cropped area is irrigated. The main source of irrigation are Tubewells and canals.

It is observed that proportionately highest irrigated land is available in Mangraura block. At village level total irrigated area is found very high in Barahapur village (Table –4) and very low total irrigated area is seen in Shankarpur village of the

Mangraura block. Details of the irrigated area through different sources of irrigation are analysed at block level in Pratapgarh district and at village level in Mangraura block of the district. Arable irrigated land is depicted in the map-20 in which general landuse pattern of Pratapgarh district is earmarked.

Map-20

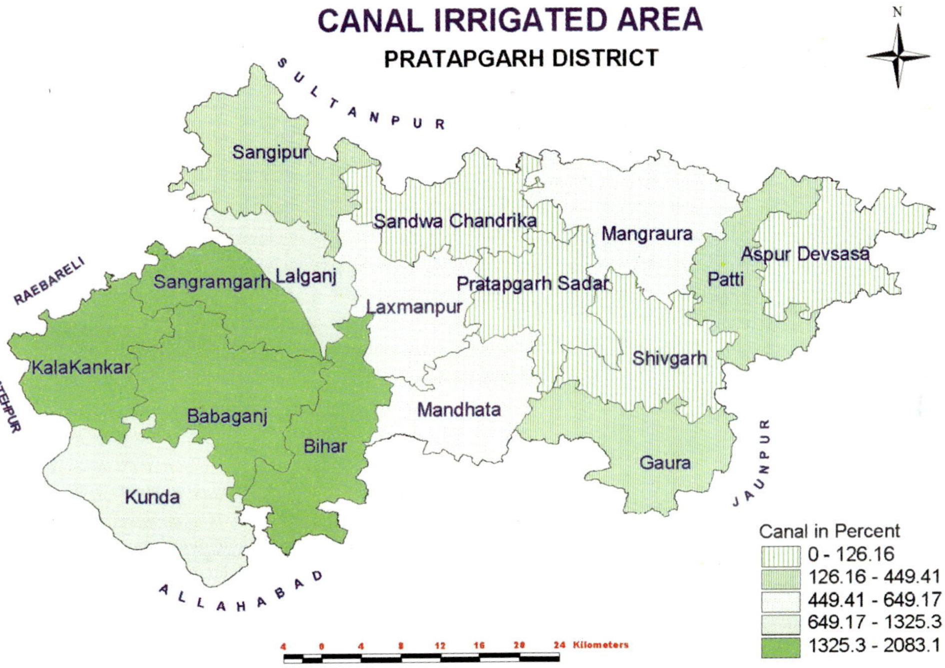

4.1 Canal Irrigation :

Canal irrigated area is 73180 ha in Pratapgarh district (Table-3) Proportionately highest canal irrigated area is observed in Bihar, Babarganj, Kalakankar and Sangramgarh blocks (map-20) while lowest canal irrigated is observed in Sondwa Chandrika block followed by Pratapgarh Sadar, Shivgarh, Aspur Devsara blocks of the Pratapgarh district.

There is 2860 ha canal irrigated area in Mangraura block out of which highest canal irrigated area is observed in Atarsand villages and lowest canal irrigated area is seen in Narayanpur, Baidupur, Madura, Raniganj villages have no canal irrigated area in Mangraura block of the Pratapgarh district.

4.2 Tube-well (Government)

Government tube wells irrigated area in Pratapgarh district is 294 ha out of which 62 ha government tubewells irrigated area is found in Sondwa Chandri block followed by Mangraura, Lalganj and Sangramgarh blocks. Most of the blocks like Babaganj, Kunda, Bihar, Sangipur, Laxmanpur, Aspur Devsara and Shivgarh blocks have no Government Tubewells irrigated area in Pratapgarh district.

Canal irrigated area in Mangraua Block is only 52 ha out of which Sarai Rajai, Mandah, Varikala, Narayanpur and Bhaidapur villages are having significant canal irrigated area followed by Sarasidih, Louli Pukhtakham, Shivpur khurd, Sarouli, Asthara, Shankarpur, Rampur and Dharauli Madapur villages which rest of the villages of Mangraura block has no canal irrigated area.

4.3 Tube-wells (Private) :

Irrigated area by the private tube-well is very significant and has an important role in the agricultural production. Total private tubewell irrigated area is Pratapgarh district is 102166 ha. Thus it is evident that approximately 63% irrigated area of the Pratapgarh district is shared by the private tubewell irrigation. Highest private tubewells irrigated area is seen in Mangraura block followed by Patti, Aspur, Devsara and Sangipur blocks while very low tube well irrigated area is found in Kalakankar block followed by Balaganj and Kunda blocks.

It has been recorded that Mangraura block is having 12122 ha of Private tube well irrigated area out of which highest private tubewells irrigated area is observed in Garauli, Parsanda, Sheshpur, Barahupur and Darchut villages as evident from Map-21 and lowest private tubewell irrigated area is found in Chandauka, Malak, Poorab patti, Hathsara, Rampur, Louli Pukhtankhan, Shivpurkhurd, Puremanikanth, Aurangabad, Shankarpur, Narharpur Saraigarh, Kanhai Madhupur, Mandah, Bojhi, Sarai Rajai, Madafespur, Sarai Jamui Sarasikham, Bhadauna, Asthara, Bhivani Chaumuri and Bhaidapur villages of the Mangraura Block.

Map-21

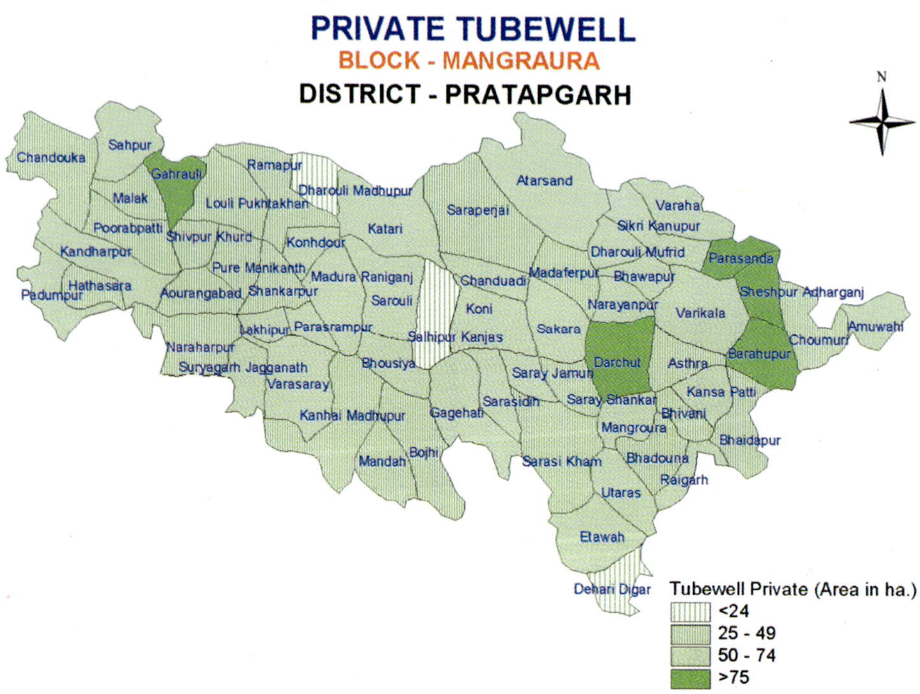

Other main source of irrigation in Pratapgarh district are well and ponds but the irrigated area under well and ponds are very insignificant. Total well irrigated area in Pratapgarh district is 16 ha while pond irrigated area is 169 ha in Pratapgarh district. Similarly irrigation through well and pond is very insignificant. Thus main source of irrigation in Pratapgarh district is private tube-well and canal while well, pond and government tube-well irrigated area is very insignificant.

5. AGRICULTURE :

Agriculture of the district Pratapgarh is characterised by mixed cropping. Agriculture is the backbone of economic activity of Pratapgarh District. Most of the population of the district is dependent on agriculture. Food grain production is the major agricultural activity in Pratapgarh District. While commercial crops has very in significant share in the agricultural production. The detailed description of food grain crops and commercial crops are analysed at block level in Pratapgarh district and also at village level in Mangraura block of the district Pratapgarh. Cropping pattern of the district is shown in the Map-22.

Map-22

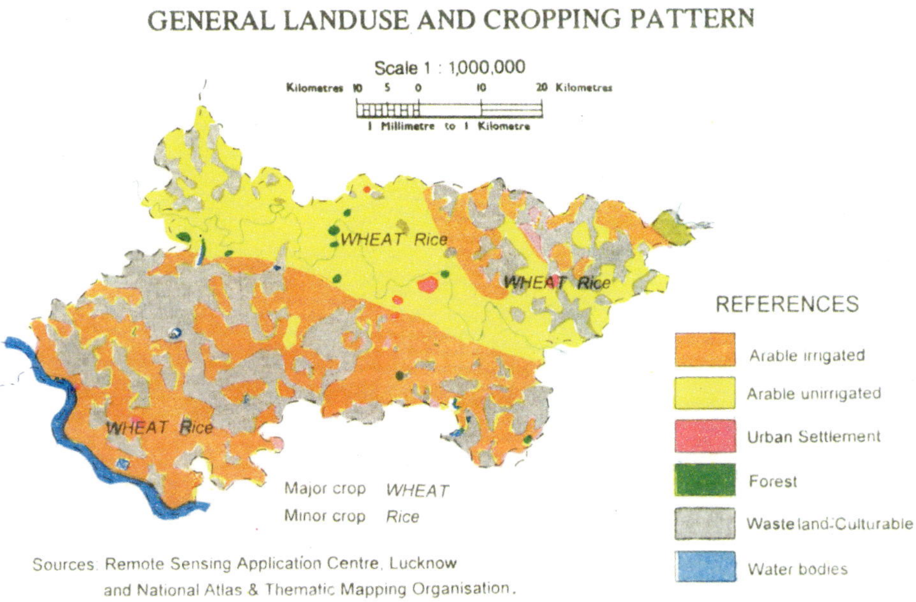

Source : National Atlas & Thematic Mapping Organisation, Dept. of Science & Technology

5.1 Wheat :

Wheat is the most important crop and wheat crop is cultivated in 40% of the cropped area in district Pratapgarh. Wheat is the main agricultural crop in Pratapgarh district. Total area under wheat cultivation is 142568 ha in Pratapgarh district. Highest area under wheat cultivation is recorded in Mangraura, Babaganj and Bihar blocks (Map-23) while lowest area under wheat cultivation is seen in Pratapgarh Sadar block of Pratapgarh district.

Mangraura block has 11015 ha of land under wheat cultivation out of which highest area under wheat cultivation is found in Shivpur Khurd village (Map-24) and lowest area under wheat cultivation is observed in Lakhipur, Asthra villages followed by other villages as shown in the Map-24. Thus wheat is main food grain crop of Mangraura block of Pratapgarh district.

Map-23

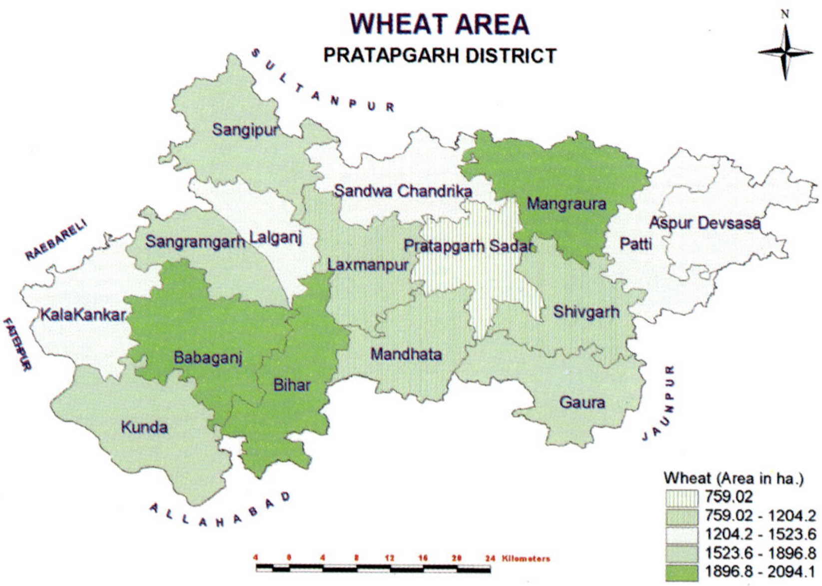

Map-24

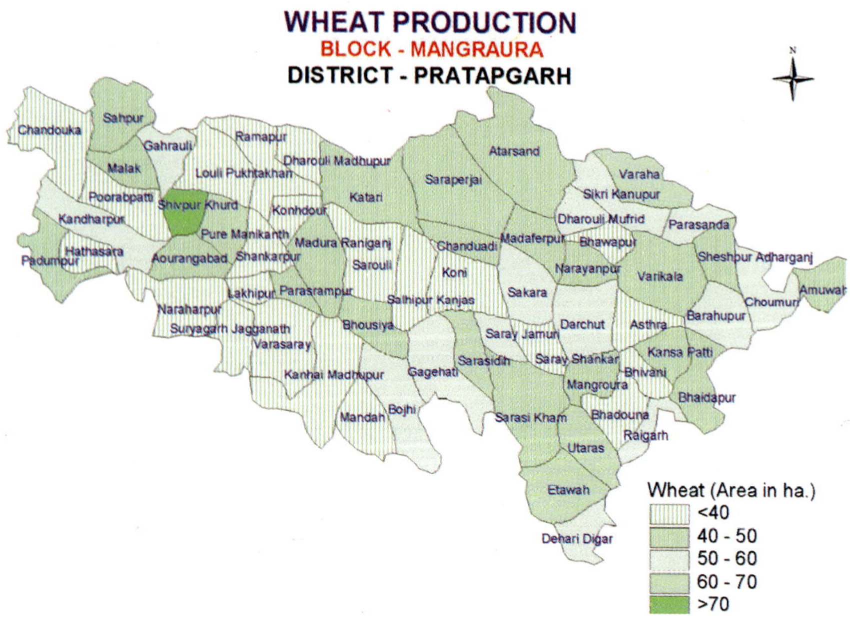

5.2 Rice :

Rice is cultivated in 34% area of total cropped land in Pratapgarh district. Rice is the second major food grain crop of the Pratapgarh district. There is 111812 ha of land under rice cultivation out of which highest rice cultivate area is seen in Sangaramgarh, Babaganj and Bihar blocks (Map-25) while lowest area under rice cultivation is observed in Pratapgarh Sadar, Laxmanpur and Shivgarh block of Pratapgarh district.

Map-25

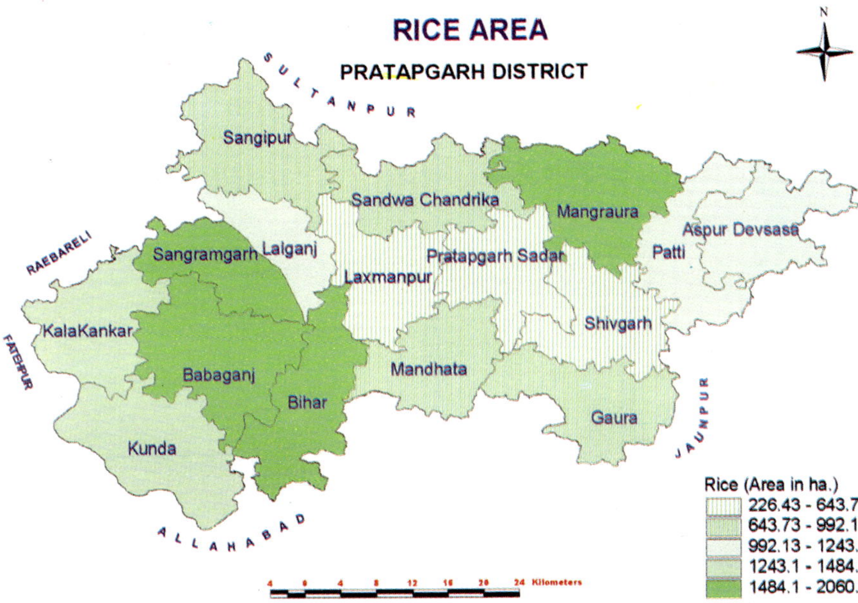

Area under rice cultivation in Mangraura Block is 10125 ha. The highest area under rice cultivation is found in Atarsand village and lowest area under rice cultivation is observed in Lakhipur village followed by Madura Raniganj, Asthara, Sarai Shankar and Raigarh villages of Mangraura block.

5.3 Barley :

Barley is cropped in 5% of the total cropped land in district Pratapgarh. Area under Barley cultivation is 2837 ha. Proportionately highest area under Barley cultivation is found in Kunda block and lowest area under Barley cultivation is seen Sangramgarh block of the district Pratapgarh.

Mangraura block is having 194 ha of land under Barley cultivation out of which highest area under Barley cultivation is found in Varaha Seraglio Lauli Pukhtakhan Varaha, Dharauli, Madupur & Shivpur Khurd villages and lowest area under Barley cultivation is seen in Baidapur, Etawah, Sarasidih, Sarai Jamauri, Sarasi kham, Sarai Shankar, Pure manikanth, Suryagarh Jagannath, Mandah Bhousiya, Kanhai Madhupur, Sikri Kanhupur, Dharauli Muplhrid, Barahupur, Bhawapur, Parastampur,, Sarai rajai, Shalhipur Kanjas, Katari, Malak, Padumpur and Kandharpur villages of the Mangraura block.

5.4 Millet :

There are 6023 ha area under Millet cultivation out of which highest area under millet cultivation is found in Sangipur block and lowest area under millet cultivation is seen in Kalakankar and Babaganj block of the Pratapgarh district.

Area under millet cultivation in Mangraura block is 246 ha out of which highest area under millet cultivation is found in Atarsand village followed by Bhawapur, Malak, Gahrauli, Sarauli villages of the Mangraura block while most of the villages has insignificant area under millet cultivation.

5.5 Maize :

Pratapgarh district is having 2121 ha of land under maize cultivation of which highest area under maize cultivation is found in Aspur Devsara block while Babaganj and Bihar block has no area under maize cultivation. Thus area under maize cultivation is very insignificant in Pratapgarh district.

There is 214 ha land under maize cultivation in Mangraura block. Highest area under maize cultivation is seen in Sarouli village while lowest insignificant under maize cultivation is recorded in most of the villages of the Mangraura block of the Pratapgarh district.

5.6 Gram :

Area under Gram crop is 7335 ha in Pratapgarh district. Highest area under gram crop cultivation is found in Sandwa chandrika block and lowest area under gram crop is seen in Sangramgarh block.

There is 825 ha of land under gram crop in Mangraura block out of which highest area under gram cultivation is found in Rampur, Dharauli Madapur, Varaha, Sarouli, Louli Pukhta khan and Shivpur Khurd villages while insignificant area under gram cultivation is seen Chandaudih, Sakara, Sarai rajai village of Mangraura block of the Pratapgarh district. Area under gram cultivation is very low due to low lying area and waterlogging in Mangraura block.

5.7 Pea :

Pea is one of the secondary crop in Pratapgarh district and area under pea crop is 4878 ha in the district. Proportionately highest area under pea cultivation is found in Sangipur block while lowest area under pea crop is seen in Kalakankar block of the district.

Area under pea cultivation is 410 ha in Mangraura block out of which proportionately highest area under pea crop is found in Dharauli, Madupur, Rampur, Varaha, Sarauli and Louli Pukhtakhan villages of Mangraura block while most of the villages are having very insignificant area under pea cultivation in Mangraura block of the Pratapgarh district.

5.8 Pigion Pea :

Pigeon pea is one of the important pulse crop in Pratapgarh district. There is 12101 ha area under pigeion pea crop in Pratapgarh district. Pigeon pea crop area is found very high in Sandwa Chandrik block followed by Sangipur, Shivgarh, Sadar blocks of Pratapgarh district while lowest area under pigeon pea crop is observed in Sangramgarh, Babaganj block of the district.

Area under pigeon pea crop is 696 ha in Mangraura block. Proportionately high pigeon pea crop area is found in Rampur, Dharauli Madapur, Bhousiya, Narharpur, Shivpur Khurd, Lauli Pukhtakhan villages of the block while most of the villages are having insignificant are under pigeon pea crop cultivation.

5.9 Mustard :

Mustard is one of the important oilseed crop under commercial crop in Pratapgarh district. Total area under mustard crop is 1453 ha in Pratapgarh district out of which proportionately highest area under mustard crop is seen in Sandwa chandrika block followed by Mangraura and Aspur Devsara blocks of the district, while lowest area under mustard crop cultivation is recorded in Kalakankar block of the Pratapgarh district.

Area under mustard oilseed crop is 157 ha in Mangraura block. Proportionately highest area under mustard crop cultivation is found in Dharauli Madapur, Varaha, Sarauli, Lauli Pukhtakhan villages of Mangraura block while maximum villages area having very insignificant area under mustard oil seed crop in Mangraura block of district Pratapgarh.

5.10 Sugarcane :

Area under sugarcane is 2108 ha in Pratapgarh district. It is observed from the map-26 that highest area under sugarcane cultivation is seen in Aspur Devsara block and lowest area under sugarcane cultivation is observed in Pratapgarh Sadar block of the district.

Sugarcane cultivated area is 357 ha in Mangraura block out of which highest area under sugarcane cultivation Varaha, Sarauli, Narayanpur, Pursenda, Dardhut Mangraura village while lowest area under sugarcane cultivation is observed in Mandah, Barhupur, Bhawapur, Lakhipur, Chanduadih, Sarai rajai, Malak and Sahpur villages of the Mangraura block. Sugarcane cultivation in block and district Pratapgarh is being cultivated as per individual requirement of byproducts of sugarcane.

5.11 Potato :

Potato is one of the important crop being cultivated as commercial crop in Pratapgarh district. Total area under potato cultivation is 6731 ha out of which highest area under potato cultivation is found in Gauranand, Lalganj block while lowest area under potato cultivation is observed in Laxmanpur, Kalakankar and Patti blocks of the district Pratapgarh.

There is 511 ha of land under potato crop cultivation in Mangraura block. Highest area under potato crop cultivation is found Berahupur, Dharauli Madapur Ramapur, Gahrauli and Sahpur villages while lowest area under potato cultivation is seen in Baidapur and Sarai rajai villages of the Mangraura block.

Map-26

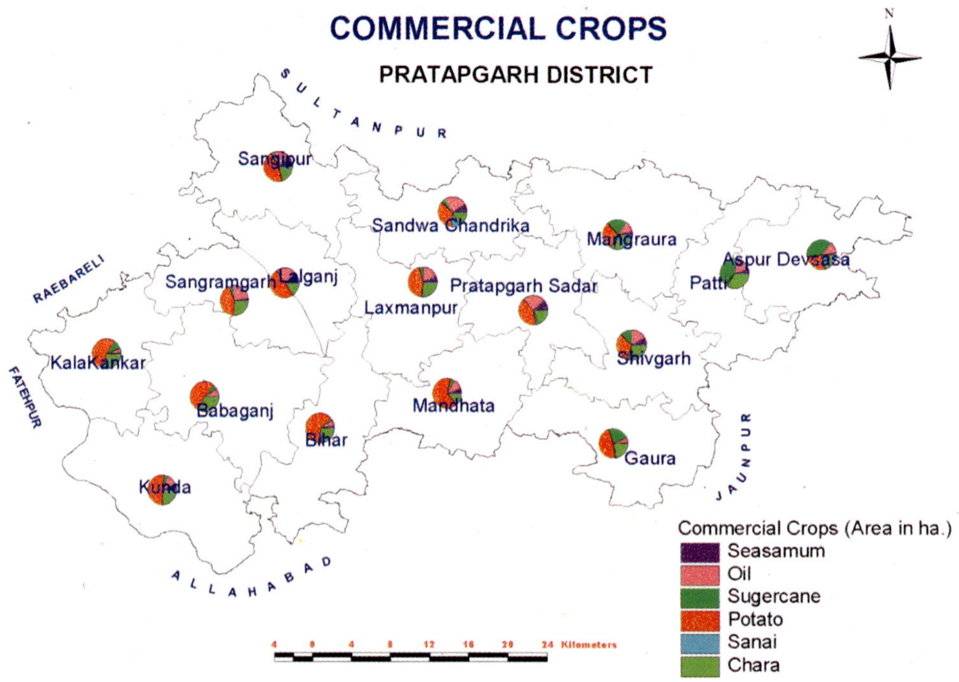

5.12 Sanai :

Sanai is being cultivated as green manuring to increase the fertility status of the soil and the bye product of Sanai is being used for making rope and other uses. There is Sanai Research Institute, at Pratapgarh established by Indian Council of Agricultural Research (ICAR), Government of India, New Delhi. Total area under Sanai cultivation is 249 ha in Pratapgarh district. The details of area under various commercial crops cultivation is depicted in the Map-26. It is recorded that highest area under sanai cultivation is available in Sandwa Chandrika block while Babaganj, Kunda and Sangramgarh blocks are having insignificant area under sanai cultivation in the Pratapgarh district.

There is 51 ha of land under Sanai crop cultivation. Proportionately highest area under sanai cultivation is found in Kandharpur and Sahpur villages of the block while approximately one ha of land under Sanai crop is recorded in the maximum villages of the Mangraura block of the Pratapgarh district. Sanai crop cultivation is being done for individual rope, requirement for household use green manicuring and commercial utility of rope. Thus it has commercial importance in the agricultural productivity for inversing the income of the deprived multitudes. 5.13 Chara :

Chara is an important cattle feed in the Pratapgarh district. Total area under chara is 3851 ha of land out of which highest area under chara cultivation is recorded in the

Mangraura block and lowest area under chara cultivation is recorded in Kalakankar block of the Pratapgarh district which is depicted in the Map-26.

It is observed that area under chara cultivation is 485 ha in Mangraura block. Highest area under chara cultivation is observed in Rampur and Varaha villages of Mangraura block and Lowest area under chara cultivation is found in Madura, Raniganj block of Mangraura block. The chara cultivation is being carried by the farmers for their individual cattle needs. Various grasses and green cattle feed is being sown to meet the increasing demand of cattle feed. Only few farmers neighbouring the city are utilizing the green cattle feed for sale purposes to meet the growing demand of urban cattle owners.

6. AGRICULTURE IMPLEMENTS :

Agricultural implements plays an important role to increase the agricultural productivity of the land. There are approximately 24780 agricultural implements in Pratapgarh district. Highest number of agricultural implements are being used in Bihar block while lowest number of agricultural implements are used in Kunda of the Pratapgarh district.

Map-27

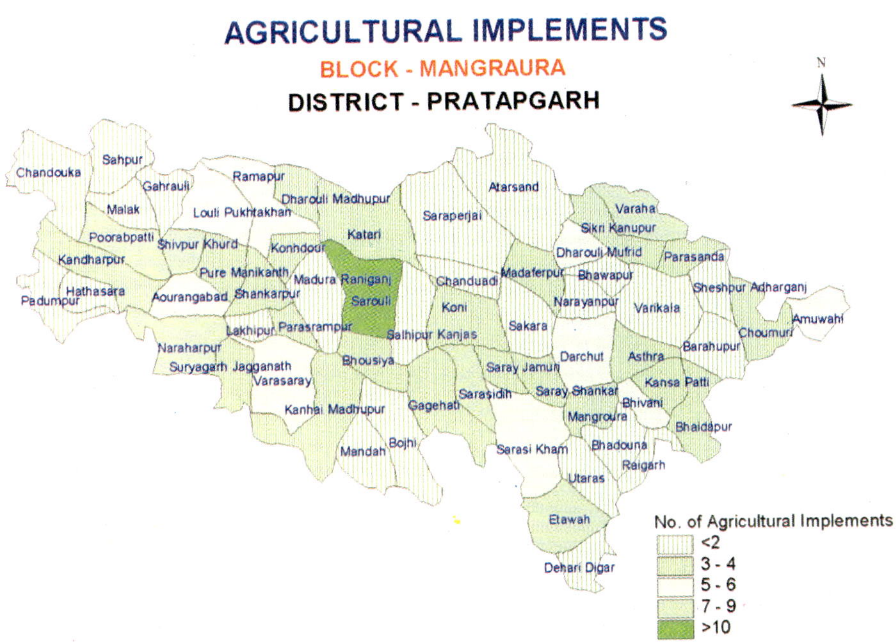

There are 1607 agricultural implements being utilized in Mangraura block out of which proportionately high number of agricultural implements are used in Etawah, Sarasidih, Sarouli Narharpur, Poorabpatti and Shivpur Khurd villages while nominal numbers of agricultural implements are used in most of the villages of Mangraura block. Very poor distribution of agricultural implements in the various villages of the block and district indicates that the farmers are still utilizing the traditional system of agriculture, which has led to low agricultural productivity. Maximum number of newly developed agricultural implements are being used in Sarouli village of Mangraura block which shown in Map-27. An attempt has been made to analyse distribution of various agricultural implement at village level in Mangraura block and at block level in district Pratapgarh.

6.1 Cultivator :

Proportionately wood cultivator is used at larger scale in Pratapgarh district. There are 101822 wood cultivator and 29327 iron cultivator being used in Pratapgarh district.

Highest number of 14342 wood cultivator and 4603 iron cultivator is used in Bihar block while lowest 1490 number of wood cultivator and 501 number of iron cultivator is used in Shivgarh block of the district Pratapgarh.

There are 9031 number of wood cultivator and 1774 number of iron cultivator being used in Mangraura block out of which highest number of wood cultivator is used in Sakara village and iron cultivator in Sarouli village of the Mangraura block. Maximum use of wood cultivator indicates that the farmers are still utilizing the traditional system of agriculture which has cause low agricultural production.

6.2 High-tech cultivator :

High-tech cultivator is comparatively less utilised due small size of land holding and backwardness. There are 310 high-tech cultivator in Pratapgarh district. Highest number of high-tech cultivator is being used in Bihar block while application of high-tech cultivator is very insignificant in Kalakankar, Babaganj, Shivgarh and Gaura block of the Pratapgarh district.

It is recorded from the district statistical hand book, Pratapgarh that there are 8 high-tech cultivator being used in Mangraura block. High-tech cultivator is used in Atarsand, Gahrauli. Aurangabad, Bojhi, Narharpur, Ketari, Shivpur Khurd and Parsanda villages of Mangraura block of Prasanda villages of Mangraura block of Pratapgarh district.

6.3 Tractor :

Tractor is being used very nominally in Pratapgarh district. There are 2174 number of tractor being used in Pratapgarh district. Highest number of tractors are used in Pratapgarh Sadar block while lowest number of tractors are being used in Mangraura block.

There are only 18 tractors in Mangraura block which are being utilized for agricultural activity, utilization of tractor is found in Konhdaur, Atarsand, Katari, Malak, Gohrauli, Parsanda, Dharouli Muphrid, Bojhi, Varanasi, Sarouli, Aurangabad, Narharpur, Shivpur khurd, Darchcut, Ramapur villages of Mangraura block of the district Pratapgarh.

6.4 Sprayer :

There are 84158 sprayer in tool district Pratapgarh which is being used as per agricultural crop protection. The highest number of sprayer is used in Bihar block while very low number of sprayer is being utilized in Sangipur block of the Pratapgarh district.

It is recorded that 1607 number of sprayer is utilized in Mangraura block out of which highest number of sprayer is used in Konhdaur, Varaha, Sarouli, Atarsand, Shivpur khurd, Dharouli Madapur villages of the Mangraura block.

7. FERTILIZER :

Fertilizer application in Pratapgarh district is 36296 ton out of which Nitrogen share is 48438 ton, Phospherous 7050 tone and Potash 672 tone. Proportionate application of fertilizer as per the gross sown are is nominal. Scientific and balanced application of fertilizer in Pratapgarh district is not utilized which has cause low agricultural productivity. Highest application of Nitrogen fertilizer is applied in Babaganj block and lowest Nitrogen fertilizer is used in Sangramgarh block of the district Pratapgarh. Proportionately highest application of phosphorus fertilizer is used in Mangraura block and lowest phosphorus fertilized is applied in Lalganj block of the district Pratapgarh. Potash fertilizer application is very high in Aspur Devsara block and lowest Potash fertilizer application is observed in Sangramgarh block.

It is observed that Nitrogen fertilizer application is 2037 tone, Phosphorus 638 ton, and Potash 44 ton in Mangraura block. Highest Nitrogen fertilizer is applied in Kanhai Madhupur village and lowest Nitrogen fertilizer is used in Shivpur Khurd village of Mangraura Block. Highest Phosphorus fertilizer is used in village Atarsand and lowest Phosphorus fertilizer is applied in Shivpur khurd village. Similarly potash fertilizer is maximum used Atarsand village and lowest potash fertilizer is used in Rajgarh, Sarai Shankar, Asthara and Madura Raniganj villages of Mangraura block of district Pratapgarh.

In view of the above it is recorded from the Map-28 that fertilizer application is comparatively very nominal is Mangraura block of Pratapgarh district. Balanced application of NPK fertilizer is not used as per the fertility status of the soil and common minimum requirement of the soil to increase the agricultural productivity because saline and alkaline soils and ravine soils fertilizer requirement is different. Highest total fertilizer application is observed in Barahapur village and lowest total fertilizer is applied in Raigarh and Sarai Shankar villages of Mangraura block. The ignorance of the farmers soil testing is not applied and with the intention to increase agricultural productivity often fertilizer application is increased. The excess fertilizer application has caused deterioration of the fertility status of soil, henceforth leading to decrease the agricultural productivity of the land. Thus scientific and balanced application of fertilizer as per requirement of the soil plays an important role in increasing the agricultural productivity.

Map-28

NITROGEN/PHOSPHORAS/POTAS
BLOCK - MANGRAURA
DISTRICT - PRATAPGARH

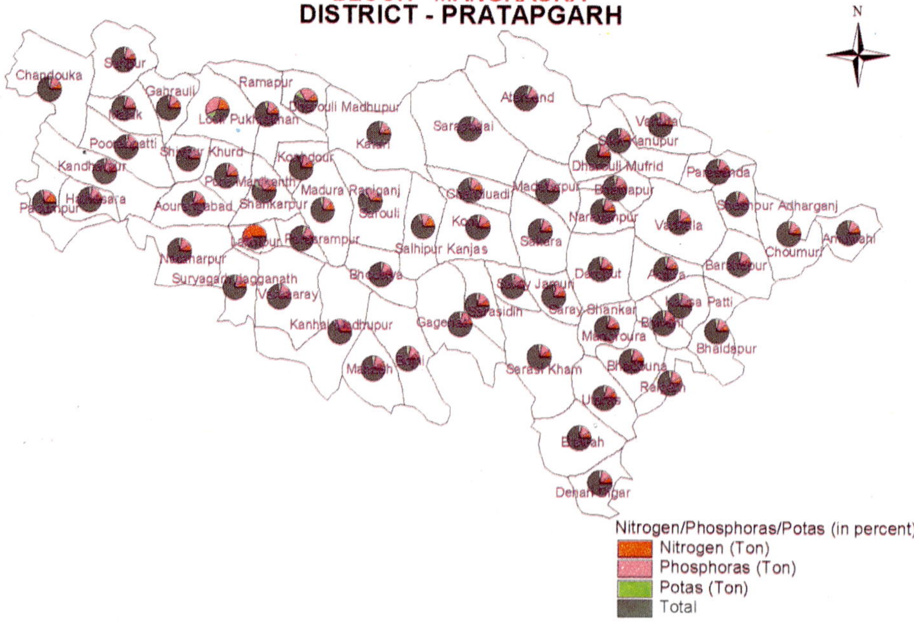

8. INSECTICIDES & PESTICIDES :

There are 19 insecticides and pesticides depot in Pratapgarh district. Pratapgarh Sadar block has 3 insecticides and pesticides depot and two depots are established in Lalganj and Laxmanpur block while there is no insecticides and pesticides depot in Sangram garh block but rest of the blocks are having one insecticides and pesticides depot.

Total use of insecticides and pesticides in Pratapgarh district is 1040 qtls out of which highest 500 qtls insecticides and pesticides are used alone in Pratapgarh Sadar block of the district. As per the available information through district statistical Hand book, Pratapgarh district.

There is only one insecticides and pesticides depot in Mangraura block. Use of insecticides and pesticides in Mangraura block is 25 qtls. Villages-wise consumption of insecticides and pesticides are very nominal and insignificant in Mangraura block.

9. BIO-GAS :

There are 4787 Bio-gas being established in Pratapgarh district. Highest number of Bio-Gas is established in Pratapgarh Sadar and Patti block, while lowest Bio-Gas centers are found in Kalakankar and Sangramgarh block of the Pratapgarh district.

There are 303 number of bio-gas being established in Mangraura block. Highest number of Bio-Gas is established in Atarsand, Kandharpur and Darchut villages while there is no bio-gas in Dehari Digar, Raigarh, Bhaidapur, Bhadauna, Etawah, Sarasidih, Sarasikham, Poorbpatti, Gagehati, Bhousiya, Kanhai Madhupur, Sikari Kanhupur,

Varikala, Varahupur, Choumuri, Gahrauli, Sarairajai, Bhawapur and Shankarpur villages of Mangraura block.

10. ANIMAL HUSBANDARY :

The dominant animals in Pratapgarh district are cow, buffalo, sheep, goat, horse, pig and Hen/cock. The available secondary sources data through district statistical Handbook, Pratapgarh provides that there are highest number of cows available in the district followed by buffalo, sheep and goat. The detailed analysis and distribution of different animals at block level in Pratapgarh and at villages level in Mangraura block is attempted with the assumption that the animal husbandry may play an important role in the economy of the district, henceforth it may be one of the decisive factor in the planning process and also in the implementation of various developmental programmes at village-block and district level development planning.

10.1 Cow :

Cow is one of the important animal in Pratapgarh district. Cow is significantly available at various levels in the district Pratapgarh due to its religious importance viz. (Pooja of go-mata) worshipping the Mother cow and also for milking purposes of female cow and use of male calf for agricultural cultivation and other household activities. There are 537511 number of cows in Pratapgarh district out of which highest number of cows are found in Sandwa Chandrika block and lowest number of cows are observed in Gaura block of the Pratapgarh district.

There are 35329 number of cows in Mangraura block out of which highest number of cows are seen in Sarouli, Ramapur, Dharouli, Madapur and Atarsand villages while lowest number of cows are observed in Narharpur village of the Mangraura Block.

10.2 Buff allow :

It is recorded that there are 1,85690 number of buff allow in Pratapgarh district. Highest number of buff allow is found in Bihar block and lowest number of buff allow animal is seen in Mangraura block of the district Pratapgarh.

It has been observed that there are 3421 number of buff allows are found in Mangraura block out of which highest number of buff allows are seen in Barahupur, Varaha villages and lowest number of buff allows are observed in Gagehati, Puremanikanth and Kandharpur village of the Mangraura block of district Pratapgarh.

10.3 Sheep :

The distribution of sheep is significant in Pratapgarh District. There are 53565 number of sheep in the district. Highest number of sheep is seen in Bihar block and lowest number of sheep is observed in Patti, Shivgarh and Gaura blocks of the Pratapgarh District.

There are 7723 number of sheeps in Mangraura block out of which highest number of sheeps are found in Varaha, Ramapur and Atarsand villages while lowest number of sheeps are seen in Lakhipur, Chaumuri, Dharauli Muphrid, Hathsara, Narayanpur, Mangraura, Utaras village but Sarouli, Mangraura, Utaras villages but Saraouli Suryagarh, Jagannath, Aurangabad, Narharpur, Shivpurkhurd, Bhawapur, Parasrampur villages are having insignificant sheeps because there is Gadaria i.e. Pal backward caste whose traditional occupation is sheep animal husbandry, villages which are out of Gadaria caste are not having sheep reusing is the main occupation of Gadaria caste in the respective villages of the Mangraura block of the district Pratapgarh.

10.4 Goat :

Goat is an important animal in Pratapgarh district. Proportionately goat is the second animal in Pratapgarh district. There are 225310 number of goats in Pratapgarh district. Highest number of goats in Pratapgarh district. Highest number of goats are found in Madhata block while lowest number of goats are seen in Patti, Gaura and Shivgarh blocks of the district Pratapgarh.

It is observed that there are 18186 number of goats in Mangraura block. Highest number of goats are seen in Dharouli Madapur villages while lowest number of goats are found in Bhivani, Gagehati, Varaha and Rampur villages of Mangraura Block.

10.5 Horse :

It is observed that there are 3933 number of horses in Pratapgarh district. Highest number of horses are seen in Bihar block and lowest number of horses are found in Pratapgarh Sadar block of the district Pratapgarh.

There are 112 number of horses in Mangarura block out of which highest number of horses are found in Louli Pukhtakhan, Varaha, Mandah, Aurangabad, Kohndaur and Ramapur villages of Mangraura block. It is observed that Bhivani, Sarasidih, Mangraura, Hathasara, Choumuri, Asthra, Amuwahi, Dharouli Muphrid, Bojhi, Bagehati, Narharpur, Sarai Shankar, Dharouli Madapur, Bhawapur, Madura Raniganj, Parasrampur, Lakhipur, Chanduadih, Koni, Sarai Rajai, Salhipur Kanjas villages are not having horses.

10.6 Pig :

Pig is an important animal husbandry in Pratapgarh district. There are 138178 number of Pigs in Pratapgarh district, out of which highest number of pigs are seen in Kalakankar block while lowest and Shivgarh block of the Pratapgarh district.

It is observed that there are 2762 number of pigs in Mangraura block. Highest number of pig are seen Sakara village and village Dharouli Madapur, Bhawapur, Madura Raniganj Villages are not having pigs while most the villages are having significant pig animal husbandry activity in Mangraura block.

10.7 Hen/Cock :

Hen/cock is the fourth important animal husbandry activity in the Pratapgarh district. There are 177377 number of hen/cock in Pratapgarh district. Highest number of hen/cock is seen in Mandhata Pratapgarh Sadar block and Kunda blocks observed in Shivgarh Gaura and Patti blocks of the Pratapgarh District.

It is recorded that there are 18182 number of hen/cock in Magraura block out of which highest number of hen/cock is seen in Dharouli Madapur village and lowest number of hen/cock is found in Katari, Padumpur, Malak, Dharouli Muphrid, Narayanpur and Utaras village of the Mangraura Block of the district Pratapgarh.

11. CONCLUSION :

The agriculture is the main component of the economic activity in Pratapgarh. Most of the population of the district is dependent on agriculture. Planning process for economic development has been implemented crimping sustainable development of village with a focus on enhancing the livelihoods workers and vulnerable sections of the society. Attempt has been made to analyse the various agricultural activities at village level in Mangrauna block and at block level in Pratapgarh district because the agriculture plays an important role in economic development henceforth in the process of planning and implementation of developmental programmes for sustainable rural development.

Agricultural cultivation is the main occupation of the people because nearly 61% of the total area is under agricultural cultivation. It is also observed that approximately 76& of the population is analysed in agricultural activity at village level in Mangrauna block and also at block level in Pratapgarh district.

Land ownership pattern in Pratapgarh districts different and land concentration in the district is very high due to kingship, zamindari/talukedari traditions, few people are owning larger area of land while maximum number of people are owning less area of land which has led to small size of land holding. Thus it is observed that small size of land holding is found among maximum number of farmers while large size of land holding is with very less people causing land concentration. Land concentration has also affected the agricultural economy of the district because most of the people are working as farm labours and existing farmers are having small size of land holding which has badly affected the agricultural activity in the economic development of the district Pratapgarh.

Canal and private tube well is the main sources of irrigation. Most of the irrigated area is being covered under canal and private tube well irrigation, while other sources of irrigation and insignificant in Pratapgarh district.

Agriculture is the backbone of the economic activity of Pratapgarh district. Food grain production is the major cropping of the Pratapgarh district. Wheat and rice is the main crop of the food grain production, followed by Barley, Millet, Maize, Gram, Pea, Pigeon Pea. Cropping of the commercial crops are nominal in district Pratapgarh. Mustard, sugarcane, potato are the major commercial crops being cultivated in the village Mangaruna block and also in the district Pratapgarh. Foodgrains and commercial crops are being cultivated as per the individual requirements of the people but excess agricultural produce is also marketed, henceforth contributes an importance role in the economic development of the district Pratapgarh.

Agricultural implements are used in a traditional system. High tech agricultural implement applications is very significant in the Pratapgarh district. Use of traditional wood cultivator is dominant in the district while high-tech cultivator and tractor application in the cultivation is significant. Sprays as agricultural tool is applied in most of the villages of the district.

Fertilizer application is used without soil testing. Maximum application of NPK fertilizer is used with the view to increase fertility status of the soil. Balanced and scientific application of fertilizer in Pratapgarh district is very insignificant. Excess use of fertilizers has deteriorated fertility status of the soil. High yielding variety of seeds and application of insecticides and pesticides are not appropriate as per the requirement which has adversely affects the agricultural productivity.

Bio-gas has been promoted in the Pratapgarh district due to exceeds animals. Animal husbandry is an important occupation in Mangrauna block and Pratapgarh district. Cows and buff allows are an important animals in Pratapgarh district followed by sheep, goat, horse pig, hen/cock and other animals. Animal husbandry is being done to meet the individual requirement of the people and excess of it is being used for commercial purposes in Mangrauna block and Pratapgarh district.

Thus agriculture and animal husbandry are the main occupation in the Pratapgarh district and it plays an important role in the economic developments . Therefore agriculture and animal husbandry should be given due importance in the planning process and implementation of planned developmental programes as per the need and traditional occupations of the local people and for their continued participation in the planning and developmental schemes and sustenance of the implemented programes with the peoples involvement.

Table -3 : Natural Resources Data Management System (NRDMS)
Pratapgarh district
A - Economic Indicators

Sl. No.	*Block*	*Area in Hectare*	*Land Ownership 0.5 to 1.00 hac.*		*1.00 to 2.00 hac.*		*2.00 to 4.00 hac.*		*4.00 to 10.00 hac.*		*Above of 10.00 hac.*	
			No.	*Area*	*No.*	*Area*	*No.*	*Area*	*No.*	*Area*	*No.*	*Area*
1	*2*	*3*	*4*	*5*	*6*	*7*	*8*	*9*	*10*	*11*	*12*	*13*
1	KalaKankar	4301	5523	3651	2875	3826	1038	2742	172	315	8	106
2	Babaganj	4820	6190	4092	3222	4287	1163	3073	193	1027	8	106
3	Kunda	5718	7343	4854	3822	5086	1380	3646	229	1219	10	133
4	Bihar	5062	6501	4297	3383	4501	1222	3229	203	1080	9	120
5	Sangipur	6292	8080	5346	4205	5595	1519	4013	252	1314	11	146
6	Lalganj	4002	5139	3391	2675	3559	966	2552	160	852	7	93
7	Laxmanpur	3665	4706	3111	2449	3259	884	2336	147	782	6	80
8	Sandwa Chandrika	4241	5443	3599	2834	3771	1023	2703	170	905	7	93
9	Pratapgarh Sadar	3291	4221	2793	2199	2926	795	2100	132	703	6	80
10	Mandhata	5085	6528	4316	3378	4522	1227	3242	202	1075	9	120
11	Mangraura	5318	6826	9513	3554	4729	1283	3390	213	1134	10	133
12	Patti	3898	5003	3307	2604	3465	940	2483	156	830	8	106
13	Aspur Devsasa	4672	5999	3960	3122	4154	1127	2978	186	990	8	106
14	Shivgarh	4687	6019	3979	3132	4167	1132	2992	188	1001	8	106
15	Gaura	5123	6578	4348	3424	4556	1236	3263	205	1091	9	120
16	Sangramgarh	4783	6152	4067	3197	4254	1154	3149	191	1017	8	106
	Total	74958	96251	68624	50075	66657	18089	47891	2999	15335	132	1754

Sl. No.	*Block*	*Source of Irrigation Canal*	*Tubewell Govt.*	*Tubewell Private*	*Pond*	*Food Production (Area in ha.) Total*	*Rice*	*Wheat*	*Barley*	*Millet*	*Maize*	*Gram*
1	*2*	*14*	*15*	*16*	*17*	*18*	*19*	*20*	*21*	*22*	*23*	*24*
1	KalaKankar	10307	4	1805	103	12219	8167	8273	183	67	2	203
2	Babaganj	10198	0	1905	0	12103	10754	10553	56	70	0	43
3	Kunda	8045	0	2085	0	10130	9009	10330	556	306	2	447
4	Bihar	12103	0	2266	10	14379	11685	12167	103	86	0	84
5	Sangipur	2031	0	10528	0	12559	4945	9693	131	1495	3	477
6	Lalganj	5085	49	4846	14	9994	6061	7358	97	225	4	113
7	Laxmanpur	3934	0	4650	39	8623	3901	6743	149	270	4	290
8	Sandwa Chandrika	10	62	8120	0	8192	4907	7253	302	1422	8	1403
9	Pratapgarh Sadar	390	1	5616	3	6010	1619	5427	247	570	78	1015
10	Mandhata	3941	18	6711	0	10670	7064	8574	134	180	12	225
11	Mangraura	2860	52	12122	0	15034	10125	11015	194	246	214	825
12	Patti	1506	24	10037	0	11567	6775	8223	240	173	388	410
13	Aspur Devsasa	791	0	10415	0	11206	7512	9553	116	337	1014	330
14	Shivgarh	403	0	8256	0	8659	3290	7378	227	374	254	1094
15	Gaura	2674	30	9457	0	12161	5726	10592	66	109	138	357
16	Sangramgarh	8912	54	3347	0	12313	10272	9436	36	93	4	19
	Total	73190	294	102166	169	175819	111812	142568	2837	6023	2121	7335

Sl. No.	Block	Commercial Crops (Area in ha.)							Agricultural Implements				
		Pea	Pigeon Pea	Must-ard	Suger -cane	Potato	Sanai	Chara	Cultivator		High-tech Cultivator	Agricultureal implements	Sprayer
									Wood	Iron			
1	2	25	26	27	28	29	30	31	32	33	34	35	36
1	KalaKankar	106	336	18	41	260	2	139	7227	757	0	875	617
2	Babaganj	231	223	36	32	352	0	220	8088	2723	0	475	331
3	Kunda	287	437	59	30	409	0	195	3984	1339	13	446	721
4	Bihar	247	299	39	15	580	2	222	14342	4603	174	3718	5033
5	Sangipur	608	1192	108	32	536	4	248	5387	3118	29	2038	53
6	Lalganj	265	562	123	19	694	6	225	4541	2578	15	1633	91
7	Laxmanpur	216	444	61	21	251	8	150	5305	3103	25	1935	58
8	Sandwa Chandrika	354	3186	173	57	391	93	199	6536	641	25	1698	141
9	Pratapgarh Sadar	238	1228	89	6	305	22	154	5993	448	2	1623	39
10	Mandhata	309	632	82	48	709	4	141	8600	1683	2	2116	378
11	Mangraura	410	696	157	357	511	51	485	9031	1774	8	1607	2337
12	Patti	364	492	129	389	201	13	325	3301	656	8	638	907
13	Aspur Devsasa	396	481	146	582	398	2	346	7092	669	7	1870	1849
14	Shivgarh	295	1326	115	152	384	28	331	1490	501	0	627	617
15	Gaura	342	362	59	294	612	14	285	3539	1042	0	601	736
16	Sangramgarh	210	205	59	33	319	0	186	7366	3692	2	2880	230
	Total	4878	12101	1453	2108	6912	249	3851	101822	29327	310	24780	14138

Sl. No.	Block	Tractor	Seeds Depo		Rural Godam		Insecticides/ pesticides		Fertilize			
			No.	Capa-city	No.	Capa-city	De-po	Capa-city	Nitro-gen	P	K	Total
1	2	37	38	39	40	41	42	43	44	45	46	47
1	KalaKankar	106	29	3590	9	900	1	25	1520	442	39	2001
2	Babaganj	130	28	4290	10	1000	1	30	2255	448	38	3739
3	Kunda	168	35	5380	12	1200	1	50	2106	438	42	2580
4	Bihar	114	28	4000	11	1100	1	25	1860	462	43	2365
5	Sangipur	202	39	5700	12	1200	1	25	1686	396	45	2129
6	Lalganj	162	38	5700	11	1100	2	100	1447	254	40	1841
7	Laxmanpur	200	28	4000	9	900	2	100	1208	308	40	1556
8	Sandwa Chandrika	153	35	5380	11	1100	1	25	1603	428	38	2069
9	Pratapgarh Sadar	208	35	5380	12	1200	3	500	1548	458	36	2042
10	Mandhata	53	38	5700	13	1300	1	25	2068	660	45	2773
11	Mangraura	18	45	6000	11	1100	1	25	2037	638	44	2119
12	Patti	150	655	6500	10	1000	1	25	1908	428	41	2317
13	Aspur Devsasa	103	28	4000	11	1100	1	25	1934	440	51	2425
14	Shivgarh	180	39	5700	12	1200	1	30	1993	444	50	2487
15	Gaura	123	35	3550	10	1000	1	30	1983	468	48	2499
16	Sangramgarh	115	30	2080	10	1000	0	0	984	338	32	1354
	Total	2174	1165	76950	174	17400	19	1040	28140	7050	672	36296

Sl. No.	Block	Bio-gas Centre	Husbandary: Cow	Buffallow	Sheep	Goat	Horse	Pig	Hen/ Cock
1	2	48	49	50	51	52	53	54	55
1	KalaKankar	105	32084	13162	4590	17292	425	23815	9071
2	Babaganj	362	31186	11141	5620	17463	294	18384	9841
3	Kunda	232	39015	14452	6292	17571	508	13683	22890
4	Bihar	278	46436	20322	9131	23546	587	20312	19223
5	Sangipur	293	39720	6321	2957	11176	232	9889	7412
6	Lalganj	181	30994	13692	1760	8531	165	12603	5625
7	Laxmanpur	289	39256	10356	3105	12456	242	9806	7353
8	Sandwa Chandrika	301	56111	17876	2132	12327	169	2822	6449
9	Pratapgarh Sadar	469	29735	18882	1190	10462	98	1430	23670
10	Mandhata	279	32960	13692	1028	44572	213	5729	25371
11	Mangraura	303	35329	3421	7723	18186	112	2762	18182
12	Patti	400	20914	10170	203	4213	255	1180	2991
13	Aspur Devsasa	272	28007	4805	3932	6735	107	1889	6491
14	Shivgarh	417	18499	4685	496	3344	116	1712	2048
15	Gaura	439	16825	9483	403	3829	125	1113	2343
16	Sangramgarh	167	40440	13230	3003	13607	285	11049	8417
	Total	4787	537511	185690	53565	225310	3933	138178	177377

Table -4 : Natural Resources Data Management System (NRDMS)
Mangraura Block, Pratapgarh district
A - Economic Indicators

Loc_ code	Vill_Name	Junior	Inter	Land_ A_hec	Canal	Tube_ Gov	T_Privat	Total	Rice	Wheat
1	Konhdour	887	669	176	19	0	153	176	121	96
2	Ramapur	1074	867	220	20	2	180	204	110	120
3	Dharouli Madapur	612	612	250	32	1	71	109	125	125
4	Bhawapur	614	719	157	33	0	124	157	116	83
5	Shankarpur	405	315	150	38	2	66	63	130	80
6	Madura Raniganj	708	792	92	4	0	86	90	81	76
7	Parasrampur	413	405	110	26	0	84	110	91	82
8	Lakhipur	321	299	56	14	0	42	56	39	26
9	Atarsand	3021	1207	750	133	0	619	753	692	460
10	Madaferpur	446	304	235	77	0	157	234	201	180
11	Chanduadih	343	217	264	11	0	253	264	244	176
12	Sakara	514	166	350	76	0	274	350	321	262
13	Koni	618	298	325	44	0	281	325	296	203
14	Sarairajai	596	207	322	0	1	131	321	269	189
15	Salhipur Kanjas	913	459	132	0	0	110	132	102	87
16	Katari	396	208	258	8	0	250	258	199	186
17	Malak	481	306	237	61	0	173	235	205	167
18	Padumpur	471	273	144	21	0	121	142	134	102
19	Gahrauli	399	293	250	47	0	230	250	204	158
20	Sahpur	607	299	300	26	0	272	300	282	168
21	Kandharpur	478	326	290	92	0	198	290	241	191
22	Chandouka	745	300	293	121	0	172	293	186	134

Loc_ code	Vill_Name	Junior	Inter	Land_ A_hec	Canal	Tube_ Gov	T_Privat	Total	Rice	Wheat
23	Parasanda	446	140	446	26	0	420	446	398	271
24	Choumuri	853	120	246	99	0	148	247	199	170
25	Varaha	400	203	151	0	0	148	125	210	180
26	Barahupur	935	10	546	10	0	536	546	456	360
27	Varikala	404	13	456	0	6	450	456	368	289
28	Asthra	356	58	93	14	1	78	93	84	59
29	Amuwahi	290	166	210	43	0	167	210	184	126
30	Dharouli Muphrid	304	262	336	84	0	252	336	298	206
31	Sikri Kanupur	913	463	354	15	0	339	354	320	298
32	Sheshpur Adharganj	346	138	162	7	0	155	162	124	96
33	Kanhai Madupur	920	1276	307	57	0	250	307	285	209
34	Bojhi	403	314	137	49	0	86	136	122	98
35	Bhousiya	960	503	165	22	0	143	165	113	100
36	Mandah	466	381	146	0	7	81	146	103	87
37	Varasaray	541	309	208	30	0	178	208	185	119
38	Gagehati	650	340	287	20	0	267	287	204	186
39	Sarouli	800	600	472	80	1	444	281	155	170
40	Suryagarh Jagannath	871	413	174	46	0	127	173	143	99
41	Aourangabad	800	314	197	60	0	137	197	149	121
42	Naraharpur	698	469	434	169	0	265	434	354	210
43	Pure Manikanth	150	54	116	38	0	78	116	86	72
44	Poorabpatti	300	85	190	87	0	100	190	180	146
45	Shivpur Khurd	406	150	54	26	2	25	82	180	160
46	Saray Shankar	359	140	103	39	0	64	103	82	72
47	Hathasara	514	417	295	105	0	190	295	156	106
48	Louli Pukhtakham	900	300	322	30	2	145	56	170	120
49	Darchut	489	396	162	10	0	152	162	143	102
50	Narayanpur	450	378	321	3	10	307	321	290	205
51	Sarasi Kham	743	517	272	87	0	182	270	224	198
52	Mangroura	800	494	166	9	0	157	166	123	99
53	Saray Jamuari	944	389	452	54	0	395	452	368	301
54	Utaras	671	320	384	35	0	349	384	323	316
55	Sarasidih	512	298	339	60	2	277	339	307	298
56	Etawah	444	287	514	58	0	454	514	414	396
57	Bhadouna	780	260	151	14	0	136	150	129	100
58	Bhivani	475	286	162	26	0	136	162	143	112
59	Bhaidapur	466	360	100	3	11	86	100	89	80
60	Kansa Patti	289	270	124	24	0	100	124	100	83
61	Raigarh	389	209	96	7	0	89	96	82	72
62	Dehari Digar	396	260	310	296	0	14	310	296	217

Loc_ code	Vill_ Name	Barley	Maize	Gram	Pea	Pig_Pea	Mustard	S_cane	Potato	Sanai
1	Konhdour	0.8	3	2.45	3.25	1.1	2	1.95	4.25	1.25
2	Ramapur	10	4	12	10	7.0	8	6	30	2
3	Dharouli Madapur	15	7	15	17	9.0	12	5	35	4
4	Bhawapur	1.5	1.5	2	2.35	2.4	1.75	3.5	3.5	2.5
5	Shankarpur	6	0	16	5	4.0	8	1.6	14	3
6	Madura Raniganj	1.5	1.52	3	1.25	3.3	2	1.2	6.5	1.5
7	Parasrampur	2	0	2.5	2.45	3.4	1.25	6.5	6.5	2.5
8	Lakhipur	1	0	1.75	1.25	2.0	2	7	4.5	2
9	Atarsand	1.75	0	4.75	3	3.5	4	10	11	1.65

Loc_ code	*Vill_ Name*	*Barley*	*Maize*	*Gram*	*Pea*	*Pig_Pea*	*Mustard*	*S_cane*	*Potato*	*Sanai*
10	Madaferpur	1.75	0	3.75	0	0.0	4.5	4	9	2.45
11	Chanduadih	2.5	0	0	0	0.0	6.5	5	6	1.24
12	Sakara	1.5	0	0	0	0.0	4.75	3	7	1.25
13	Koni	1.75	1.5	10	3	2.5	2.35	2.75	4.3	0.5
14	Sarairajai	2.4	0	0	4.5	2.1	1.75	1.25	2	1.5
15	Salhipur Kanjas	3	2.5	1.5	2	1.5	1.5	8	13	3
16	Katari	1	0	2	1	2.7	0.75	2.6	5.5	1.5
17	Malak	0.81	0	1.75	0	1.9	1.25	1.3	12.5	2
18	Padumpur	0.5	0	0.75	0	1.9	1.25	6	13	1.5
19	Gahrauli	1.34	2.5	1.25	3.5	4.0	2.75	2.1	24	5
20	Sahpur	2	3.8	0.85	2.4	3.8	3.25	3	21	6.5
21	Kandharpur	1.5	4	4	3	1.3	1.24	2.6	17	8.5
22	Chandouka	2	1.5	4.2	3.8	6.0	2.4	3.4	13	1.5
23	Parasanda	4	2.5	5	4.3	4.4	3.1	16	24	2
24	Choumuri	0.6	0.75	2.42	2	0.0	2.8	8	6	1.5
25	Varaha	20	0	12	16	0.0	17	24	16	7
26	Barahupur	4	0	3	1.5	0.0	1.2	15	26	3.5
27	Varikala	1.25	1.5	2	2.5	1.0	2.3	1.4	17	2.5
28	Asthra	0.75	0.75	1.5	1.3	0.0	1.25	13	3	1.5
29	Amuwahi	2	1.25	2.4	2.4	0.0	2	7	6.5	2
30	Dharouli Muphrid	1.75	0	1.25	4.6	0.0	1.75	10	3.5	1
31	Sikri Kanupur	1.23	0	5.65	1.8	0.0	1.85	2	4	3
32	Sheshpur Adharganj	2.24	0	1.6	2.25	0.0	2.35	4	6.5	2
33	Kanhai Madupur	2.18	2.5	3.7	1.85	0.0	1.8	11	10	4
34	Bojhi	1.85	0.5	1.25	4.15	1.3	2.4	12	9	5
35	Bhousiya	2.75	2.5	5.7	2.15	5.5	1.5	1.6	19	7
36	Mandah	1.5	0	2.7	1.75	0.0	1.82	5	13	6
37	Varasaray	0.75	0	2.4	4.6	2.4	2.45	3	8	3
38	Gagehati	1.52	1.5	1.4	1.25	1.5	1.9	4	9	4
39	Sarouli	9	12	16	14	0.0	12	18	14	1
40	Suryagarh Jagannath	0.5	0	4	2.4	0.0	1.2	6	13	2
41	Aourangabad	1.5	2.15	6.25	3	0.0	2.45	8	10	1
42	Naraharpur	2.5	1.7	3.45	1.9	5.5	2.45	6	12	4
43	Pure Manikanth	2.8	1.5	4.5	1.25	1.8	1.75	9	4.5	1
44	Poorabpatti	3	2.75	4.5	7.14	2.1	3	10	9.5	2
45	Shivpur Khurd	11	0	12	1.3	8.0	9	16	14	7
46	Saray Shankar	3.5	1.5	3.5	2	0.0	1.5	11	6.5	4
47	Hathasara	1.5	2	1.5	1.75	0.0	4.2	13	7	2
48	Louli Pukhtakham	10	2	10	11	6.0	12	1.5	12	3
49	Darchut	0.5	2.75	4.2	2.3	0.0	1.95	14	3	1
50	Narayanpur	1.5	1.8	5	4.5	1.5	2.46	17	4	3
51	Sarasi Kham	2	3	3.8	2.4	0.0	1.8	12	5	2
52	Mangroura	1.5	2.45	2	1.5	0.0	2.4	13	8	1
53	Saray Jamuari	2.75	1.45	3	2.5	0.9	1.5	9	9	2
54	Utaras	1.25	1.24	4	1.5	0.0	2.1	8	3	1
55	Sarasidih	3.5	2.4	7	4.75	0.0	1.75	7	4	2
56	Etawah	0.5	4.2	6	5.6	3.5	1.8	11	5	3
57	Bhadouna	1.75	1.8	2	1.5	0.0	2.4	9	6	1
58	Bhivani	2.75	2	2.5	1.25	0.0	4	14	8	3
59	Bhaidapur	1.9	4.1	2.75	2.25	1.3	1.25	8	1.5	1
60	Kansa Patti	3	3.2	3.15	2	0.0	2.45	9	2.5	2
61	Raigarh	1.8	1.8	2.4	1.8	0.7	3	7	3	3
62	Dehari Digar	2.4	1.5	1.24	1.75	2.5	5	6	4	1

Loc_ code	*Vill Name*	*Chara*	*Cul_ wood*	*Cul_ iron*	*Ag_imple*	*Sprayer*	*N*	*P*	*K*
1	Konhdour	4	12	13	3	10	21.12	31	10
2	Ramapur	11	32	28	5	6	27	39	13
3	Dharouli Madapur	9	25	20	4	9	19	45	15
4	Bhawapur	3	21	19	1	1	18	29	10
5	Shankarpur	5	36	38	3	4	11	27	9
6	Madura Raniganj	3	13	18	2	2	13.5	16	6
7	Parasrampur	1.5	9	14	3	3	6.7	19	7
8	Lakhipur	2	12	10	1	0	91	11	4
9	Atarsand	7.5	85	50	2	0	28	136	45
10	Madaferpur	3.5	31	13	3	1	31.5	42	14
11	Chanduadih	1.9	14	14	1	2	42	47	15
12	Sakara	2	58	39	2	0	39	63	21
13	Koni	3	36	48	3	0	38.5	58	19
14	Sarairajai	4	34	19	1	1	15	57	19
15	Salhipur Kanjas	5	13	9	2	2	30	23	8
16	Katari	3	32	28	3	0	29	46	15
17	Malak	2	29	24	1	0	18	43	13
18	Padumpur	1	31	40	2	0	30	25	7
19	Gahrauli	5	35	14	2	0	36	45	15
20	Sahpur	9	27	22	1	1	34	54	18
21	Kandharpur	6	36	39	3	2	39	52	17
22	Chandouka	3.5	36	27	17	1	35	52	18
23	Parasanda	4	26	25	4	2	53	81	26
24	Choumuri	2.5	19	18	3	0	29	44	15
25	Varaha	12	18	25	7	8	18	28	10
26	Barahupur	6	47	60	1	1	65	98	32
27	Varikala	4.5	52	50	2	3	54	82	27
28	Asthra	3.5	13	19	3	2	12	16.18	6
29	Amuwahi	4	40	35	5	1	25	37	13
30	Dharouli Muphrid	3	32	30	6	0	40	60	20
31	Sikri Kanupur	7	52	48	3	1	42	63	21
32	Sheshpur Adharganj	8	27	29	1	2	19	29	10
33	Kanhai Madupur	6	19	13	4	1	86	55	18
34	Bojhi	4	13	17	2	0	16	25	9
35	Bhousiya	5	18	14	3	2	19	30	10
36	Mandah	5	29	19	1	1	17	26	9
37	Varasaray	4	16	24	5	0	24	37	12
38	Gagehati	4	24	26	3	4	34	51	17
39	Sarouli	3	50	75	27	10	56	84	28
40	Suryagarh Jagannath	7	26	35	4	7	20	31	10
41	Aourangabad	6	34	30	6	6	23	35	11
42	Naraharpur	5	29	31	7	4	52	78	26
43	Pure Manikanth	3	24	13	3	1	13	20	7
44	Poorabpatti	2	29	7	7	2	22	34	11
45	Shivpur Khurd	9	26	28	8	8	7	9	3.5
46	Saray Shankar	4	38	27	4	0	12	18	6
47	Hathasara	6	30	24	2	1	35	53	17
48	Louli Pukhtakham	6	12	18	5	4	38	57	19
49	Darchut	5	41	12	6	3	19	29	10
50	Narayanpur	4	17	17	1	0	38	58	19
51	Sarasi Kham	6	18	18	5	2	32	48	16
52	Mangroura	3	26	31	3	0	19	29	10

Loc_ code	Vill Name	Chara	Cul_ wood	Cul_ iron	Ag_imple	Sprayer	N	P	K
53	Saray Jamuari	8	40	41	4	0	54	81	27
54	Utaras	6	14	17	2	0	46	69	23
55	Sarasidih	3	18	21	8	1	40	61	20
56	Etawah	4	37	14	9	3	61	92	30
57	Bhadouna	2	15	20	1	2	18	27	9
58	Bhivani	8	45	35	5	1	19	29	10
59	Bhaidapur	7	31	14	4	0	12	18	7
60	Kansa Patti	6	17	19	3	0	15	22	8
61	Raigarh	7	14	13	2	0	12	17	6
62	Dehari Digar	8	19	19	1	0	37	55	18

Loc_ code	Vill_Name	Total	Bio-gas	Cow	Buffalow	Sheep	Goat	Horse	Pig	Hen/ cock
1	Konhdour	62.12	3	12.5	80	125	35	4	143	120
2	Ramapur	79	2	250	120	350	18	3	10	180
3	Dharouli Madapur	79	1	250	129	60	210	0	0	300
4	Bhawapur	57	0	85	37	0	46	0	0	66
5	Shankarpur	47	0	190	80	40	66	1	25	160
6	Madura Raniganj	35.5	1	89	47	15	70	0	0	74
7	Parasrampur	32.7	2	125	36	0	61	0	19	16
8	Lakhipur	106	3	80	54	16	72	0	15	26
9	Atarsand	209	11	250	120	350	61	3	180	37
10	Madaferpur	84	4	125	20	39	75	2	19	38
11	Chanduadih	103.5	3	86	35	36	125	0	24	42
12	Sakara	126	2	129	67	90	120	3	260	150
13	Koni	116	1	55	24	20	45	0	35	35
14	Sarairajai	114.5	0	96	56	25	50	0	135	110
15	Salhipur Kanjas	46.3	2	58	26	120	24	0	16	20
16	Katari	91	1	125	80	76	125	1	70	10
17	Malak	85	3	56	40	125	78	1	19	13
18	Padumpur	50	4	135	70	86	110	1	24	10
19	Gahrauli	140	0	80	73	120	125	2	14	116
20	Sahpur	106	1	120	39	118	110	1	24	56
21	Kandharpur	108	10	59	31	35	125	2	20	326
22	Chandouka	105	3	125	32	125	60	1	56	45
23	Parasanda	160	4	110	86	96	120	3	85	40
24	Choumuri	88	0	115	36	16	100	0	61	125
25	Varaha	55	1	210	185	300	18	4	20	85
26	Barahupur	195	0	85	312	112	103	3	35	120
27	Varikala	163	0	90	120	40	24	1	61	65
28	Asthra	34.18	2	168	39	46	46	0	35	20
29	Amuwahi	75	1	120	45	61	62	0	35	16
30	Dharouli Muphrid	120	3	105	61	12	89	0	26	14
31	Sikri Kanupur	126	0	107	56	27	34	2	65	90
32	Sheshpur Adharganj	58	1	108	71	42	42	1	115	62
33	Kanhai Madupur	109	0	96	78	45	41	1	56	42
34	Bojhi	50	3	116	53	44	55	0	16	31
35	Bhousiya	59	0	85	60	133	65	2	17	19
36	Mandah	52	1	56	55	103	85	5	35	92
37	Varasaray	72	2	112	61	56	84	1	15	61
38	Gagehati	102	0	86	12	35	19	0	16	56

Loc_ code	*Vill_Name*	*Total*	*Bio-gas*	*Cow*	*Buffalow*	*Sheep*	*Goat*	*Horse*	*Pig*	*Hen/ cock*
39	Sarouli	168	2	290	167	0	106	3	115	187
40	Suryagarh Jagannath	61	3	112	71	0	86	1	10	112
41	Aourangabad	69	4	113	35	0	56	4	22	125
42	Naraharpur	156	4	35	36	0	120	0	12	35
43	Pure Manikanth	40	2	110	22	35	120	2	125	125
44	Poorabpatti	67	0	120	35	53	122	1	56	65
45	Shivpur Khurd	19.5	1	210	125	0	60	2	45	170
46	Saray Shankar	36	3	216	36	61	125	0	260	65
47	Hathasara	105	3	162	38	17	71	0	35	55
48	Louli Pukhtakham	114	1	178	152	140	180	4	105	160
49	Darchut	58	10	125	56	41	62	1	20	35
50	Narayanpur	115	3	103	61	15	150	2	15	15
51	Sarasi Kham	96	0	96	63	51	110	1	30	39
52	Mangroura	58	4	116	55	16	62	0	40	31
53	Saray Jamuari	162	3	115	35	61	79	1	17	20
54	Utaras	138	1	62	29	17	86	2	10	15
55	Sarasidih	132	0	69	39	71	71	0	110	30
56	Etawah	183	0	55	42	55	103	3	35	61
57	Bhadouna	54	0	74	24	86	36	1	40	56
58	Bhivani	58	2	87	56	80	19	0	17	45
59	Bhaidapur	37	0	112	61	81	116	2	20	65
60	Kansa Patti	45	1	103	40	82	112	1	25	56
61	Raigarh	35	0	108	35	56	56	2	15	100
62.	Dehari Digar	110	0	96	42	43	40	2	125	120

CHAPTER - V

INFRASTRCTURAL RESOURCES

1. INTRODUCTION :

Infrastructural availability of an area plays an important role in the overall development of an area. Available infrastructure of an area will play a key role in the planning process. The process of integrated approach to planning requires detailed knowledge of the interrelations and inter dependencies between various sectors to resolve often-conflicting requirements and available infrastructure of the region.It leads to a requirement for appropriate data management specially the sectoral data on Infrastructural resources. Thus it becomes necessary to analyse the available Infrastructural resources of Pratapgarh district, because based on the available Infrastructural resources common minimum requirement of the down trodden people can be realized and based the need of the people planning process can be initiated. Plan without peoples participation and with out need base plan, the planning process can not be made successful. Therefore available Infrastructural resources must be considered before initiation of the planning process. An attempt is made to analyse the available Infrastructural resources of the Mangraura block and Pratapgarh district, because it will be a backbone of the planning process.

District Pratapgarh has no important minerals. There are 17 small scale industries of cotton textiles, drugs and pharmaceuticals, light engineering and printing besides there are 4345 household (furniture, bamboo, and cane work) and agro-based industries which has been shown in the map-29 and agro-based industries (oil mill and rice mills) which are concentrated in the different parts of the Pratapgarh district.

Transport and communication network is well developed in the district. District Pratapgarh has historical, religious and cultural importance. There are important tourists places in the District.

It has been realized that the Pratapgarh District has potentialities to develop small scale/agro based industries and tourism by utilizing the available local infrastructural resources. Therefore it needs a proper planning for the growth and development of the socio-economic cum tourism infrastructure of the district Pratapgarh. In view of the above an attempt is made to analyse the available infrastructure of Mangraura block and Pratapgarh district.

2. HISTORICAL INFRASTRUCTURE

Historically it is found that the Chinese traveler Hieuntsiang visited the tehsil Kunda during Deventh Century A.D., since then Buddhist, monasteries are found here. Manikpur is the district had been a note place for its historic past. The district Pratapgarh was under the rule of Rajputs, Muslims,Hindus and the British. The district took a courageous stand against the British rule during the first was of independence.

Archeological remains of a Buddhist monastery is found here. Mankipur, the ancient town stands by the river Ganga, is full of ruins palatial residences built during the reign of Akbar. Aruined brick fort exists in Ranki. In Yahiapur stands the temple of

Belkharnath. Besides Dehiawan and Daudpur are noted for bloodshed during the mutiny. A building of great antiquity exists here which was the residence of Raja Pratap Bahadur Singh. District Pratapgarh needs a proper planning for the growth and development of socio-economic cumtourism infrastructure of the district. Rocky Ka Tila is located in the Sangipur block at the distance of 6 miles away from Sangipur village. The Rocky Ka Tila is having 2 miles length, 1 mile width and 30 feet height, Rocky Ka Tila has historical and archaeological importance.

Ajagara is located 15 kms away in the west on Varanasi-Lucknow National highway near Raniganj. Ajagara has also historical importance.

Sun's statue is found in the west of the Pratapgarh city while digging for house building and it has historical and religious importance.

Handaur is located at the distance of 24 km. on the west of Pratapgarh city at on Varanasi-Lucknow National highway. Handaur village is famous historical place.

Dih Hardo is located at the distance of 20 km on the south-west of Pratapgarh city on the Pratapgarh Kunda way and one km away Naubasta market, Dhi Hardo an ancient Tila has archaeological importance.

Sandwa Khas Tila is located about 15 km west from Pratapgarh city on Pratapgarh Kunda way and 3 km away from Sarai Anadev market in the worth of the village Sandwa khas, is one of ancient monuments and it has the historical importance in the district Pratapgarh.

Kahala Shaheed Place is located at the distance of 32 km in Raniganj tehsil & in Gaura block on the Lucknow-Pratapgarh-Varanasi national highway at 190 km distance through Gazika bagh Mubarakpur way about 6 km distance village Kahala is located in the Pratapgarh district is noted for bloodshed during the mutiny and freedom struggle.

3. RELIGIOUS INFRASTRUCTURE

Religious infrastructure is very important and famous. Various religious important places are as follows –

- Belha Devi temple located in Pratapgarh city.
- Chandrikan Devi temple in Sandwa Chandrika block.
- Chauhar Jan Devi temple is Kalakankar block.
- Ghuisar Nath temple in Sangipur block.
- Shani Dev temple Sadar block of Pratapgarh.
- Belkharnath temple in Belkharnath Dham block.
- Bhaihasan nath temple in Mandhata block.
- Hodeshwar nath temple in Kunda block.

Religious temples located in Pratapgarh district can be developed and promoted for religious tourist centers.

4. ADMINISTRATIVE INFRASTRUCTURE :

Pratapgarh Sadar is Parliamentary constituency of the district while Machhali shahr Parliamentary constituency has part area in Pratapgarh district. There are seven constituency of Member of legislative Asember and also Member of Legislative council of Uttar Pradesh.

There are 5 Tehsils viz., Prarapgarh, Sadar, Kunda, Patti, Lalganj and Raniganj. There are 17 block developments and 171 Nyaya Panchayat, 2181 number of habited villages and 38 inhabitated village and 1105 villages Panchayats in district Pratapgarh.

Mangraura block is backward block of the Pratapgarh district located in the north of the district. There are 62 villages Panchayats in Mangraura block.

There are 7 town area and one Nagar Palika Parishad and 6 Nagar Panchayat in Pratapgarh district.

There are 25 police station in Pratapgarh district out of which 20 police stations are located in rural areas and 5 police stations are located in urban areas.

There are 112 Bus station/stops in Pratapgarh district and 15 Railway stations including railway halt.

5. ROAD :

Total length of road in Pratapgarh district is 2822 km, out of which 2343 km road has been constructed by Public works Department of district Pratapgarh. Under the integrated rural development programmes, construction of roads and link roads are being implement. The road construction is being done under special component plan and Member of Parliament Local Area Development and Member of Legislative Assembly Local Area Development programmes in the Pratapgarh district.

Highest constructed Kuchha road in the Pratapgarh district shown in map-30 is found in Babaganj, Kunda,, Sangipur and Mandhapa Blocks while lowest constructed kuchha road is seen in Lalganj, Sandwa Chandrika, Laxmanpur, Bihar, Shivgarh, Patti and Aspur Devsara blocks of the Pratapgarh district.

Pucca road construction is recorded high in Mangraura block evident from map 31 and lowest pucca road construction is seen in Lalganj and Bihar bock.

Proportionately highest constructed kachha road is seen in Chaumuri, Amuwahi, Sikari kanupur, Varasaray and Aurangabad villages (Table-6) while very low constructed kachha road is seen in Bhawapur, Shankarpur, Shahpur, Kandharpur, Varaha, Saray Shankar, Hathasara, Etawaha, Bhadauna and Raigarh villages of the Mangraura block.

Constructed Pucca road is found higher in Narayanpur, Sakara, and Katari villages while lowest constructed pucca road in seen in Madura Raniganj, Narharpur, Hathasara villages of Mangraura block.

Chak road construction is found maximum in Kohndaur, Rampur, Bhawapur, Shankarpur, Parasrampur, Madura Raniganj, Atarsand, Chanduadih, Sakara, Koni, Sarai rajai, Shalhipur kanjas. Malak, Gahrauli, Shashpur, Kandharpur, Chaumuri, Barahupur, Larikala, Gagehati, and Raigarh villages while lowest constructed chak road is seen in Narayanpur, Kanhai Madupur, Suryagarh Jagannath, Aurangbad, Poorabpatti villages of the Mangraura block.

Proportionately maximum construction of bridges are recorded in Sekara, Sahipur Kanjas Sahpur, Sarauli and Dehrai Digar villages of block. Some of the villages like Kansa Patti, Sarasikham, Mangraura, Hathasara, Sarai Shankar, Aurangabad Mandeh, Varasarai, Ashara, Varikala, Chaumuri, Varaha, Parsanda, Gahrauli, padumpur, Malak, Koni, Sarai Rajai, Katarsand, Lakhipur, Madura Raniganj, Bhawapur and Shankarpur villages are not having bridge and rest of the villages are having approximately one or two bridges constructed as per the requirement.

6. COMMUNICATION :

Transport communication network is well developed in the district. Total length of road ways 1797 km and railways 148 km connecting all important places of the district. There are 14 Post offices in the urban area and 336 post offices in the rural villages of the district Pratapgarh. There are 7 telegram center in the district and approximately 39027 number of telephone connections in the district Pratapgarh. There are 112 Bus station and stops for facilitating transport communication and 15 railway stations are for railway communication.

7. DRINKING WATER :

Drinking water mission programme is being implemented in 104 villages of the district out of which 6 villages are already saturated and 176 India Mark-II Hand pump installation has been earmarked in the rest of the 98 villages for which completion and saturation of the programme is being implemented.

It is observed that proportionately maximum number of India Mark II Hand pumps are installed in Aspur Devsara and Patti blocks of the district while lowest number of India Mark-II handpump is installed in Sandwa , Chandrika, Sangramgarh and Lalganj block of the Pratapgarh district.

Maximum number of India Mark-II handpump is installed in Hohndaur, Madura Raniganj, Atarwand, Amuwahi, Bhausia, Ramapur, Dharauli Medapur, Sakara, Koni villages of the Mangraura block (table-6) and very insignificantly only one India mark-II handpump is installed is Dachhut, Bhivani, Gagehati and Aurangabad villages of the Mangraura block.

8. ENERGY :

There are 1488 electrified and habitated villages in Pratapgarh district. Urbanized 7 villages are also electrified and 1472 scheduled caste colonies have also been electrified in Pratapgarh district.

It is evident from the map-34 that highest number of houses are electrified in Pratapgarh Sadar, Babaganj and Kunda blocks of the district Pratapgarh and lowest number of electrified houses are observed in Aspur Devsara, Patti blocks of the Pratapgarh district. Non-convention energy sources are also facilitated in the district.

Distribution of electrified houses in Mangraura block has been depicted in the map-35. Proportionately highest number of electrified houses are recorded in Ramapur, Kohndaur, Suryagarh, Jagannath, Kanhai Madhupur, Mendah, Sarai Rajai, Atarsand, Koni, sakara and Sarasi Kham villages of the Mangraura block. Lowest number of electrified houses are observed in Gahrauli, Poorbpatti, Aurangabad, Varasarai, Sarai Jamuari, Dharauli, Muphrid, Shespur Adharganj and Asthara villages of the Mangraura block.

Commercial electricity consumption in Mangraura block is insignificant village

Kohndaur, Ramapur, Dharouli Madapur, Atarsand, Madaferpur, Kandharpur, Parsanda, Charmuri, Amuwahi, Dharouli Muphrid, Bhousiya, Mandah, Sarouli, Poorabpatti, Louli Pukhtakham and Sarasi Kham villages are having commercial electricity consumption.

9. Medical/health :

There are 10 community health centers in Pratapgarh district, block level 8 Primary health center and 166 sub centers. There are 49 new Primary Health Centers and 360 new sub centers in district Pratapgarh. Total number of Doctors in the district is 139 and Male health Supeervisor-83, Female Health supervisor-47 in the district. There are 68 male Health workers and 397 female health workers in the district who are engaged in providing health services.

Maximum number of health centers including sub centers are found in Mangraura,Patti and Shivgarh block while minimum number of health center are seen in Pratapgarh sadar, Bahaganj, Sangramgarh, and Aspur Devsara blocks of the Pratapgarh district.

There are 25 health centers in Mangraura block. Village wise location of health center is shown in map-36. The old health centers are 16 in number and 9 health sub centers are also operational in Mangraura block. Thus 25 health centers are engages in providing health services to 62 villages Panchayats of Mangraura block.

Map-29

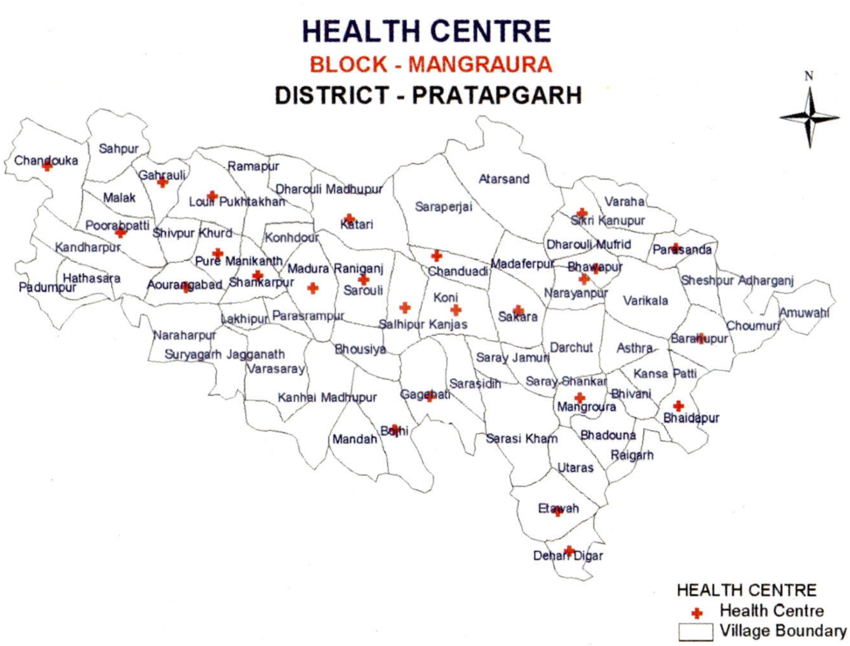

10. AGRO-INDUSTRIES :

Small industries units are 2893 in Pratapgarh district in which 8473 workers are employed (Table-5). Highest number of small industry units are seen in Mangraura,

Lalganj and Sangipur blocks while lowest number of small scale industry units are recorded in Sangramgarh block. Maximum number of small scale industry workers are seen in Pratapgarh Sadar block and lowest workers are found in Sangramgarh block which is shown in the Map-31 in the from of pie diagram.

Khadi gramodyog units are 2671 in Pratapgarh district in which 3566 workers are employed. Highest number of Khadi Gramdyog units are seen in Kunda, Laxmanpur, Pratapgarh Sadar, Patti, Shivgarh, and Gaura blocks while lowest number of khadi gramodyog units are found in Kalakankar and Babaganj blocks of Pratapgarh district. Proportionately highest number of Khadi Gramodyog workers are found in Pratapgarh Sadar block and lowest number of workers are found in Babaganj block of the district Pratapgarh.

There are 17 small scale industries of cotton textiles, drugs and Pharmaceuticals, light engineering and printing. Besides there are furniture, bamboo, and cane work 4345 household workers including oil mill & rice mill – agro-based industries workers are concentrated in the different parts of the district Pratapgarh which is shown in the Map-30.

Proportionate distribution of industrial workers in Pratapgarh district is 1% to the total workers and 4% other workers. There is potential to develop small scale and agro-based industries infrastructure of the district Pratapgarh.

Agro-industries are found in Barahupur, Sikari Kanupur, Bojhi, Varasarai, Narharpur, Pure manikanth Shivpur khurd, Hathasara, Narayanpur, Mangraura, Bhadauna, Bhaidapur, Dehari Digar villages of Mangraura block. Detailed distribution of Agro-industries and Gramodyog units are mentioned in the Table-6.

Map-30

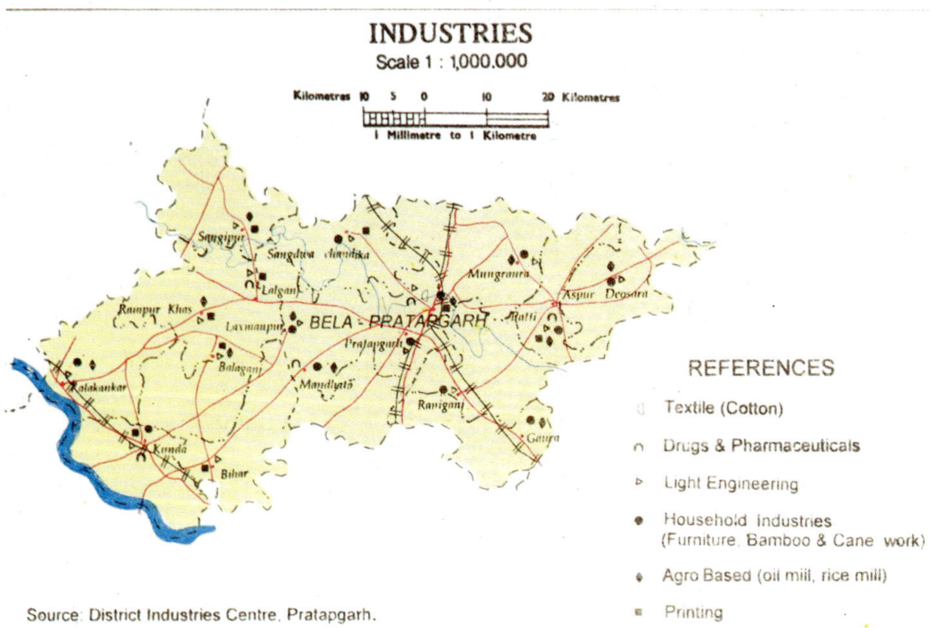

Gramodyog units are found in Kohndaur, Ramapur, Bhawapur, Parasrampur, Madaferpur, Koni, Katari, Malak, Padumpur, Shahpur, Parsanda, Barahupur, Dharauli Muphrid, Sikari Kanupur, Shespur, Adharganj, Kanhai, Medhupur, Bojhi, Gagehati, Sarouli, Aurangabad, Puremani Kanth, Sarai Shankar, Narayanpur, Utaras, Sarasidhi, Bhadouna villages of Mangraura block.

Map-31

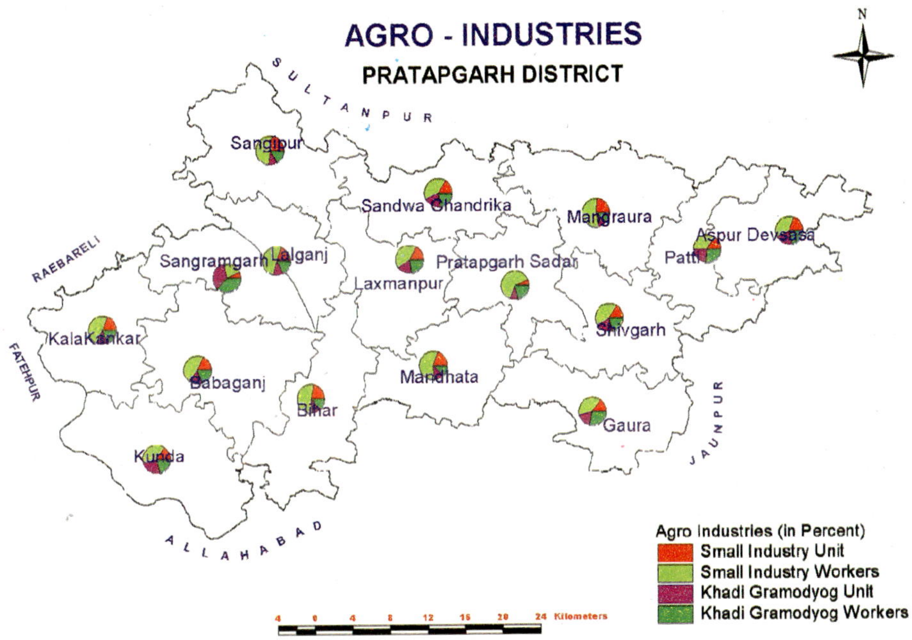

Highest more than 10 number of employed workers are found in Rampur, Dharouli Madapur, Shakarpur, Parasrampur, Madaferpur, Sakara Koni, Katari, Malak, Shahpur, Barahupur, Sikari Kanupur, Kanhai Madhupur, Gagehati, Pure Mani Kanth, Shivpur khurd, Narayanpur, Mangraura, Sarasidih, Bhadauna, and Dehra Digar villages of the Mangraura block, while rest of the villages where Agro-industries and Gramodyog units are functioning has less than 10 numbers of employed workers.

11. ANIMAL HOSPITALS :

There are 45 animal hospitals in Pratapgarh district and 49 animal health service centers, 12 artificial insemination centers and 55 artificial inseminization sub centers in District Pratapgarh. Thus there are 151 animal hospitals and animal development centers in Pratapgarh district.

Proportionately maximum 15 numbers of animal health and development center are found in Mangraura block and lowest 6 numbers of animal health and animal development centers are recorded in Babaganj block. Details of the distribution of animal health centers and animal hospitals are mentioned in Table-5. It is observed that in comparison to number 06 animals the animal hospitals and animal health & development centers are very nominal in Pratapgarh district. Thus animal hospitals and animal development centers infrastructure potentialities has to be developed in district Pratapgarh and also in Mangraura block.

12. HOUSING :

Low cost housing scheme is known as Indira Awas Yojana, Housing scheme is being implemented under Integrated Rural Development Programme of the district. In this scheme 104 villages of the district have been selected in which 2672 low cost houses are being constructed in the Pratapgarh district.

Indira Awas Yojana is being implemented by the Government of India and State Government of Uttar Pradesh having 75% and 25% financial contribution respectively. Indira Awas Yojana is being provided to the below poverty line people and without housing poor families. Scheduled caste, Bonded labours, widow, Handicapped persons are given due priority for Indira Awas Yojana. Besides the Integrated Rural Development Programme of Indira Awas Yojana another housing facility for 1607 houses construction has been also supported for the identified selected beneficiaries and mostly the construction of housing has been completed.

Low Cost Housing scheme has been implemented in the various villages of Mangraura block, but few villages viz., Bhawapur, Prasasram rampur, Solhipur Kanjas, Padumpur villages have not been covered center the Indira Awas Yojana because these villages are not having the beneficiaries belonging to the below poverty line, scheduled caste, widow, Handicapped bounded labour etc. category. Proportionately highest number of India Awas Yojana facilitated in the Sikari Kanupur, Sheshpur Adhasganj, Atarsand, Salhipur Kanjas, Puremani Kanth, sarasi Kham villages (Table-6) of the Block Mangraura and lowest number of low cost housing scheme has been provided in Shankarpur, Varikala, Bhousiya, Mandah, Varasarai, Gagehati, Daschhut and Dehri Digar villages of the Mangraura block.

Thus housing is the one of the basis needs of man kind in terms of safely, security, self-esteem, social status, cultural identify satisfaction and achievement. Housing for all is the goal of the government. Keeping this fact into consideration rural housing in Pratapgarh and in Mangraura block has been constructed as per the needy deprived rural multitudes and criteria laid for the selection of beneficiaries for Indira Awas Yojana.

13. BANKING :

There are 59 Nationalised banks and 4 other banks in district Pratapgarh. There are 72 rural banks and 25 co-operative banks in the district. Agriculture co-operative and Rural Development Bank is having 5 branches in the Pratapgarh district.

14. EDUCATIONAL INFRASTRUCTURE :

Pratapgarh district is having 1881 Junior Basic Schools and 488 Senior Basic Schools. There are 195 senior secondary schools and 5 Degree Colleges and 7 Post Graduate Colleges in the Pratapgarh district. There are 3 Industrial Training Institute and one polytechnic Institute in Pratapgarh District. As per the population growth number of educational institutions are nominal and it is very important to develop the educational Infrastructure of the Pratapgarh district and also Mangraura Block.

15. TOURISM :

There are some important tourist places in the Pratapgarh district. The archaeological remains of Buddhist monastery found in Pratapgarh can be developed for tourism. The Manikpur, the ancient town stands by the Ganga is full of ruins of political residences built during the reign of Akbar can be promoted for tourism. The Inyahiapur temple of Baba Belkharnath Dham can also be developed for tourism.

The district Pratapgarh has potentialities to develop the tourism infrastructure. In view of the above District Administration of the Pratapgarh has planned to develop the Belha Devi and Belkhar nath Dham temple for tourism for which suitable financial support has also been made available to the implementing agency. Financial support for tourism development has been made available to develop Jwala Mukhi temple, Ghuisarnath temple, Chauharjan Devi Dham temple. Various tourist places are developed and it beautification programme is being implemented to promote and develop the tourism infrastructure of the District Pratapgarh Common minimum requirement viz., electricity, drinking water, low cost sanitation and link road facilities are also made available to the various religious temples located in the different parts of the district Pratapgarh.

16. CONCLUSION :

Thus, the infrastructural resources plays on important role in the economic development of any area. The available infrastructure play a key role in the process of planning. Therefore, available infrastructural resources must be given due importance in the formulation of planning because the existing infrastructural resources are the backbone of economic activity and a base for the formulation of need base action plan.

District Pratapgarh has the historical, archaeological religious and cultural importance which has potentialities to develop the tourism infrastructure of the district. The archaeological remains of Buddhist monastery available in the district can be developed a truism infrastructure. The religious temples can also be developed for devotees and tourists as an infrastructure.

The transport and communication network of the Pratapgarh district is well developed . The road ways and railways network are connecting all the important places of the Pratapgarh District.

Drinking water programme is also being implement at larger scale in Pratapgarh district. Some of the selected villages of the district has been saturated under Drinking Water Mission Programme while other selected village are being saturated. It has been recorded that most of the villages have provided minimum drinking water facility but some of the villages are facing polluted under ground water source for which district Administration has initiated suitable remedies to solved the polluted water.

The most of villages of the Pratapgarh district has been electrified and most of the households have been facilitated by the electricity and commercial electricity consumption in the district is very nominal in rural areas excepting marketing centers and urbanized areas including urban areas as well. Therefore electricity infrastructure has to be promoted and developed to promote the economic growth and implementation of planned developmental programmes in the district Pratapgarh.

Medical health facilities are appropriate in the Pratapgarh district as per the population ration medical health facilities has to be promoted and developed. Animal hospitals are property distributed in the Pratapgarh district.

Banking infrastructure, animal husbandry and educational infrastructure are properly distributed in the Pratapgarh district.

Small scale industries and agro-based industries and Khadi & village industries and Gramodyog units are concentrated in the different parts of the district Pratapgarh. There are 1% industrial and 4% other workers. Temple of Belkharnath dham stands in Yahiapur. Dahiawan and Daudpur are noted for bloodshed during the mutiny.

Thus the district Pratapgarh has infrastructural potentialities to develop small scale and agro-based industries and tourism by utilizing the available local infrastructural resources. Therefore infrastructural resources, needs a proper planning for the economic growth and development of the infrastructural resources of the Pratapgarh district. Thus infrastructural resources will be an asset in the planning process at village level in Mangraura block and also at block level in Pratapgarh district and it will be helped in the implementation of planned developmental programmes with the continued participation of the people and sustenance of the successfully implemented planned village developmental programmes.

Table -5 : Natural Resources Data Management System (NRDMS)
Pratapgarh district
Infrastructural Resources

Sl. No	*Block*	*Animal Hospital / Dev. Centre*	*Agro-Industries*				*Medical/Health*	
			Small Industry		*Khadi Gramodyog*		*Centre*	*Doctor*
			Unit	*Workers*	*Unit*	*Workers*		
1	*2*	*3*	*4*	*5*	*6*	*7*	*8*	*9*
1	KalaKankar	7	137	342	97	130	11	7
2	Babaganj	6	103	256	88	111	7	6
3	Kunda	14	137	342	213	179	13	14
4	Bihar	9	203	501	105	127	11	13
5	Sangipur	10	262	611	126	196	9	4
6	Lalganj	5	252	630	148	202	8	9
7	Laxmanpur	6	209	520	202	292	8	7
8	Sandwa Chandrika	8	142	355	178	199	10	9
9	Pratapgarh Sadar	12	175	1826	278	598	7	5
10	Mandhata	11	222	612	121	131	9	7
11	Mangraura	15	285	655	117	149	16	9
12	Patti	8	142	310	211	251	15	12
13	Aspur Devsasa	13	193	370	192	216	7	8
14	Shivgarh	8	208	550	249	263	18	11
15	Gaura	9	198	521	227	394	12	9
16	Sangramgarh	10	25	72	119	128	5	9
	Total	151	2893	8473	2671	3566	166	139

Table -6 : Natural Resources Data Management System (NRDMS)
Mangraura Block
Infrastructural Resources (Village Plan)

Loc_ code	*Vill Name*	*Elect _v*	*Low _c_h*	*Agro_ ind*	*Gramo*	*Emp-loy*	*P_ Road*	*K_ Road*	*Bridge*	*Chak-road*	*Health*
1	Konhdour	367	25	0	1	8	1.50	0.70	1	1.60	0
2	Ramapur	400	31	1	1	10	2.00	0.30	1	1.90	0
3	Dharouli Madapur	160	25	3	0	15	1.50	0.90	1	1.40	0
4	Bhawapur	289	0	0	1	4	1.00	0.15	0	1.90	1
5	Shankarpur	140	8	2	0	10	2.00	0.16	0	2.50	1
6	Madura Raniganj	97	17	0	0	0	0.50	0.40	0	2.10	1
7	Parasrampur	128	0	1	1	16	0.80	0.27	1	1.70	0
8	Lakhipur	103	24	0	0	0	2.30	1.15	0	1.20	0
9	Atarsand	513	60	0	0	0	1.00	0.27	0	1.50	0
10	Madaferpur	289	10	1	1	13	1.75	1.15	3	2.50	0
11	Chanduadih	213	25	0	0	0	2.00	0.50	2	1.50	1
12	Sakara	346	21	2	0	11	3.50	0.70	10	2.00	1
13	Koni	453	12	2	2	18	1.50	0.40	0	3.00	1
14	Sarairajai	345	80	1	0	8	1.00	0.35	0	2.70	0
15	Salhipur Kanjas	270	0	0	0	0	2.00	0.60	9	2.47	1
16	Katari	196	22	1	1	12	3.00	0.45	2	1.27	1
17	Malak	188	13	2	0	11	1.00	1.30	0	2.45	0
18	Padumpur	100	0	1	0	6	2.30	0.25	0	1.24	0
19	Gahrauli	7	17	0	1	7	1.25	0.30	0	2.47	1
20	Sahpur	96	10	1	1	14	2.00	0.15	3	1.50	0
21	Kandharpur	199	25	0	0	0	1.50	0.16	1	2.45	0
22	Chandouka	300	14	0	1	8	1.25	0.37	1	1.40	1
23	Parasanda	92	27	1	0	6	1.50	1.35	0	1.20	1
24	Choumuri	90	21	0	0	0	2.50	1.65	0	1.60	0
25	Varaha	150	48	0	0	0	1.25	0.19	0	0.90	0
26	Barahupur	100	12	1	2	10	1.24	0.24	2	1.80	1
27	Varikala	81	9	0	0	0	2.75	0.36	0	1.50	0
28	Asthra	64	24	0	0	0	1.25	0.28	0	1.35	0
29	Amuwahi	100	13	0	0	0	1.45	1.50	1	1.26	0
30	Dharouli Muphrid	59	26	0	1	3	1.36	1.30	1	1.30	0
31	Sikri Kanupur	129	60	2	1	17	1.80	1.73	1	1.10	1
32	Sheshpur Adharganj	36	51	0	1	7	2.30	0.90	0	0.56	0
33	Kanhai Madupur	500	24	0	1	6	1.56	0.40	0	0.40	0
34	Bojhi	100	13	2	2	11	1.87	0.50	2	1.34	1
35	Bhousiya	147	2	0	0	0	1.24	0.78	1	1.47	0
36	Mandah	350	7	0	0	0	1.30	1.40	0	1.26	0
37	Varasaray	61	8	1	0	7	1.28	1.90	0	1.46	0
38	Gagehati	200	9	0	2	16	1.24	0.38	1	1.50	1
39	Sarouli	250	22	0	1	7	2.00	0.90	3	1.47	1
40	Suryagarh Jagannath	400	13	0	0	0	2.12	1.20	1	0.46	0
41	Aourangabad	13	25	0	1	9	1.75	1.50	0	0.38	1
42	Naraharpur	132	48	1	0	4	0.50	1.46	1	1.32	0
43	Pure Manikanth	203	65	1	1	11	1.50	0.70	2	1.30	1
44	Poorabpatti	67	25	0	0	0	1.25	0.30	2	0.40	1
45	Shivpur Khurd	160	16	2	0	11	1.35	0.93	1	1.60	0
46	Saray Shankar	85	14	0	1	7	0.75	0.15	0	0.90	0
47	Hathasara	100	12	3	0	0	0.50	0.16	0	1.20	0
48	Louli Pukhtakham	110	21	0	0	0	1.25	0.24	1	0.80	1

Loc_ code	Vill Name	Elect _v	Low _c_h	Agro_ ind	Gramo	Emp-loy	P_ Road	K_ Road	Bridge	Chak-road	Health
49	Darchut	100	6	0	0	13	2.40	0.25	1	0.56	0
50	Narayanpur	187	33	1	1	0	3.25	0.40	1	0.16	1
51	Sarasi Kham	390	65	0	0	17	2.75	0.27	2	1.17	0
52	Mangroura	158	37	2	0	0	1.70	0.30	0	1.23	1
53	Saray Jamuari	19	31	0	0	8	2.40	0.25	0	0.90	0
54	Utaras	249	62	0	1	12	2.50	0.40	1	1.20	0
55	Sarasidih	250	12	0	1	0	1.50	0.60	2	1.30	0
56	Etawah	200	24	0	0	19	1.20	0.19	1	0.65	1
57	Bhadouna	150	31	2	1	0	1.40	0.18	1	1.17	0
58	Bhivani	200	25	0	0	8	1.24	0.70	1	1.26	0
59	Bhaidapur	169	13	1	0	0	1.30	0.90	1	1.32	1
60	Kansa Patti	100	24	0	0	0	1.25	0.40	0	0.44	0
61	Raigarh	90	12	0	0	15	1.80	0.19	0	1.60	0
62	Dehari Digar	98	7	3	0	18	1.25	0.25	3	0.70	1

CHAPTER - VI

RURAL DEVELOPMENT PROGRAMME

1. INTRODUCTION :

The economic development has been realized and commendable advances have been made in the diverse field of rural development programmes would in reality be in complete, if such rural developmental programmes fail to translate into better and dignified life for the majority of people who live in remote rural areas.

Increasingly there is a talk of divided between rural urban.

- Rural Area
- Urban Area
- Rur-ban Area

It is argued that faster development is required to bridge this divide between rural, rur-ban and urban areas. Then urban areas are comparatively more developed than rural to run-ban areas (Rus ban) while rus ban area are developed more that the rural areas. Therefore appropriate and faster development of rural areas are required to fulfill the increasing demand of increasing population so that the disparities between rural to urban can be bridged, the ensure integrated development.

It has been felt that the development should be participatory and it should be planned according to the local needs of deprived rural multitudes. Development should be planned through tapping the local talent and available natural and human resources of the region in order to make the implemented developmental programmes self sustainable , various rural developmental programmes are being implemented, aiming at sustainable development of rural areas, with a focus on enhancing the livelihoods of weaker and vulnerable sections of the society. In conformity with the commitment to accord foremost priority to rural development, a number of steps have been initiated to make the implementation of ongoing programmes more effective and accelerated.

Implementation of rural developmental programmes can be made more effective through peoples participation. Thus the rural development should be for the rural people and it should be maintained and sustained through the rural people. Participatory planning and development should be initiated at grass root/village level. It has been mentioned in the constitution of India that "Governments should evolve methods to unite the village panchayat and provide such powers and and right, which can be helpful to work as an unit of Self-Government.

It has been stated by Mahatma Gandhi ji that "In the Panchayati Raj System, each village should be self sustained and in dependent, the implementation of the welfare programmes of rural masses,can be implement in a better manner in the villages of vast rural India".

In view of the above, as per policy of government of India, the State Government of Uttar Pradesh established Self Government in rural areas. Historical and revolutionary decision has been taken to allot the work, to allocate financial resources to implement the planned programmes and allocated financial and administrative rights to provide the Self-Governance of village Panchayat, Block Panchayat and district Panchayat.

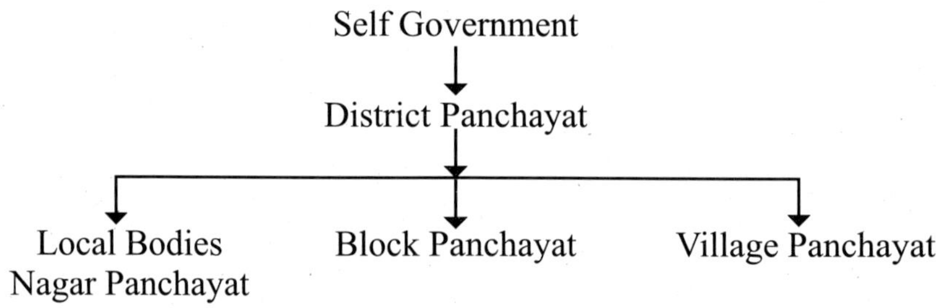

Development unit shall be the village in this new system of decentralization village shall be the Central focal print for development. Really it will be meaningful to transfer this in the planning and developmental programme and its control and management will be ensured through people participation. Planning Process will be done from bottoms top. After independence first of all revolutionary steps of decentralization will bring total change in the life of rural villagers and it will provide a new era for integrated development of rural areas.

The real meaning of democracy is the importance of the people and rural government is the main sole of rural development. Government, management, financial and administrate control of village Panchayat and continued participation and cooperation of the to establish village-Panchayat for self Government for peoples participatory planning, implementation of rural developmental programmes for sustenance.

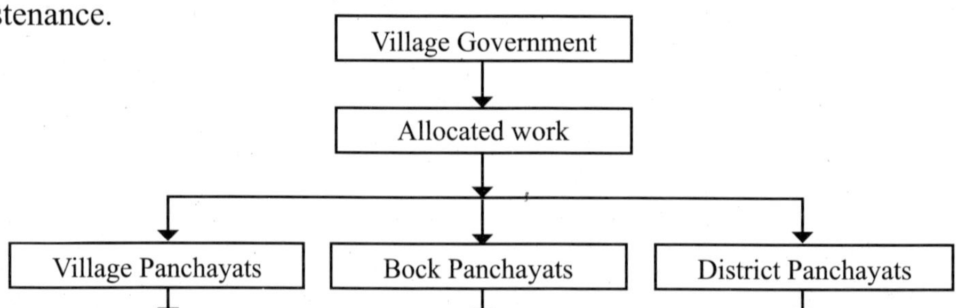

Village Panchayats	Bock Panchayats	District Panchayats
1. Education - Primary & Secondary Education	1. Rural Development Programmes	1. Medican & Health
2. Government Tubewells	2. Primary Health Centre	2. Development Programmes
3. Hand Pumps	3. Animal Hospital	3. Education
4. Youth welfare	4. Seed Centre	4. Tubewells Govt.
5. Medical & Health	5. Marketing store	5. Yourth welfare
6. Women & Child Development	6. Look of Additional villages	6. Women & child Development
7. Animal Department	7. Maintenance of Assets	7. Animal Department
8. Food supply shops		8. Food supply shops
9. Agriculture work		9. Agriculture & Horticulture Dept.
10. Rural Development		10. Panchayati Raj
11. Panchayati Raj Department		11. Jal Nigam
12. All Types of Pension & Scholorships		12. Food Supply
		13. Forest Dept.
		14. Public works Dept.
		15. Irrigation Dept.
		16. Industries
		17. Fisheries Dept.
		18. Other Departments

Allocated works of village, Block and district Panchayats including various Departmental Programmes are described. Thus, it can be said that education, tubewells, Handpumps, youth welfare, Medical Health, women & child development, Animal Food supply shops, agriculture, rural development, Panchayati Raj, Scholarship & pension related works at village level is being looks by village Panchayats.

Committees of Panchayats

Committees	Works	Constitution of Committee
Planning & Development	Plan Formulation & Agriculture, Animal & Poverty alleviation programm	1. Chairman 2. 6 other members (one member each Sc, BC & women)
Education	Primary, Sr. Secondary Education.Information EducationLiteracy etc. work	1. Chairman 2. 4 other members (SC, BC, Women) 3. Head master 4. 3 Gaurdians.
Construction	All construction works & to ensure quality work	1. Chairman 2. 4 other members (SC, BC, women
Health welfare	Medical, Health, Family welfare women & child development, Social welfare, Shaeduled case backward class development programmes	1. Chairman 2. 4 other members (SC, BC, women)
Administrative	Personnel/Staff related all works	1. Chairman 2. 4 other members (SC, BC, Women)

Block Panchayat is looks after rural development, Primary Health Centre, Seed Centre & Animal hospital, Marketing stores works of additional villages and maintenance of assets of block panchayats.

District Rural Development Agency (DRDA) is reconstituted i.e. Chairman – DRDA at present is the Chairman District Panchayat. In the Governing Body of DRDA 5 additional members are included viz. Chairman of 5 standing committees of district Panchayats. District Fisheries Development Agency is Chaired by Chairman District Panchayat including 5 Chairman of the standing committees of District Panchayat.

Chairman of Sinchai Bandhu is Chairman District Panchayat. Various Financial Schemes are being implemented by the Chief Development officer, through District Rural Development Agency (DRDA) in which various district level implementing line departments are transferred under the control of District Panchayats.

District Planning Committee has been formed which is chaired by the nominated minister of the State Government; Chairman district Panchayat is Vice-Chairman and the District headquarters. Local Body Chairman is the Vice-Chairman of the Zila Yojana Samiti, collector of the district member by post, and members of Parliament, Members of legislative assembly is the permanent member of Zila Yojana Samiti. Chief Executive Officer is the Member Secretary and District Economic & Statistical officer is the Joint Secretary of the District Planning Committee and other members are nominated by the Government. Village, block and district plan is formulated every year. Thus the decentralization of government system i.e. Self Government from village-block-district Panchayats has been ensured and those Panchayats has be provided administrative and financial rights for the formulation of various developmental programmes ensuring peoples participation its implementation and making the implemented programmes self sustained.

An attempt has been made to describe the various rural developmental programmes being implemented by the village Panchayat, Block Panchayat and district Panchayat in Mangraura block and District Pratapgarh respectively. Analysis of various rural development programmes includes schemes supported by government of India, State government of Uttar Pradesh and local bodies of the district including District-Block and village Panchayats in the various blocks of district Pratapgarh and in the different villages of Mangraura block.

Sampoorna Grameen Rajgar Yojana is being implemented to provide additional wage employment in the rural areas as also food security alongside the creation of durable community, social and economic infrastructure in the rural areas. The programme is self targeting in nature with special emphasis to provide wage employment to women, scheduled caste and parents of children withdrawn from hazardous occupations.

Pradhan Mantri Gram Sadak Yojana aims to expand and renovate rural road network which will lead to agricultural growth, increase rural employment opportunities, better access to Health, education other public services and general improvement in the quality of life, bridging the rural-urban divide.

Rural Housing is the basic needs of mankind in terms of safety, security, self esteem, social status, cultural , identity, satisfaction, and achievement "Housing for all" is the goal of government. To meet the shortage of housing in rural villages, the Indira Awas Yojana is launched as a sub-scheme of Jawahar Rojgar Yojana.

Swarn Jayanti Gram Swarozgar Yojana is a significant step to have sustained income and remove the shackles of poverty through self employment. Self employment involves procurement of raw material, marketing of goods and dealing with finance.significant step to have sustained income and remove the shackles of poverty through self employment. Self employment involves procurement of raw material, marketing of goods and dealing with finance.

Watershed Development Programme for development of wastelands/degraded lands namely Drought Prone Areas Programme (DAAP), Desert Development Programme (DDP) and Integrated wastelands Development Programme (IWDP). A new initiative called 'Hariyali' with the objective of empowering Panchayati Raj Institutions both financially and administratively in implementation of Watershed Development Programme.

Land Reforms Scheme is being implemented for computerization of Land Reforms (CLR) and strengthening of Revenue Administration and updating of Land Records (SRI & ULR).

Rural water supply Programme is being implemented for providing drinking water facilities to rural areas because water is an essential ingredient of our daily life. The importance of safe drinking water can not be under estimated. Poor quality of water causes many diseases.

Central Rural Sanitation Programme is being implemented to remove the disposal of human excrete of cess-pools, open ditches, pit latrines, bucket system etc. It is well known fact that a direct relationship exists between water, sanitation and health, consumption of unsafe drinking water improper disposal of human excreta and lack of personal and food hygiene have been the major causes of many diseases. High infant mortality rate (IMR) is also attributed largely to poor sanitation.

Pradhan Mantri Grameen Jal Samvardhan Yojana is being implemented with the objective of drought proofing the identified dry and rainfed areas through location specific water conservation measures and water storage technologies to mitigate the adverse effects of drought. Improving ground water potential and augmenting water supply especially for meeting drinking water requirements through harvesting of rain water in water stressed villages. Better management of water domain especially in over exploited areas for improving soil moisture availability and water security in holistic manner in long term.

Besides, various rural development programmes are being implemented in the district Pratapgarh. An attempt is made to describe the various rural development programme being implemented at village level in Mangraura block and also at block level in the district Pratapgarh.

2. SWARN JAYANTI GRAM SWAROJGAR YOJANA:

Self-Employment is a significant step to have sustained income and remove the poverty. An integrated Self-Employment Programme-Swarn Jayanti Gram Swarojgar Yojana (SGSY) is launched with focus on :

- Group approach
- Identification of key activities with desired backward and forward linkages.
- Developing activity clusters.

In this scheme assistance is given to the poor families living below the poverty line for taking up self employment are called as "Swarojgars". They may take the activity either individually or in groups called the Self-Help Groups. Activities are selected based on the availability of raw materials, skill, aptitude of the people and market potentiality of the product. These are called "Key Activities" and Swarojgaris get appreciable sustained income from the selected activity over a period of tie to enable the swarojgaris to cross the poverty line.

The are 6804 beneficiaries under Swarnjanti Swarojgar Yojana (SG-SY) in Pratapgarh. Highest number of SG-SY scheme beneficiaries are found in Kalakankar block (Table –7) and lowest number of SG-SY beneficiaries are observed in Baba bheltharnath Dham, Gaura and Laxmanpur block of the district Pratapgahr. Detailed distribution of Rojgar Yojana is depicted in the Map-32.

Map-32

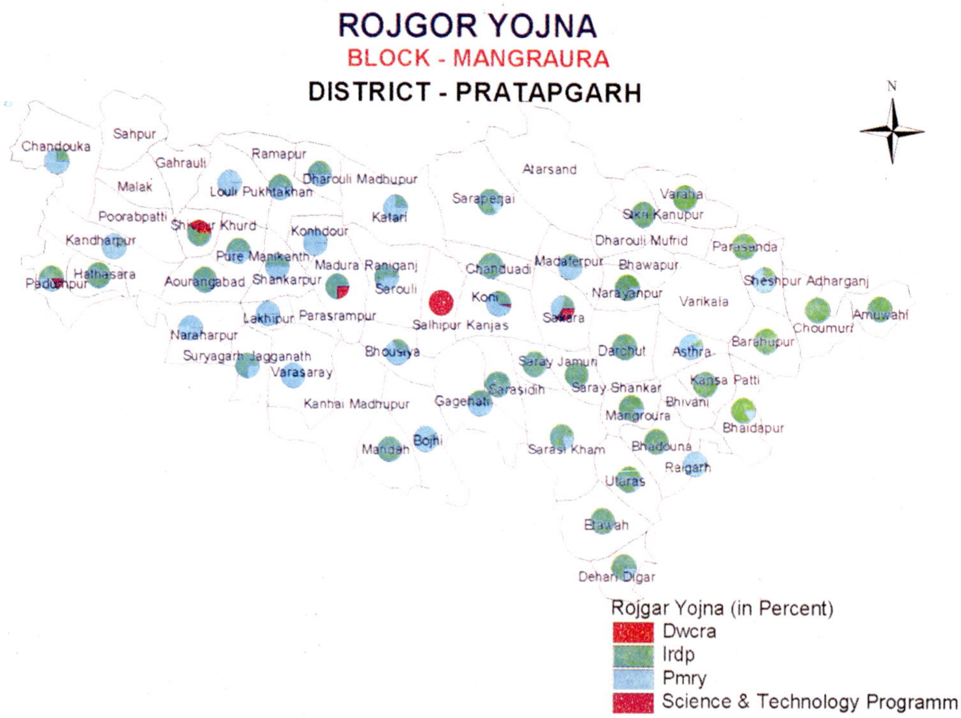

Selected number of beneficiaries in Mangraura block under Swarnjayanti Gram Swarojagar yojana are 358. The highest number of SG-SY beneficiaries are observed in Raigarh Sikari Kanpur villages (Table-8) while village- Bhousiya Bhaidapur and Sarasidih has no beneficiaries selected under the SG-SY scheme and very nominal SG-SY beneficiaries are seen in Gagehati, Narharpur, Sheshpur Adharganj, villages of the Mangraura block.

Under the Swarnjayanti Gram Swarojgar Yojana (SG-SY) 1837 groups were passed under first grade out of which cash credit limit was sanctioned for 1356 and 256 groups were passed in the second grade and 248 groups were financially supported and linked with the main activities.

3. SAMPOORNA GRAMEEN ROJGAR YOJANA:

Sampoorna Grameen Rojgar Yojna (SG-RY) has been launched to provide additional wage employment in the rural areas as also food security, alongside the creation of durable community, social and economic infrastructure, in the rural areas. The programme is self targeting in nature with special emphasis to provide wage employment to women, scheduled caste and parents of children withdrawn from hazardous occupations. The SG-RY scheme is implemented through Panchayati Raj Institutions at the district, intermediate and village level. There are 4685 beneficiaries benefited under the Samporrna Grameen Rojgar Yojana in Pratapgarh district (Table-7), out of which highest number of beneficiaries are observed in Pratapgarh Sadar and Babaganj blocks while lowest number of beneficiaries are seen in the Baba

Bhelkharnath, Sangramgarh, gaura Shivgarh, Aspur Devsara, Mangraura, Lalganj, Bihar and Kalakankar block of the district Pratapgarh.

Sampoorna Gramin Rojgar Yojana being implemented for maximum employment to facilitate wage and food so that the migration of workers are stopped and for construction of permanent assets. In this scheme food and cash is being paid to the labours. It has been recorded that 18295 lakh man day employment has been created and 13767 metri ton food has been distributed and a sum of Rs. 2981.66 lakh expenditure has been ensured.

There are 149 beneficiaries supported under the Sampoorna Grameen Rojgar Yojana in Mangraura block. Highest number of SGRY beneficiaries are found in Kohndaur, Atarsand, Katari, Dharouli Muphrid, Barahupur, Kandharpur, Chandauka village (Tabl-8) and lowest number of beneficiaries under SG-RY scheme are found in Malak, Mandah, Poorbpatti villages while Saray Shankar, Narharpur, Gagehati, Varikala, Varaha, Chaumuri, Dharouli Madapur, Madura Raniganj, Madaferpur Koni, Salhipur khas and Parsanda villages are not yet covered under the s Samporrna Grameen Rojgar Yojana in Mangraura block.

4. ENERGY :

Complete electrification of the selected rural villages under integrated rural development programme has been launched in the Pratapgarh district. The electrification programme is also implemented under the special component plan scheme. Non-conventional energy development is also promoted in the district.

There are 1,56,278 electrified houses in the Map-33 in the district Pratapgarh. Proportionately maximum number of electrified houses are seen in Pratapgarh Sadar and Babaganj blocks (Table-7) and lowest number of electrified houses are observed in Baba Bhelkharnath, Shivgarh, Aspur Devsara and Patti blocks of the district Pratapgarh.

Map-33

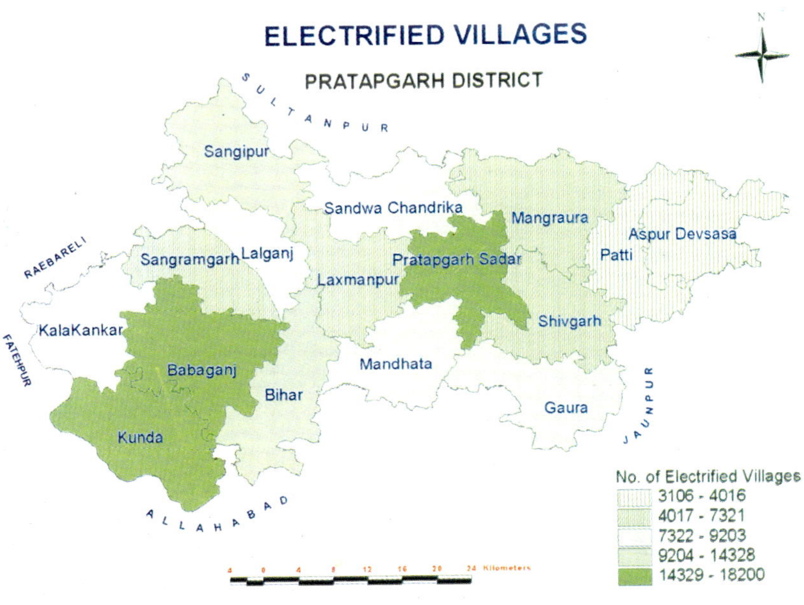

Sadar pump, Solar light and other non-conventional energy devices have been made available to the interested beneficiaries at concessional rate in the district Pratapgarh. Various demonstration, extension and training programmes on non-conventional energy sources have been implemented in the district Pratapgarh.

National Bio-Gas and fertilizer management programme is being implemented in the district with the view to provide cheap working gas and Bio-fertilizer to increase the fertility status of the soil.

There are 709 commercial electricity connection in the district Pratapgarh. Highest number of commercial electricity consumers are found in Kalakankar, Sandwachandrika, Pratapgarh Sadar and Mangraura blocks while lowest number of commercial electricity consumers are seen in Baba Bhekkhar Dham, Shivgarh and Mandhata blocks of the district Pratapgarh. The highest number of electrified houses are found in Atarsand, Rampur, Kohndour, Sakara, Kanjas, Sarsi Kham, Mandah villages of the Mangaura block. The details distribution of electrified house are depicted in the Map-33. There are 71 commercial electricity consumers in Mangraura block of the district.

Map-33

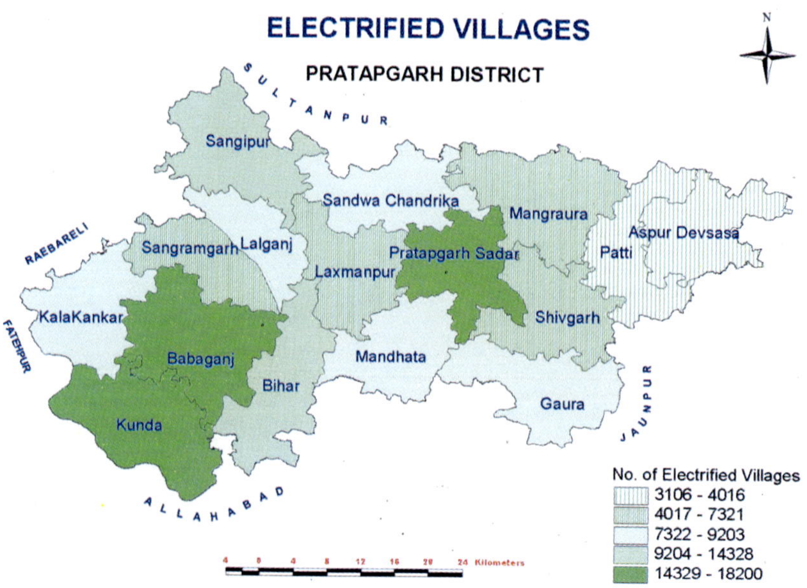

5. SMALL SCALE INDUSTRIES :

In Pratapgarh district, there are 17 small scale industries of cotton, textiles, drugs and pharmaceuticals, light engineering and printing and besides there are 4345 household – furniture, bamboo and cane work and agro-based industries – oil mill and rice mills are concentrated in the different parts of the district Pratapgarh.

There are 24 percent agricultural workers, 1% industrial workers 4% other workers, 3% marginal workers and 68% non-workers in the district Pratapgarh.

The details of the employed persons in Mangraura block at village level is shown in the Map-39. The highest number of employed persons are seen in the Lakhipur,

Dharouli Madhupur Saray Shankar and Bhadauna villages while lowest number of employed persons are found in the Amuwahi. Barahupur Asthra, Raigarh, Sarasikham, Saray Jamuri, Koni Madura Raniganj, Saouli, Bhousiya, Shankarpur, varasarya, Kanhai Madhupur, Aurangabad, Louli Pukhtakhan, Shankarpur and Poorabpatti villages.

As per available information through secondary sources of data there are 136 cottage industry in the Pratapgarh district, out of which highest number of cottage industries are found in Pratapgarh Sadar block while block Mandhata has no cottage industry but very insignificant cottage industries are found in Babaganj, Lalganj and Patti Blocks.

There are 13 cottage industries in Mangraura block. Maximum number of cottage industries are found in Kohndaur village of Mangraura block.

There are 120 Gramodyog units in Pratapgarh districts (Table-7). Maximum number of Gramodyog units are found in Pratapgarh Sadar, Shivgarh, Gaura, Kunda and Bihar blocks while lowest number of Gramodyog units are seen in Sangramgarh, Baba Bhelkharnath and Laxmanpur blocks of the district Pratapgarh.

There are 5 Gramodyog working units in Mangraura block out of which maximum number of Gramodyog units are found in Kohndaur village of the Mangraura block because Kohndaur is the main marketing centre of the blockand this village is located on the National High way from Allahabad to Faizabad. Requisite facilities for the establishment of cottage industry and Gramodyog units are also available in Kohndaur village of Mangraura block.

6. FOOD SUPPLY CENTRES :

There are 973 food supply centers in Pratapgarh district out of which maximum number of food supply centers are found in Kunda, Bihar, Mandhata, Mangraura, Patti, Aspur Devsara, Shivgarh, Babu Bhelkhar Nath Dham and Gaura blocks of the district while lowest number of food supply centers are found in Kalakankar, Lalganj and Pratapgarh Sadar blocks of the district Pratapgarh.

There are 65 food supply centers in Mangraura block. It is observed that in each village Panchayat there is food supply centre in Mangraura block is food supply Centre in Mangraura block to facilitate low cost foodgrain and other common minimum requirements of the villagers.

7. DRINKING WATER :

Water is an essential ingredient of our daily life. The importance of safe drinking water cannot be under estimated. Poor quality of water causes many diseases. Drinking water facilities to rural villages are implemented through district Rural Development Agency Pratapgarh. Reforms has been introduced in the rural water supply sector with a view to institutionalize community participation in the implementation of rural drinking water supply programmes where in the beneficiaries will have to bear partial capital cost, full operation and maintenance through Panchayati Raj Institutions. A new initiative of 'Swajaldhara' has been launched with the following key elements –

(a) Demand driven and community participation approach.

(b) Panchayats/Communities to plan, implement, operate maintain and manage all drinking water schemes.
(c) Partial capital cost sharing by the communities upfront in cash.
(d) Full ownership of drinking water assets with Gram Panchayats and
(e) Full operation, management and maintenance by the users/Panchayats.

Beneficiary groups, Gram Panchayats etc. adopting the reform will be eligible for Swajaldhara programmes. 10% community contribution of the estimated capital cost of the schemes up from (5% in case of predominantly scheduled caste habitations) will be integral part of the project and 90% of funds towards the projects excluding community contribution cost will be fully by the Central Government of India.

Thus it has been recorded that there are 24834 India Mark II Hand Pumps in Pratapgarh District installed under the various schemes through District Rural Development Agency.

Pratapgarh district highest number of India Mark-II Hand Pumps are installed in Aspur Devsara block, and Patti block and lowest number of India Mark-II Hand pumps are seen in Lalganj and Sangramgarh blocks (Map –34) of the district Pratapgarh.

Map-34

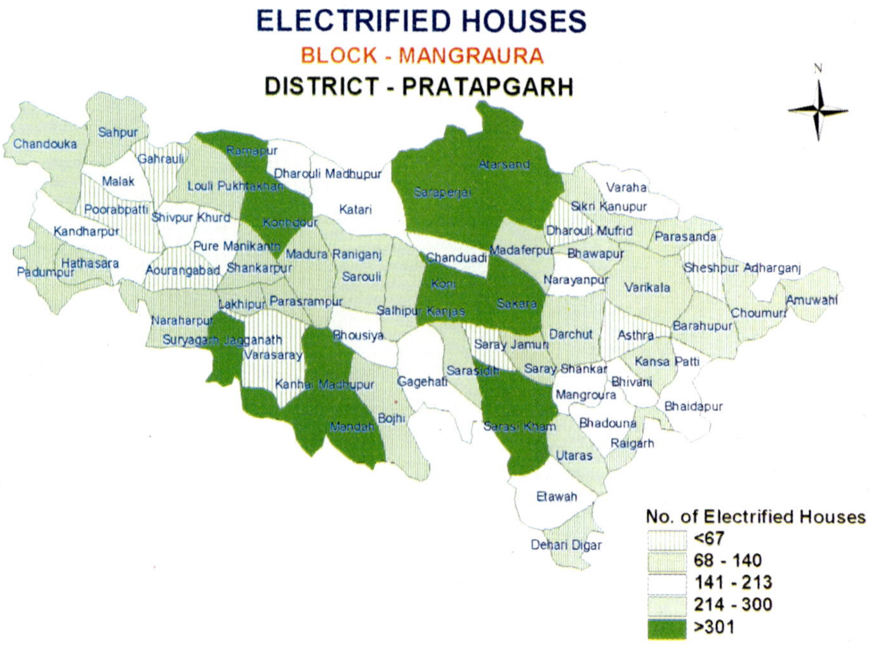

There are 1529 India Mark –II Hand Pumps installed in Mangraura block of the district Pratapgarh. Highest number of hand pumps including Local Hand Pumps and India Mark II Handpumps are installed in Atarsand, Sarairajai, Malak, Shahpur, Chandauka, Dharauli, Muphrid, Sikari Kanupur, Mandah, Gagehati, Aurangabad and Sarai Jamuari villages while lowest number of total hand pumps are seen in Madura Raniganj Dharouli Madapur, Parasrampur, Sakara, Koni, Salhipur Kanjas, Bhousiaya Saryagarh Jagganath villages of the Mangraura block.

8. SANITATION :

There is direct relationship between water, sanitation and health. Consumption of unsafe drinking water improper disposal of human excreta and lack of personal and food hygiene have been the major causes of many diseases in developing countries. High infant mortality rate is also attributed largely to poor sanitation. In view of the above Centrally sponsored Rural Sanitation Programme has been launched.

In the rural villages 22% of households are estimated to have toilet facilities. The sanitation campaign is being implemented with the following major components:

- Construction of individual households latrines.
- Sanitary complex for women.
- School sanitation.
- Awareness Generation.

In Pratapgarh district, there are 4375 rural latrines constructed, out of which maximum number of rural sanitation latrines are constructed in Aspur, Devsara and Gaura block and lowest rural latrines are constructed in Kalakankar block.

In Mangraura block 199 low cost rural latrines are constructed. It is recorded that in Rampur, Dharauli Madapur, Shankarpur, Kohndaur village, Atarsand, Lauli Pukhtakhan more than 10 latrines have been constructed while 62 rural latrines are constructed in Varaha village and Shikari Kanupur, Sheshpur Adharganj, Kanhai Madupur, Mandah Varasaray, Gagehati, Sarouli, Shivpur Khurd villages are having less than 10 constructed rural latrines but rest of the villages are not having any construction of rural sanitation. Thus it is observed that rural sanitation programme in Mangraura block is in significant and rural sanitation programme has not reached among the remote rural villages of Mangraura block.

9. RURAL HOUSING :

In terms of safety, security, self esteem, social status, cultural identify, satisfaction and achievement housing is the basic needs of mankind. "Housing for all" is the goal of the government. Indira Awas Yojana is launched to meet the shortage of housing in rural areas. Indira Awas Yojana aims at providing assistance to rural people below poverty line belonging to scheduled caste and other deprived rural multitudes.

Total number of rural housing facility have been provided to 23355 households belonging to weaker section of society. The highest number of rural houses have been constructed in Lalganj and Kunda blocks while lowest number of rural houses have been constructed in Baba Bhelkharnath Dham and Shivgarh block.

There are 1694 number of rural houses constructed in Mangraura block out of which maximum number of houses are constructed in Atarsand, Sarai Rajai, Sikari Kanupur, Puremanikanth, Sarasikham and Utaras villages while rest of the villages are having very nominal construction of rural houses for the deprived rural altitudes of Mangraura block.

10. WELFARE PROGRAMMES :

Various welfare programmes are being launched in Pratapgarh district, which includes scheduled caste, Backward caste and Minority welfare programmes. There are various schemes of the welfare programmes like scholarships, financial support for self employment and other supports for the needy downtrodden beneficiaries. Different welfare programmes being implemented in the district at block level and also at villages level are analysed.

10.1 Scheduled Caste Welfare Programmes :

Scheduled Caste welfare programmes are being implemented in the Pratapgarh district for which financial allocations have been earmarked for providing Scholarships for scheduled caste student and for the marriage health treatment atrocities etc. and sustained self-employment. Thus there are 61709 number of scheduled caste beneficiaries being benefited under the scheduled caste welfare programmes in the Pratapgarh district. Highest number of Scheduled caste beneficiaries are found in Bihar block (Tabl-7) and lowest number of scheduled caste beneficiaries benefited under scheduled caste welfare programmes. are seen in Sangipur block of the district Pratapgarh.

There are 4454 number of scheduled caste beneficiaries supported under scheduled caste welfare programmes in Mangraura block. Scholarships to the scheduled caste students have been provided to the interested needy students and other type of support including marriage and other needful support have been provided to the needy scheduled caste beneficiaries.

10.2 Backward caste welfare programmes :

Backward caste welfare programmes are being supported to the needy interested backward caste student in Pratapgarh district. There are 9522 number of backward caste beneficiaries being supported under the backward caste welfare programmes in Pratapgarh district. Maximum number of backward caste beneficiaries have been benefited in Pratapgarh sadar block and lowest number of backward caste beneficiaries supported under the backward caste welfare programmes are seen in Sangramgarh block of the district Pratapgarh.

Total 620 number of backward caste beneficiaries are supported under the backward caste welfare programmes in the Mangraura block. The scholarship have been distributed to the needy interested backward caste students under the backward caste welfare schemes in Mangraura block of district Pratapgarh.

10.3 Minority Welfare Programmes :

Various minority welfare programmes have been implemented in the district Pratapgarh. There are 35238 number of minority beneficiaries being benefited under the minority welfare development programmers. Maximum number of minority beneficiaries have been benefited in Laxmanpur block and lowest number of minority beneficiaries supported under the minority welfare programmes are found in Aspur Devsara block of the district Pratapgarh.

There are 3074 number of minority beneficiaries being supported under the minority welfare programmes in Mangraura block. Under the minority welfare scheme, scholarship to the needy interested poor minority students have been distributed in Mangraura block of the district Pratapgarh. There are 1575 handicapped beneficiaries have been supported for integrated development of handicapped beneficiaries in the Pratapgarh district.

11. RURAL ROADS :

It has been recognised that simple physical access in the form of an all weather road is itself a powerful catalyst to economic development. Rural connectivity has, therefore, become an important instrument in the strategy for alleviating poverty. As a subsidiary objective the programme also seeks to improve the condition of Rural Roads so as to ensure synergy. It is expected that an expanded and renovated rural road network will lead to agricultural growth, increase in rural employment opportunities, better access to health, education and other public services and a general improvement in the quality of life, bridging the rural-urban divide. Pucca and kacha road have been constructed in District Pratapgarh under the various programmes launched by the government of India and State Government of Uttar Pradesh.

11.1 Kaccha Road :

Under the various schemes initiated by the District Authorities of Pratapgarh 887 km. rural kaccha road have been constructed in Pratapgarh district. Maximum Kaccha road have been constructed in Mandhata block while lowest distance long kaccha road have been constructed in Lalganj and Sandwa chandrika blocks of the district Pratapgarh.

There are 53 km. long kaccha road constructed in Mangraura block. It has been recorded that in Ramapur, Chanduadih, Sakara, Bojhi, Aurangabad villages highest distance long kaccha road has been constructed while other villages very nominal distance long kaccha road has been constructed.

11.2 Pucca Road :

There are 242836 km long Pucca road constructed in Pratapgarh district. Out of which maximum distance long pucca road have been constructed in Mangraura block as shown in the Map-35 and lowest distance pucca road has been constructed in Bihar block of the district Pratapgarh.

Map-35

There are 216 km. long distance pucca road being constructed under various schemes in Mangraura block. The highest long distance pucca road has been constructed in Kohndaur, Madaferpur koni, Sariarajai, Ko gagehati, Narharpur and Rampur villages while other village are having nominal construction of pucca road under various schemes including Member of Parliament Local Area Development and Member of Legislative Local Area Development Scheme, in Mangraura block of the district Pratapgarh.

12. WOMEN AND CHILD DEVELOPMENT PROGRAMME :

Various women and child development programmes are being implemented in the district Pratapgarh. Downtrodden widows are supported through providing grants-in-aid under the woman development programme while nutrition food and health development programmes for child development have been implemented in Pratapgarh district under the women and child development programme 2013 beneficiaries have been supported in the Pratapgarh district. Maximum number of women & child development programme was ensured in Kunda and Mandhata blocks while lowest number of women and child development beneficiaries have been benefited in Kalakankar, Babaganj, Lalganj and Patti blocks of the district Pratapgarh.

There are 140 number of women and child development beneficiaries benefited under the women and child development programme in Mangraura block. Women and child development programme have been provided to the beneficiaries in Lakhipur, Madaferpur, Koni, Salhipur Kanjas Padumpur, Chandauka, Choumuri, Barahupur, Amuwahi, Bhousiya, Mandah, Surya Jagannath, Narharpur and Sarasikham villages while rest of the villages are having insignificant number of beneficiaries being support under the women and child development programme in Mangraura block of the district Pratapgarh, because child development programme is not being implemented in Mangraura block, only 6 other blocks of the district Pratapgarh have been selected under Food Nutrition and Child Development Programme in the district. Thus is women and child development programme is being implemented at a initial phase in the selected blocks of the district Pratapgarh.

13. AGRICULTURE :

High yielding variety of 6188 qtls seeds have been distributed through U.P. Agro and Agriculture co-operative. During the Rabi and Kharif cropping season 3629 M. ton nitrogen, 12105 m. ton phosphorus and 1754 m. ton potash has been distribute in the district Pratapgarh to increase the agricultural productivity.

Co-operative and commercial banks distributed Rs. 1661.77 crore loan to the farmers for kharif crops and Rs. 2930 crore loan was distributed for Rabi crops.

Kisan credit card has been distributed for 58237 farmers in the district Pratapgarh.

Macro-mode management scheme has been launched to increase the agricultural productivity field demonstration and training programme for farmers have been organised and grants-in-aid have been provided for procurement of seeds in the district. To promote the agricultural productivity various schemes are implemented in the district.

- National Pulse Development Scheme.
- National Oilseed Development Scheme.
- Special Sanai Production Scheme
- Village Seed Productivity Scheme.
- Kisan Mitra Yojana.
- Agriculture Diversified scheme.
- Macro-mode management schemem and
- National Agriculture crop Insurance Scheme.

Fertilizer is one of the costly agriculture investment in the crop production. Attempt has been mode to ensure good quality fertilizer to the farmers in the district Pratapgarh. Appropriate application of fertilizer, insecticides & pesticides and high yielding variety of seeds are provided through the concerned line departments to increase the agriculture productivity in the district Pratapgarh.

14. HORTICULTURE :

Horticulture unit has been established in the Pratapgarh district to promote horticultural activities. Aonla fruit belt have been declared for Pratapgarh Sadar and Mangraura block and Mango fruit belt for Patti, Kunda and Kalakankar block of the district Pratapgarh. Horticulture growers are financially and technically supported under the special horticulture development scheme. Seeds and special horticulture development scheme. Seeds and technical back up support are being provided to the farmers. High yielding variety of seeds are made available and cold storage facility is also provided. Extension training and demonstration programmes are being organised through Diversified agriculture support programme.

Aonla cultivation at larger extent is being done in the 28 villages of Mangraura block and 41 villages of the Pratapgarh Sadar block. Commercial set up is being provided to Aonla cultivation. During 1936 Aonla cultivation in 2 bigha land was implement in village- gode and later on the area under anole cultivation was increased from 10 bigha to 80 bigha. Aonla plant moved from religious importance to commercial and income generation stage. Later on anole have been promoted for Murabba preparation and preservation and processing of anole have been done by 25-30 entrepreneurs in the district Pratapgarh.

There are 2 government nursery and more than 50 individual nurseries established in the Pratapgarh district. High yielding variety of Aonla plants are supported to other parts of Uttar Pradesh and allow other states.

The concerned line department is assertive to promote anole cultivation. Financial support is being made available to anole producers and high quality anole plantation material is also provided training programme is being organised to train and demonstrate aonla plantation and protection for better quality & quantity aonla production.

Preservation and processing of Aonla is being done for Preparation & production of Murabba, Laddu, Burfi and pickles. To promote the preservation and processing of aonla government community fruit preservation centre has been established at Kunda and district headquarter of Pratapgarh.

Maximum portion of produced aonla is perished due to insufficient transpiration facility. It is proposed that at Chilbila railway station near gode special railway mail coach should be managed for suitable transportation of produced aonla. Aonla fruit preservation centre should be established for consumption of produced aonla. Baidyanath & Thandu commercial units should be established as per availability of aonla raw material.

15. FISHERIES :

Fisheries cultivation has been promoted in Pratapgarh with the view to provide fish food and to increase income and generate employment for the deprived rural multitudes various fisheries development programmes have been launched in district Pratapgarh.

15.1 Patta allotment of Ponds for fisheries :

Available ponds in the villages have been allotted on patta for fisheries cultivation. Fisheries related community is being preferred for ponds patta allotment including scheduled caste people and Registered fisheries co-operatives are promoted for allotment of ponds on Patta.

There are 5032 ponds in Pratapgarh district having 2826.203 hec. ponds out of which 2504 ponds having an area of 1902.31 ha. have been allotted on patta to the interested beneficiaries.

15.1 Development of Ponds :

Individual and Patta allotted ponds are developed for fisheries cultivation-requisite digging of ponds, link road construction, maintenance of funds, application of fertilizer gobar khad, medicines, fish seed, nutritious food for fish etc. are managed by district fisheries development agency, Pratapgarh after appropriate survey, project is formulated for the loan assistance to the concerned banks. Grants-in-aid for 25% is sanctioned to scheduled caste beneficiaries and 20% for other caste and rest of the amount is provided by the bank. A sum of Rs. 60,000/- per ha is sanctioned for leveling, waterlogged, uncultivable fallow land and construction of new ponds a sum of Rs. 2.0 lakh loan has been earmarked and supported in the form of loan through bank.

Maintenance of old and new ponds and other necessary materials including seed, fertilizer, medicine, diesel, fish-feed etc. are provided for which Rs. 30,000/- per ha loan is made available in which 25% i.e. Rs. 7500/- and for others 20% i.e. Rs. 6000/- subsidy is provided by the agency and rest amount is supported through bank as loan.

15.2 Fisheries Training :

Individually owned and hightech-fisheries training for which Rs. 50/- per day allowance is paid to the beneficiaries. The fishers community and scheduled caste beneficiaries are given priority for the training.

15.3 Fish Seed Production :

Extension and propagation of fish culture is ensured in the district due to which demand for fish seed has been increased. Government fish seed production centre has been established in Belha village of Lalganj block. The fish seed production capacity is 15.0 lakh. To minimize the fish seed production cost and improve the quality, it has been modernized and converted in to fish-hatchery and production capacity from 15.0 lack has been creased upto 35.0 lakh fish seed and at present it is a profitable proposition for the district Pratapgarh.

15.4 Fish See d Distribution :

To meet the increasing demand of fishers govt. Fish seed Centre, Behla and individual fish hatcheries fish seed production has been promoted. Uttar Pradesh Fish Development Corporation purchase the fish hatcheries and at a fixed price including Rs. 10/- per thousand transportation fee is charged for the distribution of fish seed to the fisherman's ponds.

15.5 Fisherman Housing Scheme :

The housing problem of fisherman is solved as Indira Awas Yojana is launched in the district. fisherman houses are construction alongwith handpump, low cost latrines. There are 71 fisherman houses constructed in Kalkankar, Shivgarh, Patti, Belkhanath dham and Mandhata blocks of the district Pratapgarh.

15.6 Fisheries Development Scheme :

Community ponds are constructed for fisherman community, scheduled caste and economically backward persons with the view to provide employment. In the Kalakankar block, in village-Andharipur 30 ponds are constructed including water facility, 30 fisherman families have been provided an employment for there livelihood.

In view of the success of the above scheme 10 ponds have been constructed in village Sarasikham of the Mangraura block under the fisheries development scheme.

15.7 Fisherman cooperative societies:

Fisherman cooperative societies are registered to develop fisherman community like other cooperative societies and its Registrar is Director-Fisheries, Uttar Pradesh. It is linked at state level with state fisherman cooperative federation and at National level with National Fishermen Cooperative Federation Cooperative Societies having 298 members in Pratapgarh district. These societies are availabling loan and grants from State Fishermen co-operative Federation. Financial subsidy is provided and priority in the Patta allotment of ponds to the Fisherman cooperative Societies are provided the concerned departments.

15.8 Fishermen accident policy scheme :

Members of the Registered Fishermen Co-operative Societies are provided Rs. 35,000/- in the case of accidental death and Rs. 17500/- in case of handicapped ness due to accident. The insurance policy facility is provided by Director. Fisheries as per recommendation of Assistant Director Fisheries.

16. DAIRY DEVELOPMENT :

Milk Produces Cooperative Federation Ltd. district Pratapgarh is collecting the milk in the remote rural areas through village level milk cooperative Federations. The milk federation was in the financial crisis few years back but recently urban the Ambedkar Scheme on the Antu Road 4 cooperatives namely –

- Pirupur
- Makai pur
- Rai Chandrapur
- Poorab gaon has been reconstituted and the milk collection has been started. In these societies there are 40 beneficiaries out of which 10 beneficiaries belongs to scheduled caste and Integrated Mini Dairy Scheme has been launched and their economic conditions are improved through milk collection. It is proposed to form milk cooperatives on the Pratapgarh to Antu and Pratapgarh-Raniganj-Patti way for the collection of the milk. It is proposed to establish milk chilling plant to promote dairy development programmes in the district Pratapgarh.

17. INTEGRATED RURAL DEVELOPMENT PROGRAMME :

Integrated rural development programme has been launched in the district Pratapgarh as per the recommendations of the local members of legislative assembly 10 villages have been selected for the complete situation of 16 development programmers. There are 7 legislative Assemblies in the district and 4 members of Legislative council and as per their recommendations 104 villages have been selected for integrated 16 rural development programmes.

In the Mangraura block village Asthara, Dahrouli Madhupur, Hathasara and Barahupur have been selected under the Integrated Rural Development Programme for complete implementation of 16 developmental programmes in the selected villages.

18. CONCLUSION :

Thus the rural development programmes have been given top priority in the district. Integrated Rural Development Programmes have been launched in 104 villages in which 16 programmes are being implemented, social welfare and other schemes are being implement on the priority basis to bridge the divide between rural to urban. It is argued that faster development is rquired to bridge this divide.

In view of the above it has been felt that the development should be participatory and it should be planned according to the local needs of the deprived rural multitudes. Development should be planned through tapping local talent and resources. Implementation of rural development programmes can be made more effective through peoples participation. Therefore self government programmes have been ensured with the view of the village as development unit. Development should start from (bottom) village to block and district onward.

The real meaning of democracy is the importance of the people and rural government is the main sole of rural development. Administrative, financial and programme formulation and implementation rights and control are provided to village Panchayats for Self- Government. Different activities of related line departments are handed over to village-block and district Panchayats and various committees have been formed to control the different rural development activities. The district Rural Development Agency (DRDA) has been reconstitute i.e. Chairman-DRDA at present is the Chairman district Panchayat forming 5 standing committees of the village-block-district Panchayat to ensure successful implementation of the planned projects.

Centrally sponsored several rural development programmes are launched in the district –

- Sampoorna Grameen Rojgar Yojana.
- Pradhan Mantri Gram Sadak Yojana
- Rural Housing
- Swarn Jayanti Gram Swarojgar Yojana
- Watershed Development Programme.
- Land Reforms
- Rural water supply programme.
- Central Rural sanitation programme.
- Pradhan Mantri Grameen Jal Samvasdhan Yojana

Swarn Jayani Gram Swarojgar Yojana is being implemented to generate self employment to have sustained in come and to remove the poverty. Assistance is given to the poor families living under the below poverty line. Selected person under this scheme is called as 'Swarojgaris'. There are 6804 Swarojgaris selected in Pratapgarh district and 358 Swarojgaris have been selected in Mangraura block, suitable technical/financial back up supported provided to the selected Swarojgaris.

Sampoorna Grameen Rojgar Yojana (SGRY) has been launched in Pratapgarh district benefiting 4685 selected beneficiaries in the district out of which 149 beneficiaries have been supported in Mangraura block.

Under the integrated rural development programme complete electrification of the selected villages are ensured. There are 156278 electrified houses in the district an 709 commercial electricity consumers in the district. Non- conventional sources of energy in the form of solar light, solar water pump, Bio-Gas etc. are also promoted in Pratapgarh district.

There are 17 small scale industries of cotton, textiles, drugs pharmaceuticals, light engineering and printing, besides there are 4345 household-furniture, bamboo and canework industries and agro-based industries oilmills, rice mills are concentrated in the different parts of the District Pratapgarh.. There are 5 Gramodyog units in Mangraura block.

There are 973 food supply centers in Pratapgarh and 65 food supply centers in Mangraura block. It has been ensured that there are at least one food supply centre in each village Panchayat of the Mangraura block of the district Pratapgarh.

Rural drinking water supply is ensured because water is an essential ingredient of our daily life. It is recorded that 24834 India Mark-II hand pumps have been installed in district Pratapgarh-Locak Hand Pump alongwith India Mark-II Hand pumps are installed to meet the increasing demand of growing population.

Rural sensation programme is launched in the district and 4375 rural latrines have been constructed. There are 199 low cost rural latrines constructed in mangraura block.

Rural Housing programme is being implemented in the district with a holistic approach of "Housing for All". Indira Awas Yojana is launched to meet the housing shortage. total 23355 houses are constructed in the district out of which 1694 number of rural houses are constructed in Mangraura block.

Various welfare programmes are launched including scheduled caste, Backward caste and Minority welfare programme in which scholarships to needy interested students including other employment generation and welfare programmes are being implemented at village level in Mangraura block and at block level in Pratapgarh district.

Construction of rural roads are ensured under various schemes in the district. There are 887 km. rural kaccha road constructed and 2428.36 km. Pucca road constructed in Pratapgarh district. Similarly 53 km. long kaccha road and 216 km. long pucca road has been constructed in Mangraura block.

Various women and child development programme have been launched in which 2013 beneficiaries have been supported under this programme. There are 140 women and child development beneficiaries in Mangraura block of the district Pratapgarh.

Various agricultural development programmes are being implemented to increase the agricultural productivity of district. Provision of high yielding variety of seeds, fertilizer, insecticides, pesticides kisan credit card including technical back up support and financial support are provided to the needy interested farmers under various schemes launched by the government.

Horticulture development is also an important source of income in the district Pratapgarh Sadar and Mangraoura block has been declare as Aonala Belt while Patti, Kunda and Kalakankar block have been developed as Mango Belt in the district.Aonla cultivation is being implemented in the 28 villages of the Mangaura block. There are several aonla fruits and vegetables preservation and processing units which has generated employment and increased the income of the deprived rural multitudes.

Fisheries cultivation has been promoted in the district and various schemes are launched to develop the fish culture in the district. Fisheries co-operatives have been formed to promote the fish culture with the view to utilize available water & land resources to generate employment and increase the income of the downtrodden section of the society. Physical, financial & technical backup support including insurance policy support are provided to ensure integrated development of fishermen of the district. In Mangraura block 10 ponds are developed to promote fish culture in the waterlogged villages of the block.

Dairy Development programme is being implemented in the district through formulation of Milk produces co-operatives in pirupur, Makaipur, Rai Chandapur and Poorabgaon through involving 40 beneficiaries. Integrated mini diary scheme has been launched to improve the collection of milk and new milk producers co-operatives are formed on the Antu road and Pratapgarh to Patti road.

Integrated Rural Development Programmes being implemented in the district as per recommendation of the local peoples representatives in which 104 villages have been selected for complete implementation of 16 activities of rural development. Village-Asthara, Dharouli Madhupur, Hathasara and Barahupur have been selected under the Integrated Rural Development Programme for saturation of earmarked 16 rural development activities.

The rural development programmes are being implemented in the district in which peoples participation are not properly ensured and improper implementation of sanctioned programmes and maintenance of the implemented programmes has led to the least sustainability of the implemented programmes because successful implementation of rural development programmes will lead to generate employment and increase the income of deprived rural multitudes and improve the socio-economic conditions of the poor people living in the remote rural areas.

●●●

Table -7 : Natural Resources Data Management System (NRDMS)
Pratapgarh district
Rural Development Programmes

Sl. No.	*Blocks*	*Swarn Jayanti Swarojgar Yojana*	*PMRY*	*Energy Electrified Houses*	*Energy Commercial Electrification*	*Cottage Industry*	*Gramodyog*	*Food Supply Centres*	*India Mark 2 Hand pump*	*Sanitation*
1	*2*	*3*	*4*	*5*	*7*	*8*	*9*	*10*	*11*	*12*
1	KalaKankar	995	145	8563	60	7	5	45	1155	85
2	Babaganj	440	1160	17300	36	3	8	52	1180	163
3	Kunda	502	186	16134	57	11	10	71	1627	230
4	Bihar	383	146	14328	19	8	10	63	1169	257
5	Sangipur	390	169	12200	39	5	8	55	1200	229
6	Lalganj	384	140	8314	13	3	7	41	1046	463
7	Laxmanpur	272	180	7316	27	6	3	59	1110	147
8	Sandwa Chandrika	440	160	8031	90	9	8	35	1015	236
9	Pratapgarh Sadar	375	1220	18200	79	39	10	41	1783	206
10	Mandhata	457	166	9203	13	0	4	76	1572	184
11	Mangraura	358	149	6211	71	13	5	65	1529	199
12	Patti	366	180	4016	26	2	7	61	2088	408
13	Aspur Devsara	446	145	3106	50	6	4	62	2169	599
14	Shivgarh	317	146	7321	17	8	15	67	1928	155
15	Gaura	286	103	9036	53	5	10	60	1745	508
16	Sangramgarh	358	145	6709	46	7	3	53	1024	166
17	Bobabhel Khernath	213	142	3217	13	4	3	67	1574	140
	Total	6704	4685	156278	709	136	120	973	24834	4375

Sl. No.	*Blocks*	*Rural Housing*	*SC Programme*	*BC Programme*	*Minority Programme*	*Women & Child Dev.*	*Pucca Road*	*Kaccha Road*
1	*2*	*13*	*14*	*15*	*16*	*17*	*18*	*19*
1	KalaKankar	1398	5910	580	1424	101	163.5	59
2	Babaganj	1659	2645	488	1428	110	166.3	64
3	Kunda	1713	6319	620	2878	156	142.75	63
4	Bihar	1510	10645	510	2080	135	92.0	39
5	Sangipur	1530	1114	680	1627	133	178.65	63
6	Lalganj	1919	3294	530	1253	86	99.63	36
7	Laxmanpur	1424	1850	480	4656	113	150.5	43
8	Sandwa Chandrika	1376	3638	710	1407	141	119.3	39
9	Pratapgarh Sadar	1431	4660	924	3184	135	116.0	59
10	Mandhata	1608	4893	340	2061	150	112.376	71
11	Mangraura	1694	4454	620	3074	140	216.0	53
12	Patti	1243	1855	440	2132	103	125.0	47
13	Aspur Devsara	1418	1832	730	633	116	177.0	35
14	Shivgarh	728	2398	460	1678	133	150.0	44
15	Gaura	1134	1416	710	2508	139	147.0	56
16	Sangramgarh	1278	2603	130	1124	122	158.53	59
17	Bobabhel Khernath	713	2183	670	2091	113	113.5	57
	Total	23355	61709	9522	35238	2126	2428.36	887

Table -8 : Natural Resources Data Management System (NRDMS)
Mangraura Block, Pratapgarh District
Rural Development Prograrmmes

Loc_ Code	*Vill_Name*	*SwarnJayanti Gram Swarojgar Yojana*	*Sampoorna Gramin Yojana*	*India Mark-II Hand pump*	*Sanitation*
1	*2*	*4*	*5*	*6*	*7*
1	Konhdour	5	16	30	0
2	Ramapur	4	5	18	11
3	Dharouli Madapur	5	0	14	15
4	Bhawapur	2	4	0	0
5	Shankarpur	3	3	21	12
6	Madura Raniganj	2	0	0	0
7	Parasrampur	4	2	0	0
8	Lakhipur	6	5	18	0
9	Atarsand	5	80	65	0
10	Madaferpur	4	0	21	0
11	Chanduadih	4	10	18	0
12	Sakara	4	3	0	0
13	Koni	3	0	0	0
14	Sarairajai	5	2	53	0
15	Salhipur Kanjas	2	0	0	0
16	Katari	2	25	26	0
17	Malak	6	1	85	0
18	Padumpur	5	7	36	0
19	Gahrauli	4	2	28	0
20	Sahpur	2	5	82	0
21	Kandharpur	6	10	40	0
22	Chandouka	3	13	65	0
23	Parasanda	4	0	45	0
24	Choumuri	5	0	35	0
25	Varaha	5	0	16	62
26	Barahupur	2	11	31	0
27	Varikala	3	0	35	0
28	Asthra	4	5	39	0
29	Amuwahi	6	3	46	0
30	Dharouli Muphrid	3	16	51	0
31	Sikri Kanupur	11	0	63	2
32	Sheshpur Adharganj	1	4	40	3
33	Kanhai Madupur	4	11	45	1
34	Bojhi	7	2	25	0
35	Bhousiya	0	5	15	0
36	Mandah	6	1	55	0
37	Varasaray	0	3	36	1
38	Gagehati	1	0	65	4
39	Sarouli	2	2	30	6
40	Suryagarh Jagannath	3	5	10	0
41	Aourangabad	3	3	84	0
42	Naraharpur	1	0	35	0
43	Pure Manikanth	5	3	30	0
44	Poorabpatti	3	1	38	0
45	Shivpur Khurd	4	5	18	8
46	Saray Shankar	4	0	46	0

Table -8 : Contd.....

Loc_ Code	*Vill_Name*	*SwarnJayanti Gram Swarojgar Yojana*	*Sampoorna Gramin Yojana*	*India Mark-II Hand pump*	*Sanitation*
1	*2*	*4*	*5*	*6*	*7*
47	Hathasara	5	13	17	0
48	Louli Pukhtakham	6	3	18	12
49	Darchut	8	14	26	0
50	Narayanpur	2	15	32	0
51	Sarasi Kham	4	15	32	0
52	Mangroura	0	61	17	0
53	Saray Jamuari	3	20	53	0
54	Utaras	3	15	30	0
55	Sarasidih	0	31	26	0
56	Etawah	2	12	19	0
57	Bhadouna	6	35	41	0
58	Bhivani	2	7	27	0
59	Bhaidapur	1	0	18	0
60	Kansa Patti	3	13	44	0
61	Raigarh	10	0	26	0
62	Dehari Digar	2	7	31	0

CHAPTER - VII
VILLAGE PLANNING

1. INTRODUCTION :

Planning is a means to achieve the development or it can be said that planning is an organised process by which the people achieves its developmental goals. If the intentions and objectives of development are distorted, then the planning also becomes an distorted exercise. Planning is done without willing consent of the local people and without involving peoples participation because the planning is talk of the people in which planners can provide technical back up support to achieve their planning goals. The government is stressing for the involvement of people in the planning process and implementation of need base developmental programmes.

The planners have to provide developmental planning, scientific technical backup support to the grass root village level peoples representatives, villagers and officials involved in village development and planning. The planners should assist villagers as a social scientist who can easily understand the basic grass root level need of the villagers, so that the need of the people is planned and developmental activities are implemented with the participation of road village people to ensure to achieve the planned target of development.

The development should be participatory tapping the local talent and resources in order to be sustainable. Effort is being made to implement various rural development programmes with a focus on enhancing the livelihoods of weaker and vulnerable sections for sustainable development. Fore most priority has been given to rural development for which a number of steps have been initiated to make the implementation of ongoing schemes and programmes more effective and accelerated.

In view of the above government is stressing to organize the village Panchayats and decentralization for village panchayats have been organised. Three tier Panchayati Raj i.e. village-block and district Panchayat have been organised and the administrative and financial powers have been allocated to Panchayats. Self-government in the rural areas and autonomy to the local bodies, administrative and programme responsibilities, financial resources allocation, transfer of related line departments staff to Panchayats and administrative and financial rights has been provided to village-block and district Panchayats with the view that it will have good and positive results.

Villages is the development unit in the new system of decentralization. Local development will be done by the local people. Faster development will be ensured assuming village as a centre for development. Real administration is transferred to the local rural bodies in which planning development works, its management and control is ensured through peoples participation.

Planning will be done from bottom to top. Revolutionary step of decentralization will have complete change among the villagers life and it will have new era of integrated rural development of the rural area.

In view of the above decentralization of administrative and financial powers of village Panchayats, block and district Panchayats have been ensured in Pratapgarh district. Village Panchayats have been hand over education, Govt. Tube wells, Hand Pump, Youth welfare, Medical & Health, women & child development, animal, food supply shops, agriculture, rural development, Panchayati raj and pension & scholarships activities. The village Panchayat in its open meeting are able to decide the village plan, ensure implementation of developmental activities and also maintenance of the created assets for its sustainability. There are 5 standing committees of the Panchayats viz., Planning & Development, Education, Construction work, Health & Welfare and Administrative committees, are responsible for the formulation of plan and implementation of planned developmental activities and maintenance & sustenance of the completed project.

The village, block and district Panchayats have been given requisite responsibilities, administrative control, physical and financial powers and concerned line departments have also been handover to the Panchayats to ensure Self-Government of village-block-district Panchayats.

In view of the 'Self Government' of Panchayats at village level in Mangraura block and at block level in Pratapgarh district need base peoples participatory action plan has been formulated to fulfill the dreams of self-government i.e. Panchayati Raj to Lokraj to Garm Raj to establish the Ram Raj which has been the dream of Mahatma Gandhiji.

2. DISTRICT PLANNING : PRATAPGARH :

District Pratapgarh has historical cultural archeological and religious importance. Various developmental schemes are implemented in which successful results has been obtained. The planning process and implementation of sanctioned programmes and implementation of sanctioned programmes are being finalized through District Planning Committee.

District Planning Committee has been constituted as per the Uttar Pradesh District Planning Committee Act 1999 –

- District Planning Committee is chaired by the nominated Minister of the cabinet of government of Uttar Pradesh.
- The Chairman District Panchayat is the Vice-Chairman.
- Chairman of the urban local bodies at district headquarter is the Vice-Chairman.
- District Panchayat and Municipalities 4/5 are the members,
- District Magistrate as Members.
- Other member of Parliament & Members of Ligislative assembly are the Permanent invited Members.
- Over all Member of district Panchayat is between 20-40 members.
- Chief Executive officer of the District Panchayat is the Secretary of District Planning Committee
- District Economics & statistics officer as joint Secretary of District Planning Committee.

Activities of the District Planning are as follows :

- Finalization of local needs and aims under the National and state level objective.
- Collection, collation & updation of natural and human resources data for planning and preparation of block-wise available resources outline.

- Indexing of available resources at village-block-district level.
- Finalization of policies, programmes & priorities of development through optimum justified utilization of natural and other resources.
- Formulation of Annual and five year plan, amendment, consolidation of the Plan format based on the objectives of the Plan.
- Preparation of the Employment Plan for the District.
- Evaluation of financial resources for the Financial support of the District Plan.
- Follow up, monitoring and evaluation of all the programmes being implemented in the district.
- Allocation of expenditure for sect oral and sub-sect oral programmes under the total infrastructure for District Development Planning.
- Meeting of the district Planning Committee will be called at least once in three months.

Planning process of the District Pratapgarh are as follows :

- Village Panchayat will formulate its own development planning every year.
- Block Panchayat will include development planning of village Panchayat and formulate Block Development Planning.
- District Panchayat will in corporate for mulated Block Development Planning and formulate the District Development Planning for District Planning Committee.
- Development Plan of urban bodies are referred to District Planning Committee.
- District Planning committee is authorized to consider the Development Plan received from Panchayats and urban local bodies.
- District Plan is finalized by the District Planning Committee as per Development Plan formulated by District Panchayat and Municipalities based on mutual interest, specially regional planning, water and other physical and natural resources, considering integrated development, establishment and environment of the district.
- Formulated finalized district plan –2006-07 by the District Planning Committee, Pratapgarh are as follows :

2.1 Agriculture :

Various programmes for agricultural development has been initiated in Pratapgarh district. Cultivation of oilseed and pulses has been propagated and promoted in the Pratapgarh District in which 260 qtls certified seed distribution, 150 ha field demonstration, 10 number of agricultural tools distribution, 20 sprinkler distribution, 30 ha land seed processing, 700 numbers agricultural protection equipments, 1900 phosphorous solublizing Bacteria culture, 3 training programmes, and agricultural chemicals for 25 ha land, 15 number irrigation piple, Nitrogen, phosphorus and potash for 10 ha and Integrated Pest Management will be demonstrated on 10 ha land under the National Pulses Development Scheme in the district Pratapgarh.

Maiz project has been also implementation in which 10 qtls certified seed, seed distribution for 33 ha. Land, 210 mini-kit distribution, 10 field demonstrations, Integrated pest management on 2 ha land, agriculture protection chemicals for 10 ha land, manually operated 100 agricultural equipments, 10 culture phosphorus solublizing Bacteria, gypsum and pyrite for 90 ha land, farmers one training programme, agriculture irrigation 10 pipes, target has been earmarked under Maiz Development Programme in District Pratapgarh.

National oil seed development programme has been implemented in which 25 qtls seed distribution, field demonstration on 30 ha, 1650 culture, 7 training programme for farmers, integrated pest management of 30 ha of land, Bio-technological demonstrations on 5 ha land, agriculture protection chemical demonstration on 35 ha land, distribution of 10 sprinkler set for irrigation, agriculture protection 200 equipments, 10 agricultural tools and equipments and one Kisan Mela and one field day demonstration programmes have been earmarked to promote agricultural activities in the district Pratapgarh. Besides, 10 agricultural field demonstration 5 sprinkler irrigation set distribution, crop protection 77 equipment and 25 vermi-compost bio-fertilizer support facility for agricultural development has been earmarked to promote and develop agricultural activities in the Pratapgarh district.

Approximately 599 ha land development programme have been proposed (Table-9) under the various schemes launched by the State Government of Uttar Pradesh and also under the centrally sponsored schemes under the other schemes approximately 19523 qtls high yielding variety seed distribution has been earmarked which is depicted in the table –9. Proportionately in Pratapgarh Sadar block while maximum seed distribution for agricultural development has been earmarked for Kunda block of the district Pratapgarh as per the local farmers need.

Fertilizer and seed distribution programmes has been properly implemented in the District Pratapgarh but to ensue the cropping intensity crop loan facilities are provided. To make the farmers self sustained about 61400 kisan credit cards have been also distributed.

Field demonstrations and farmers training programmes are organized to increase the agricultural productivity under the macro-mode-management programme and grants are made available to farmers for availability of high yielding variety of seeds.

National Pulses Development Programme and National Oil seed Development Programme as mentioned above are implemented in which seeds agricultural equipments distribution and field demonstrations & farmers training programmes are organized.

In Pratapgarh district special Sanai Production scheme is launched in which farmers are technically demonstrated for increasing sanai productions in Pratapgarh district.

Village seed production schemes are implemented in which Rs. 500/- grant per ha is provided for seed production and the developed seed is certified through seed certification organization.

Kisan Mitra Yojana is being implemented in which agriculture graduate person is selected and trained to impart training for Kisan Mitra at village level in Pratapgarh district.

Uttar Pradesh Agriculture Diversified support Project is being implemented in Mangraura block, Patti, Aspur, Devsara, Gaura, Shivgarh and Sandwa Chandrika blocks of district Pratapgarh, in which vermin-compost and integrated pest management programmes are demonstrated.

National Agriculture Crop Insurance Programmes are launched in Pratapgarh district in which farmers are facilitated for crop insurance for Rabi & kharif crops in which in the circumstances of natural calamities, loss of crops of farmers are supported by the government.

2.2 Horticulture :

Horticulture development programme has been implemented in the district because of the Aonla belt and Mango belt blocks declared in the district. It is proposed to distribute approximately 45618 number of plants. (Table –9) in Pratapgarh district out of which maximum number of plants distribution are proposed in Lalganj and Bihar blocks through individual private and government nurseries.

It is proposed to modernize government nurseries and horticulture plant production units and to product 30,000 grafted fruits plants and 30,000 fruit seed plants and one ha horticulture field maintenance has been earmarked in the district 1500 grafted plants and 92576 horticultural seed plants through government horticultural nurseries have been produced in the district Pratapgarh to promote declared aonla fruit belt of Mangraura and Pratapgarh Sadar block and Mango belt in Kunda and Kalakankar blocks under the special horticultural development programme. Technical back up support and seeds are provided by the Department of horticulture and cold storage are controlled for Potato storage and private horticultural nurseries are promoted to promote the horticultural activities in the district. Uttar Pradesh diversified Agriculture support project is also implemented in which horticultural development programmes are being implement in the Pratapgarh district.

Intensified horticultural belt and for the integrated field fruits & vegetables development technical awareness training programme and supply of plants are ensured by the Department of horticulture under this programme 20 ha Mango field extension and Integrated development of fruit belt scheme is being implement in the district Pratapgarh.

It is proposed to organize 50 vegetables field demonstrations and 50 field demonstrations rose etc. flowers cultivation and one day horticultural training programme for 2000 horticultural growers in the district Pratapgarh.

Fruits, vegetables and spices development schemes are technically implemented in the district Pratapgarh in which 250 field demonstrations are vegetables cropping out of which 85 special component plan vegetables cropping has been proposed in the district plan of the Pratapgarh.

2.3 Financial support for small and marginal farmers :

To increase the agricultural productivity financial support is provided to small and marginal farmers in which free tube-well boring for 3070 small and marginal farmers are proposed in which 442 farmers are proposed under the special component plan programmes in the district Pratapgarh.

2.4 Animal husbandry :

Animal husbandry, animal health & disease treatment services, animal development and extension services are provided in Pratapgarh district. There are 9 incomplete animal hospitals located at Gangapur, Dhakawa, Kohndaur, Patti, Prithviganj, Birsingpur, Atheha, Shivgarh and Jamtali which has to be completed for which requisite financial support has been allocated and sanctioned under the district plan. It has been approved in the district Plan for construction of 7 new animal hospitals at Kunda, Baghrai, Rahtikar, Raniganj, Kaithola, Madhupur, Bhagwatganj, Chhitapganj and Lalganj. It has been proposed to construct 33 new residential houses for the staff. It has been also proposed to construct new Animal service centers at Jogipur, Delhupur, Diwanganj, Teunga, Gadwara, Jethwara, Kushuwapur, Saifabad, Kotia, Dhindhuai, Baijalpur, Aurangabad, Katara, Madaniganj, Lawana, Pure nauti, Kanewara, Atraura, Subansa, Rocky, Sankar daha, Bharcheck, Sarai Anadev, Rajgarh, Haripur Bardaita. Dilippur, Newadia Bandupur, Kadrau, Pachras Samshergarh for animal service center and arrangements of medicines for animal hospitals Rs. 789 thousands have been sanctioned to strengthened and facilitate animal hospitals and animal service centers in Pratapgarh district.

Budget allocation has been ensured to control the various diseases of animals. Production of new variety of animals calf through artificial inseminisation and quality improvement of animals specially Buffalo and cow. The artificial inseminisation support is provided through BAIF (Bharatiya Agro-Industries Foundation) . It has been proposed to artificially inseminise 60500 cows and buffalo out of which 36800 cows and buff allows will be artificially inseminise under the special component plan scheme of the government. It has been also proposed to establish animal production and extension centers. It is has been proposed to establish 10 pigs development center in Pratapgarh for which financial budget allocation has been earmarked. It has been proposed to establish animal production field and provide animal health services including community animal medicine support center, in which it is planned to provide medicines for 1500 sheep's in Pratapgarh district. Grass production and grazing land development scheme has been planned in the district to provide nutritious cattle feed in the district Pratapgarh for which suitable financial support has been allocated.

2.5 Dairy Development :

Strengthening, reconstituting and extension of Dairy cooperative federations and societies and Pratapgarh district has been planned in the district Pratapgarh for which Rs. 17.0 lakh has been allocated. It is proposed to constitute 152 Dairy cooperative societies and production of 5500 litre upto 4568 and to provide 517 metric ton cattle feed and 1500 liter milk arrangement for sale in cities. Besides it is proposed to increase the members of milk societies upto 10200 members and register 126 milk societies and provide 517 metric ton cattle feed. It is planned to supply 4600 milk per day for milk consumers and presently milk production through dairy is 3000 liter milk per day. Thus reconstitution of Dairy co-operative Societies, availability of cattle feed and increase the milk production to meet the increasing demand of growing population has been planned in the district Plan of Pratapgarh.

2.6 Fisheries Development :

Fisheries development programmes are being implemented by the District

Fisheries Development Agency, Pratapgarh. It is proposed to train 100 fishermen and development of 100 ha ponds and ensure fish seed distribution in the district Pratapgarh for which appropriate financial support has been allocated. National welfare scheme of the fishermen has been launched and installation of India Mark-II hand pump has been proposed in the areas of fishermen. It has been also planned to facilitate accidental insurance for 310 fishermen in the district Pratapgarh.

2.7 Forest :

Social forestry has been promoted in the urban and rural areas of the Pratapgarh district. It has been proposed to construct 557 brickguard in the urban areas, and 2.0 lakh plant protection and maintenance of 810 brick-guard in the urban areas of district Pratapgarh.

Social forestry programmes are launched in the rural areas, in which it has been proposed to ensure plantation on 170 ha of land for advance soil work and 170 ha land plantation under scheduled caste special component plan. Advance soil work on 200 ha land and 75 ha land soil work under special component plan for social afforestation has been planned in the district Pratapgarh. It is planned to raise 4.0 lakh nursery plants and large scale propagation and extension of social forestry and Agro-forestry programmes at block level in district Pratapgarh for which training programmes and organization of workshops have been proposed. It has been also planned to protect 9.0 lakh plants and 3.5 lakh plants under special component plan scheme of the district.

2.8 Co-operative :

Cooperative programmes are being implemented in the district Pratapgarh, Various financial support are provided the district co-operative Banks under the control of district co-operative Department. It is planned to provide interest free loan to scheduled caste farmers and poor section people for the purchase of part item for their self employment and sustenance. A sum of Rs. 2.0 lakh has been allocated for financial support to facilitate 10,000 poor scheduled caste beneficiaries for interest less loan to purchase part material under the co-operative scheme launched by the government for interest grant for the crop loan to the scheduled caste beneficiaries.

2.8 Rural Development :

Various rural development programmes are being implemented under the different schemes launched by the government.

(i) **Swarn Jayanti Gram Swarojgar Yojana :** Integrated Self-employment programme-Swarn Jayanti Gram Swarojgar Yojana (SGSY) is launched for the poor families living below the poverty line. Persons taking up self employment are called Swarojgaries. Different activities are selected for individual persona and groups called the Self-Help Groups. Proposed target under Swarn Jayanti Gram Swarojgar Yojana is 1964 beneficiaries out of which 354 scheduled caste beneficiaries will be facilitated under the special component plan scheme of the government, in which administrative and training programme has been included. Selected Swarjojgaris will be trained and suitable technical & financial back up support will be provided under the Swarn Jayanti Gram Swarojgar Yojana.

(ii) Integrated Wasteland Development Programme : Integrated wasteland Development Programme has been launched under drought prone area development scheme of the government in Rs. 936 thousand has been allocated for the successful implementation of the project.

(iii) Integrated Rural Energy Programme : Integrated rural energy programme has been launched in the district Pratapgarh in which light and housing electrification financial budget of Rs. 105 thousand has been allocated for 130 lights and 20 piece lights under special component plan of the government. Other programmes including organization of training and peoples awareness programme has been planned. Expenditure for the organization of 5 awareness & 01 training and seminar programme has been also allocated. 10 streetlight facilities and 2 light lender special component plan has been also earmarked in which a sum of Rs. 176 thousand has been allocated out of which Rs. 35 thousand had been allocated under the special component Plan scheme of the government. (iv) Indira Awas Yojana : Indira Awas Yojana is being implemented to meet the shortage of housing in rural areas. District Panchayat Pratapgarh and district Rural Development Agency Pratapgarh has planned to construct 1290 low cost rural houses for deprived poor section of society out of which 774 low cost rural houses construction have been allocated for scheduled caste beneficiaries under special component plan scheme of the government.

(v) Sampoorna Grameen Rojagar Yojana : Sampoorna Grameen Rojagar Yojana is launched to provide additional wage employment in the rural areas, as also food security alongside the creation of durable community, social and economic infrastructure in rural areas. The special emphasis is to provide waste employment to women, scheduled caste and parents of children with drawn from hazardous occupations. It is proposed to generate 15.93 lakh man days employment under the Sampoorna Grameen Rojagar Yojana out of which 7.97 lakh man day employment generation for scheduled caste beneficiaries under special component for scheduled caste beneficiaries under special component plan of the government.

(vi) Panchayat Raj : Panchayati Raj Institutions have been playing an important role in making rural development programmes peoples participatory, attracting the rural people, developing plan as per the local need and optimum utilization of available local resources. Panchayati Raj institution have been provided constitutional protection to perform constitutional responsibilities under the three tier i.e. village-block and district level Panchayati Raj system.

(vii) It is planned to construct 25.89 km. kharanza and nail in the selected Ambedkar villages for integrated development for which a sum of Rs. 70.58 lakh budget has been allocated. It is proposed to construct multipurpose welfare center and 17 Panchayt Bhawan in the district, for this purpose a sum of Rs. 9.08 lakhs have been allocated in the district plan of Pratapgarh.

(viii) Community Development : Community Development programme has been implemented to strengthen various rural development programmes in the district. It is proposed to construct official buildings at block development offices and at District Development office including electrification programmes for which Rs. 89.63 lakh has been allocated for strengthening various rural development programmes. It is planned to type IV houses in Babaganj, Sangipur, Shivgarh, Laxmanpur blocks and construction of Type-II houses and construction of house building and meeting hall in Pratapgarh Sadar block and Meting hall & boundary wall in Belkharnath dham block and office of the block Pramukh in gaura block in Pratapgarh district.

(ix) **Land use :** A sum of Rs. 25 thousand has been allocated to organize workshops, seminars and awareness camp for planning land use pattern of the district Pratapgarh.

(x) **Economics and statistics :** Strengthening the office of the district statistics and economics a sum of Rs. 80 thousand budget has been allocated for the purchase the computer, machinery & equipments and other requisite furnitures.

(xi) **Additional sources of energy :** Emphasis has been given in generate additional sources of energy through utilizing human excreta / night soil, provision for 30 solar light and 5 solar light under special component scheme has been made for which a sum of Rs. 33 thousand has been allocated in the district plan. To create awareness for generation of additional sources of energy 8 training programme has been earmarked in the district plan of Pratapgarh.

(xii) **Rural small scale industry :** Rural small scale industries establishment has been promoted in the district. Pratapgarh entrepreneurship development training programme and research for entrepreneurial development had been priorities for which a sum of Rs. 172 thousand has been earmarked in the district plan of Pratapgarh to facilitate 26 beneficiaries and 10 beneficiaries under special component plant scheme of the government.

(xiii) **Khadi and village Industries :** Khadi and village industries programmes are promoted by government for optimum utilization of available natural and agro-base products and generation of employment and to increase the income of deprived rural poors in the district under this programme Chief Ministers Rural Industry Employment scheme for which a sum of Rs. 20.87 lakh has been allocated in the district plan of Pratapgarh to provide benefit for 85 beneficiaries under the Chief Minister's Rural Industry Employment scheme of the government.

(xiv) **Road and Bridge :** Construction of general roads in the district has been given topmost priority for the construction of general roads a sum of Rs. 872.59 lakhs has been allocated. Ambedkar Gram and Integrated rural development programme has been launched in the district, for the successful implementation of the programme appropriate financial budget allocation has been made in the district plan of Pratapgarh. It is planned to construct 36.02 km Earth work, 45.07 km. kharanja work and 54.07 km. pacca road construction including construction of 72 bridges.

2.9. Irrigation :

Irrigation is the one of the major input in agricultural production. Various schemes have been launched to facilitate irrigation to increase the agriculture productivity in the district Pratapgarh.

(i) **Private Minor Irrigation :** Private minor source of irrigation have been promoted in the district for which medium deep tube-well boring for the installation of 10 tube-wells and 2 deep tube-well boring have been proposed in the district for which 6.8 lakh and Rs. 1.58 lakh financial budget has been allocated respectively ground water charging check dam have been also proposed under this scheme 34 ponds and 4 check dam construction has been proposed for which as. 19.20 lakh financial budget has been allocated in the district plan.

(ii) Government Minor Irrigation and Government Tube-well : Irrigation through government minor irrigation and government tubewells have been promote in the district in which installation of general tubewells, re-installation of failure 6 tubewells and re-maintenance of 10 km long irrigation Nali/Goa and replacement of 15 P.V.C. pipe has been proposed. It is also planned to establish 20 pump sets and establishment of 400 starters and establishments of 50 T.P. Switches and provision of flat cables. Construction of new tub wells under chaudhari charan singh scheme have been launched in which construction of 2 new tube wells have been proposed in the district plan for which Rs. 12.38 lakh has been earmarked. It has been also proposed to modernize the installed tube wells in which reconstruction of 6 failure tube wells establishment of 20 pump sets, 400 starters, 50 T.P. switches establishment has been proposed and M.S.pipe 6 inches and Mechanical improvement, reconstruction of 10 km. old irrigation gul/nail and 15 piece P.V.C. pipe line for its reconstruction have been proposed for which a sum of Rs. 40.99 lakh budget has been allocated in the district plan of Pratapgarh.

2.10 Environment Programmes :

Various environment programmes in the district Pratapgarh are implemented in which environment awareness training programmes has been proposed. It includes development of environment development and Archaeologically important tree's maintenance and construction and Raniganj Ajafara and progration & extension of environment programmes. Environment Training and extension programme have been also proposed in which purchase of popularization materials of different important environmental items, installation of boards & banners and other training programmes have been proposed. Popularization and training programmes have been proposed on Prithvi Divas-2 world environment day one, Van Mahatasava-2, Exhin\bition one, and one plant sole install an cleaning of Malin Dasti and one aforestation programme as been proposed for which Rs. 1.80 lakh financial budget has been allocated.

2.11 Trouism :

Tourism has been promoted in the district due to historical, cultural, religious and archaeological importance of the district Pratapgarh in which water and electricity facility and local tourism development has been proposed. Financial allocations has been mode for beautification and development of tourist places in the district. Budgetary allocations has been made to organize tourism melas and functions to promote tourism activity in the district Pratapgarh.

2.12 Education :

Development of educational infrastructure and encouragement of students has been one of the top priority of the government. Various education programmes have been promoted in the distinct Pratapgarh.

(i) **Primary Education :** In the primary education, Shiksha mitra yojana have been launched for which a sum of Rs. 117.37 lakh financial support has been allocated and an other Sarv Shiksha Abhian i.e. Education for All has been implemented for which a s sum of Rs. 170.28 lakh has been allocated in the district Plan of Pratapgarh.

(ii) **Secondary Education :** Secondary education is being promoted in the district in which construction of building extension, electrification, purchase of building and land for government higher secondary schools have been proposed for which Rs. 81.16 lakh financial budget has been allocated. Special facilities have been made available to the girls studying in the secondary schools in remote rural areas has been proposed and Rs. 1.20 lakh financial budget has been allocated. Non-Government higher secondary schools subject matter specialist teachers remuneration have been proposed for which a sum of Rs. 6.00 lakh have been allocated in the district plan of Pratapgarh.

Financial support for construction of science laboratory in government higher secondary schools and modernization of Inter level government High Schools have been proposed in the district Plan. It is proposed to open additional classes in the government schools and introduction of new subjects in the government schools have also been proposed in the district plan of Pratapgarh.

2.11 Pradeshik Vikas Dal :

Pradeshik Vikas Dal scheme is launched in the district to promote rural sports and organization of rural sports programmes at block and district level a sum of Rs. 4.86 lakh financial budget has been allocated. A sum of Rs. 14.31 lakh has been allocated to establish stadium in the rural areas in the district Pratapgarh to promote and propos gate sports interest among rural youths in the district. District level sports officer and district Pradeshik Vikas Dal officer and block level officers and engaged in the promotion and propagation of sports programmes in the rural areas.

2.12 Health and family welfare :

Various health and family welfare programmes are launched in the district. To promote the family welfare programmes construction of family welfare sub-centre have been proposed in the district.

(i) **Allopathic :** Allopathic medical and health facilities are promoted in the district in which construction of building for primary health center have been proposed and financial budget has been also allocated for the construction of community health centers and construction of building for community health center has been proposed in the district plan. It is also proposed to facilitate plastic surgery/burn unit and pathology division of the hospital. It is proposed to provide special facilities for medicine & surgical divisions of the hospital. It is planned to develop Intensive care unit/ new burn care unit of the government hospitals of the district Pratapgarh.

(ii) **Homeopathic :** Homeopathic medical health facilities are promoted in the district in which establishment of 12 government Homeopathic hospitals have been proposed in the district for which necessary financial support has been allocation the district plan of Pratapgarh.

(iii) Aurvedic & Unani : Aurvedic and Unani medical facilities are provided in the district in which establishment of 10 Ayurvedic/Unani hospitals and construction of hospital building for unani hospitals are proposed in the plan and necessary financial support has been allocated in the district plan of Pratapgarh.

2.13 Jal Nigam :

Rural drinking water general programmes are being implemented by Jal Nigal implanting agency in district Pratapgarh. It is planned to complete 21 incomplete projects at kandhai madhupur, saifabad, udaiyadih, Ramganj, Narharpur, Menhadia, Handaur, Agai, Sangipur, Pichura under common minimum programme of the district and repair & maintenance of the tube-well installed at Bhupiamau, Panigo, Kalakankar, gotani during the correct financial year under the maintenance scheme. Reboring work at Patti under the Rural drinking water shame has been proposed in the plan. It is proposed to repair and maintain the tube wells during the current financial year installed at Lalganj, Silaudhi and Sangramgarh. It is planned to construct drinking water tube wells at Senapur, Kailidih, Derwa and Mangarh during the current financial year and other programmes under the centrally financed scheme 340 new hand pump, 600 rebore for the already installed handpumps and replacement of defective 8000 meter G.I. Pipe has been proposed during the current financial year in the proposed plan of district Pratapgarh. Thus under the rural drinking water scheme establishment of new handpumps, rebore-of defective hand pumps and completion of the impolite work has been proposed in this financial year of the district plan.

Urban drinking water programme has been launched in which rebore of the tube-well installed at Manikpur, Bela Pratapgarh Municipality and installation of 75 India Mark- II handpumps has been proposed for the urban areas of the district.

It is proposed to install 310 new India mark-II hand pump in the rural areas under Rural Drinking water scheme of the Department of Rural Development in the District Pratapgarh. Rural sanitation programme have been launched in the district in which construction of 17832 low cost latrines and 4458 low cost latrines construction under special component plan have been proposed in the district plan of the Pratapgarh.

It is also planned to construct type-IV four housed under the pooled housing scheme of the public works department of the district Pratapgarh.

2.14 Information :

Information and population programmes are launched in the district in which organization of 25 kisan meals and exhibitions are proposed and organization of 50 song & drama programmes are proposed to popularize the various schemes of the government. Strengthening of district information center, publication and photography scheme has been proposed for which appropriate financial support has been allocated in the plan budget of the district Pratapgarh.

2.15 Welfare schemes :

(i) Schedule castes : Various scheduled caste welfare scholarships schemes are launched in the district in which scholarship for 7731 students studying in class 9-10 and 17938 scheduled caste students scholarships for class 6-8 and 36080 scheduled caste students scholarship for class 1-5 has been earmarked in district plan of Pratapgarh.

It is proposed to provide scholarships for 72 students studying in the Industrial Training Institute (I..T.I.) at Pratapgarh. It has been proposed to provide grants for 850 beneficiaries for the marriage of the daughters of the sick persons and financial support for the 850 persons suffering from various exploitation and atrocities.

(ii) General caste : Scholarships for general class students has been proposed in the district in which scholarships for 18615 general caste students belonging to below poverty line has been proposed studying in class 1 to 10 in the district Plan of Pratapgarh.

(iii) Backward caste : Scholarships for backward caste students have been proposed in the district plan in which 11284 backward students scholarships studying in the above high school classes and below high school backward caste 228690 students scholarships have been planned for which suitable financial support has been allocated in the district plan of Pratapgarh.

(iv) Minority : Minority welfare schemes are launched in the district Pratapgarh in which 1580 minority students scholarships have been proposed in the plan budge of the district Pratapgarh.

(v) Employment : Employment programme has been launched in the district in which building construction of employment office, instructor/educational guidelines center, scholarships for the training beneficiaries, purchase of books and arrangements for technical subjects have been proposed in the district plan of Pratapgarh.

(vi) Hand craft Training : Handicraft training programme has been proposed in the district plan in which extension and strengthening of present industrial training institutes have been proposed. It is proposed to purchase the equipments for the refrigeration, air conditioning mechanic embroidery cutting, short -hand and electrician trade in industrial training institutes at Patti and Pratapgarh for which requisite financial support has been also allocated. (vii) Strengthening of government polytechnic: It has been proposed to strengthen the government polytechnic in the district in which financial support for the purchase of equipments and strengthening the government polytechnic has been proposed in the district plan of Pratapgarh. (viii) Social Welfare: Social welfare schemes are launched in the district in which pension for2251 old age persons have been proposed and 1126 old age persons pension is allocated under special component plan of the government in the district Pratapgarh.

(ix) Handy Capped Welfare: Handicapped welfare schemes are implemented in the district in which 1260 beneficiaries belonging to eye less, deaf and dumb, physically and mentally handy capped persons maintenance and management grants have been allocated in the district plan. It is also proposed to support 750 schedule caste handy capped beneficiaries under the special component plan scheme of the government.

It is also proposed to provide grants for training and education to different categories of handicapped persons and handy capped students have been selected and proposed for financial grants for education and training in plan-budget for district Pratapgarh.

(x) It has been proposed to grants for the purchase of artificial physical parts for physically handicapped persons in which 200 physically handicapped persons are selected and

782 physically handy capped persons will provided grants for the purchase of physically handicapped persons under special component plan of the government.

(xi) Women Welfare: Women welfare schemes are being implemented in the district in helpless widows are provided financial grants. During current financial year 1999 widow women beneficiaries are selected for the financial grants in aid and 782 women widow helpless scheduled caste beneficiaries are selected for grants-in-aid under the special component plan scheme of the government.

(xii) Nutrition: Nutrition support under child development scheme are being launched in the district in which transportation expenditure of the nutrition food has been allocated for Sandwa Chandrika Rampur sang ramgarh, Pratapgarh Sadar and Belkhar Nath Dham block of the district Pratapgarh in the district plan.

(xiii) It has been also proposed to strengthen the road and transport system of the district in which generator set, photo stat machine water cooler,, fax machine and other items including furniture etc. has been supplied to strengthen the office of the transport in the plan-budget of the district Pratapgarh..

Thus the major, important activities at district and block level including various line departments and as per the policy and guidelines laid by the state government activities plan are formulated, incorporated and finalized by the district planning committee but there are certain main activities which are perceived by the local people but at district level it is difficult to incorporate all programmes and proposals in the district plan. Therefore, it becomes necessary to describe such need base action plan realized and desired by the people which can be implemented and successfully completed by the various non-government organizations and local bodes i.e. village panchayats, municipalities, block panchayats and district panchayats because the local body institutions are also involved in the implementation of such need base programmes to fulfill the increasing demand of the growing population. In view of the above an attempt is made to analyse the need base plan activities perceived by the local people for its implementation through various sources and resources in the district Pratapgarh.

(xiv) Need Base Planning: Pratapgarh District: District plan of the Pratapgarh has been analysed. District plan proposals are formulated by the District Panchayat in association with district economic and statistics office. In the district plan some of the planned proposals of block are incorporated while most of the work proposals are incorporated as per the recommendations of the concerned line departments. It has been informed the Block Panchayat incorporates need base demand rural developmental activities proposed by the village panchayats but members of the block development committee of the block plays an important role in the formulation of the block plan and incorporation of their recommendations in the block plan.

Thus it can be said that village Panchayat decides their need base plan work through their village panchayat members and block development committee members involvement and recommendations are incorporated at certain extent in the block plan. The members of district panchayat committee recommendations are incorporated in the district Panchayats plan while Chairman of the urban local bodies and district panchayats and concerned implementing line departments plays an important role in the formulation and finalization of district plan which is chaired by the Nomination Minister of the State Government.

3. WASTELANDS DEVELOPMENT

Wastelands development programmes in the district Pratapgarh are implemented by Uttar Pradesh Bhoomi Sudhar Nigam in certain selected villages of the district and other line departments related to agriculture. The wastelands in Pratapgarh district are categories as user land, waterlogged land, ravine land, banjar and fallow land. Thus it is proposed to reclaim about 599 hectares of wastelands (table-9) in district Pratapgarh to meet the increasing demand for food grain, fodder, fuel wood, fiber, fruits and fisheries in the district. It is recorded that maximum programme has been demarked in the Pratapgarh Sadar and Patti blocks while minimum wastelands development programme has been identified in the Kalakankar, Kunda, Yaura and Baba Bhellcher Nath Dham blocks of the district Pratapgarh.

3.1 Agriculture Development:

The overall productivity on an area depends on high yielding variety i.e. good quality seeds besides other agricultural inputs. Irrigation integrated pest management, agricultural implementation, etc. production various schemes are launched in the district to strengthen the agricultural production system. It has been observed that high yielding variety of seeds for different crops are required by the farmers. It has been recorded that about 19523 qtls. High yielding variety seeds are required in the district out of which maximum quantity high yielding variety of seeds are required Kunda, Lalganj, Pratapgarh Sadar blocks while low quantity high yielding variety of seeds are need in Baba Bhelkhar Nath Dham, Kalakankar, Songipur Laxmanpur, Sangramgarh and Yaura blocks of the district Pratapgarh.

3.2 Horticulture Development:

Horticulture is an other importance agro-base activity in the district Pratapgarh is farmers for aonla production and some of the villages of Mangraura block and Pratapgarh Sadar block has been declared as aonla belt.. Kunda and Kalakankar blocks has been declared as special horticultural zone for mango fruits for which special package including technical and financial back up support are provided to the interested horticultural growers in the district. I the horticultural development high yielding variety seeds of the fruits and grappled nursery plants are important in determining the quality and quantity production of fruits and vegetables. Thus good developed quality 45618 plants are required to strengthen the horticultural activity in the district Pratapgarh, out of which maximum horticultural plants are required in Bihar and Langanj block which low quantity plants are needed in the Aspur Devsara block of the district Pratapgarh.

Preservation and processing of fruits and vegetables is another important activity because it provides value addition to the horticultural produce and generate employment and increase the income of the deprived rural multitudes. In view of the above an integrated food products orders (FPO) license based minimum 5 fruits and vegetables preservation and processing units establishment are required in the district at Kunda, Mangraura and Pratapgarh Sadar blocks of the district Pratapgarh.

3.3 Gramodyog:

Establishment of Gramodyog units are necessary in Pratapgarh district with the view to optimum utilization of available agro-base products natural and human resources of the district. Thus it is planned to establish 85 gramodyog units in the district Pratapgarh out of which more than 10 gramodyog units establishment is need in the Mangraura and Pratapgarh Sadar block of the district while lowest gramodyog units are required in Babaganj and Yaural blocks of the district.

3.4 Sampoorna Gramin Rojgar yojna;

Besides the district plan it has been observed that 3118 beneficiaries are deserving needy and interested avail the facilities under the sampoorna gramin rojgar yojna launched by the government, out of which maximum number of need beneficiaries are seen in the Kalakankar, Babaganj, Kunda and Bihar blocks while lowest number of beneficiaries under sampoorna gramin rojgar yojna are found in Baba Phekhar Nath Dham, and Mangraura blocks of the district. Thus the benefits of the scheme under sampoorna gramin rojgar yojna should reach to more deserving interested below poverty line beneficiaries at village, block level in the district Pratapgarh.

3.5 Swarn Jayanti Gram Swarojgar yojna:

Swarn Jayanti Gram Swarojgar yojna is an important employment generating scheme of the government. Self employment is the basic aim of the scheme, under this scheme selected beneficiaries are trained and financial & technical back up support is provided for establishment of their working units. Thus such beneficiaries are call as Swarojgaris. It has been observed that there are 11972 interested, deserving Swarnrojgari beneficiaries in the district to whom requisite support can be provided under Swarn Jayanti Gram Swarojgar yojna being implemented in the district Pratapgarh. Maximum number of self-employment beneficiaries are found in Kalakankar block while lowest number of Swarojgaris beneficiaries are observed in Yaura Block under the Swarn Jayanti Gram Swarojgar yojna launched by the Government.

3.6 India Mark II Hand Pump:

India Mark II Hand Pump is one of the main system to obtain good quality drinking water in the rural areas. Government is also striving hard to meet the minimum demand of the rural drinking water and various schemes are launched to fulfill the growing demands of rural drinking water to control the health hazards in remote rural areas. It has been observed that approximately 676 more India Mark II hand pumps installation are required in the district out of which maximum number of India Mark II hand pumps are required in Kunda and Pratapgarh Sadar blocks while lowest number of India Mark II hand pumps are needed in the Sangipur, Lalganj and Bala Bhellchar Nath Dham blocks of the district Pratapgarh.

3.7 Road and Bridge and Chackroad:

Rural road is an important infrastructure to ensure integrated development of the village. It has been observed that approximately 1330 km. Pucca road construction is required in the district Pratapgarh which includes already constructed earth work and kharanza road in the district. It is recorded that maximum pucca road construction is required in Bihar block while lowest length pucca road construction is needed in Lalganj block of the district Pratapgarh.

Similarly 1111 km kharanza road construction is need in the district Pratapgarh including already completed earth work roads maximum distance kharanza road construction is required in Mandhata and Mangraura blocks and lowest length kharanza road construction is needed in Kunda and Songipur blocks of the district.

It has been observed that to connect the various villages and the farmers field approximately 1294 km chackroad construction is required in the district. Maximum distance chackroad construction is required in Lalganj and Laxmanpur block while minimum length chackroad construction is needed in the Kalakankar and Shivgarh blocks of the smooth movement of the farmers to their agricultural field.

Small bridges and pulias are required in the remote rural villages of the district to across the canals and rain water flow. It has been observed that atleast 76 bridges/pulias construction is required in district out of which maximum 10 bridges are required in Kunda block followed by Pratapgarh Sadar and Bihar blocks while lowest bridges are required in Patti & Aspur Revara blocks of the district Pratapgarh.

3.8 Health:

Primary health services are very important to the common people within limited distance common minimum health and medical facilities are required. Besides the existing health services available in the district, there are common minimum 28primary health centers or sub-primary health centers are required in the district Pratapgarh. It has been observed that maximum 3 numbers of primary/sub health centers are required in the Kunda and Pratapgarh Sadar blocks of the district while minimum one primary/sub-health center are required in Babaganj, Bihar, Sangipur, Laxmanpur, Mandhata, Mangraura, Patti, Shivgarh and Sangramgarh blocks of the district Pratapgarh to fulfill the common minimum health services to the deprived rural multitudes living the remote village of the district.

4. VILLAGE PLANNING – MANGRAURA BLOCK:

Various administrative and financial rights have been provided to the village-panchayats block panchayats and district panchayats under the decentralization system of panchayati raj. Panchayati Raj institutions have been strengthened and made more autonomous for the formulation of need base planning, implementation and maintenance of the planned programmes various developmental works have been handed over to the Panchayats.

Block Panchayat have been given responsibilities for the implementation of rural development programmes at Block level. Medical, health and family welfare programmes including availability of requisite financial medicines etc. are made available to primary health centers through block panchayats. Similarly animal hospitals management. Block level seed centers are also in the control of block panchayat. Block level marketing stress are supervised by block panchayats for smooth functioning of public distribution system. Works covering more than one Gram Panchayats are also implemented by the Block Panchayats and handed over related line departments assets are also maintained by the block panchayats.

Village Panchayats are provided the work responsibilities of education in which primary, senior secondary and non-formal education activities are transferred to village panchayats. School teachers, Head Masters and instructors are working in the control of village panchayat for which requisite financial support is directly provided to the village panchayats. Government Tube-wells are also handed over to the village panchayats, its maintenance agreement has been made available to the irrigation department. Hand pumps are the assets of village panchayat for repair, maintenance of the hand pumps as per the norms of the finance is provided by the government directly to village panchayats. Youth welfare and sports programmes are being implemented by the village panchayats for which financial support and materials are provided by the government to village panchayats. Medical, health & family welfare programmes are implemented under the control of village panchayats. Village level women and child development programmes are implemented under the control of village panchayats. Animal service center and 'D' category animal hospitals are implemented by the village panchayats. Food supply shops distribution and allotment rights are given to village panchayats. Village level agricultural programmes are implemented by village panchayats. Village level rural development programmes are implemented by village panchayats for which financial support is provided by the government. Village level related works of Panchayati Raj are implemented by the village panchayats. Village Panchayats are also distributing the pensions and scholarships in the open meetings of the village panchayats.

(i) Block Planning:

It has been already discussed that there are 62 village panchayats in Mangraura Block. Most of the villages of the block are backward and located the remote rural areas. It is evident from the above discussions that primary health center, animal hospitals, seed censer, marketing stores, works covering more than one village panchayats and maintenance of the assets are under the control of Block Panchayats for which necessary financial budgets and material are directly provided the Government and being implemented and controlled by Block Panchayats. Various block level rural development programmes implementation, monitoring and evaluation are done by the block panchayats. Concerned block level officers and staff are working under the control of Block Panchayat. Block level implementation of rural development programmes requisite budgets are provided directly by the government.

Various rural development programmes being implemented by the block panchayat Mangraura are mainly construction of link roads, nail/kharanza, low cost latrines, free boring, Indira Awas, rural drinking water, repair and maintenance of community assets viz., schools, hospitals etc.

There are only two sources of financial support like implementation of rural development programmes under Sampoorna Gramin Rojgar Yojna and 10th & 12th Finance Commission of the State.

Tenth Finance Commission of the State provides financial assistance to the block panchayats for functioning of the office of the block panchayats, staff and repair and maintenance of the state as per recommendations of the block panchayats. Various rural development programmes are also implemented as per the formulated and finalized plan and allocated budgetary provisions of the 10th Finance Commission of the State Government.

Sampoorna Gramin Rojgar yojna is one of the important scheme of the Government, to provide additional wage employment in the rural areas as also food security alongside the creation of durable community, social and economic infrastructure in the rural areas. Sampoorna Gramin Rojgar Yojna is being implemented through Panchayati Raj institutions and the resources are shared in the ratio of 20:30:50 between District Panchayat, Block Panchayat, and Gram Panchayats respectively.

Allocations of funds/food grains from the government is on the proportionate basis of the rural poor and index of backwardness formulated on the basis of proportion of rural scheduled caste population of agricultural workers. Thus 60% weight age is given to the scheduled caste population and 40% to the total population of the Gram Panchayat. The minimum allocation of Rs. 25,000/- to each Gram Panchayat is provided and total food grain is allocated in proportion to their cash component.

Every worker seeking employment under Sampoorna Rojgar yojna is provided minimum 5 kgs. Of food grains (in kind) per man day as part of the wages and balance of the wages are paid in cash. Minimum of 25% wages are paid in cash.

In this programmes block Panchayat Mangraura formulated the need base action plan and proposed to implemented the construction of nail, pulia, chackroad, kharnaza and other need base programmes in various villages of the block as per recommendations and proposals of the block development committee members of the Mangraura block.

Construction of chuckroad, kharanza and nail and earth work have been planned in Kohndaur, Ramapur, shankarpur, Lakhipur, Starrand, Sakara, Sarai rajai, Katari, Gaurauli, Chandauka, Parpanda, Chaumri, Asthara, Kanhari Madupur, Dhousiua, Gagehati, Narharpur, Poorabpatti, Shivpur Khurd, Sarayshankar, Narayanpur, Mangraura, Sarasidin, Etawaha, Bhaidapur, Raigarh villages of the Mangraura block. Under this scheme maximum employment to scheduled caste and persons belonging to below poverty lines are provided. It is also planned to construct 25% works benefiting directly to the scheduled caste population under the special commitment plan scheme of the government.

(ii) Village Planning:

Village level planning of Mangraura block have been planned as per the need base recommendations of the 62 village panchayats of the Mangraura block. It has been observed that at village level most of workers are b being implemented for the construction of nail, kharanza, chuckroad, pulia, repair and maintenance of the community assets for which maximum financial support to village panchayats are made available at the 50% ratio under the Sampoorna Gramin Rojgar yojna of the government with the view to provide 50% cash wage to generate employment and food grain in kind for food security to the scheduled caste and weaker section people living below poverty line in the respective village panchayats.

Need base Action Plan is approved from the Gram Panchayat in which planning execution, monitoring and supervision is also considered. Monitoring committee is formed involving scheduled caste and women as member. Thus the Sampoorna Gramin Rojgar yojna is demand driven and allocation of food grains is based on the requirements of the local needs.

The major need base action plan of the village panchayats are mainly nail, kharanza, chuckroads, earth work and maintenance of the community assets, besides there are several other need base programmes which can increase the agricultural productivity and generate more employment and increase their income through optimum utilization of available natural and human resources in the respective village panchayats. Therefore, an attempt is made to analyse need base action plan village panchayats of Mangraura block of district Pratapgarh.

4.1 Land Development:

Land development including reclamation of wastelands are an important activity in the various villages of Mangraura block because most of the land of the villages are badly affected by usarization i.e. salinity & alkalinity soil, water logging and undulated land. Calcareousness of the soil is the major problem due to which percolation of the surface water approximately at one meter depth is restrained, which causes usarization and main hindrance in the growth of the plants and poor agricultural cropping. It has been seen that aonla plantation in user land is successful due to which approximately in 28 villages of the block aonla plantation is very successful in the Mangraura block. Seeing the good quality aonla production concerned villages of the block have been declared as aonla belt. Keeping the above facts into consideration more than 10 hectares land development programme have been proposed in Kharouli Madapur, Shankarpur, Atarsand, Sakara, Varaha, Sikari Kanhupur villages of the block while there 28 villages in which land development programmes have not been proposed and rest of villages are having nominal need base land reclamation plan. Thus the reclamation of wastelands in the mangrauna block will be milestones in increasing the agricultural productivity of the various villages of the block.

4.2 Waterlogged land Development:

Waterlogged development is another problem in few villages of the Mangraura block. It has proposed to reclaim the waterlogged for developing ponds for fisheries culture. Thus more than 5 hectares of waterlogged land development for fisheries have been proposed in Chandauka, Saikari kanupur, Pure Manikanth, Bhaduna and Raigarh villages while less than 5 hectares waterlogged land development has been planned in ampur, Madura Raniganj, Atarsand, Koni, Katari, Gehrauli, Sahpur, Chaumuri, Dharouli, Muphrid, Sarouli, Mendah, Narharpur, Poorab patti, Shivpur Khurd,

Sarashankar, Hathasara, Naryanpur, Sarsikhan, Mangraura, Sarai Jamuari and Dehri Digar village while rest of the villages are not having any action plan for the reclamation of waterlogged land.

4.3 Agriculture Development:

The village farmers are able to manage irrigation, fertilizer and pest mangement even at certain extent application of agricultural implements as well but the availability of high yielding variety of seeds is the major problems. Therefore in most of the villages it has been need base demand for availability of seeds to increase the agricultural productivity of the area. It has been planned to provide more than 5 qtls of high yielding seeds in Satara, Atarsand, Asthara, Sheshpur, Adharganj and Sarai Zamuari villages while in rest of the villages less than 5 qtls. of high yield variety seeds have been required to increase the agricultural productivity of the villages so that the produced foodgrain may be procured for it utilization as seeds with the view to multiply and increase the agricultural productivity.

4.4 Horticultural Development:

Some of the villages of Mangraura block have been selected for special package to promote aonla horticultural plantation and this area has been declared as aonla belt by the government. In view of the special package under aonla belt Kohndaur, Ramapur, Madura Raniganj, Madaferpur, Padumpur, Kandharpur, Parsonda Basahupur Pharauli Muphrid, Lauli Pukhtakhan villages have proposed more than 5 hectares of land to develop for aonla cultivation (Table-10) about 31 village panchayats have no action plan for aonla plantation but rest of the villages have proposed to develop less than 5 hectares of land for aonla cultivation. Thus the aonla cultivation has been adopted as one of the commercial horticultural cultivation in most of the villages of the Mangraura block for which special package and financial support have been provided to the aonla horticultural growers.

4.5 Agro-Industries:

The promotion of agro-industries establishment in Mangraura block is very insignificant while during the primary survey and meetings alongwith concerned village panchayat secretaries, village pradhan, members of the village and block panchayat in different villages establishment of agro-industries have been proposed for which necessary technical back up support and financial assistance have been sought by the villagers. It has been observed that more than two agro-industries units have been proposed in Bhawapur, Chanduadih, Sakara, Malak, Sikari, Kanupur, Bojhi, Narharpur, Shivpur Khurd, Hathrara, Narayanpur, Mangraura, Bhadauna, Dehri Digar and Kohndaon villages of the Mangraura block and 30 village panchayats have not planned to develop agro-industries units while rest of the villages have planned and proposed to established atleast one or two agro industries in their respective village panchayats for optimum utilization of available natural and agro-base resources to generate employment and increase the income of deprived rural multitudes for their self sustenance.

4.6 Gramodyog:

Establishment of Gramodyog units have been proposed in Kohndaur, Ramapur, Bawapur, Prasrampur, Madaferpur, Koni, Katari, Gahrauli, Shahpur, Chandauka, Parsonda, Barahupur, Sikari Kanupur, Bijhi, Bjousiya, Varasaray, Gageheti, aurangabad, Prumanikanth, sarayshankar, Narayanpur, Utaras, Sarasilih, bhadauna villages while rest of the villages are not having any planned proposal for the establishment of Gramodyog units. Undoubtedly the establishment of Gramodyog in the various villages of Mangraura block will be mile stone in the utilization of available natural and agro-base and human resources to generate employment and increase the income of the rural peoples of the concerned village panchayats.

4.7 Swarn Jayanti Gram Swarojgar yojna:

Self employment is a significant step to have sustained employment, income and remove the shackles of poverty. Integrated self-employment programme- Swaran Jayanti Gram Swarojgar yojna is launched in which assistance is given to the poor families living below the poverty line for taken up self-employment. The persons taken self employment are called swarojgaris. Technical back up support and financial assistance are provided to the selected saarojgaris to generate employment and increase their income and to make them self sustained. It has been recorded that various village panchayats have proposed swarojgari for self employment, under this scheme maximum 30 numbers of swarojgaris have been proposed in Ramapur, Dharauli Madapur, Lakhipur, Sakara, Katari, Sarayshankar and Bhadauna villages, while lowest less than 10 swarojgaries have been proposed in Lauli Pulchtakhan, Sarasi Khan, Sarai Jamuari, Raigarh, Barahpur, Asthara, Amuwahi, Dharauli Muphrid, Bhauriya, Varasarai, Sarauli, Augangaba, Narharpur, Shankarpur, Madura Raniganj, Kono villages of the Mangraura block. Thus it is evident that most of the unemployed rural youths are interest to be the swarojgaries and are interested available necessary support being provided by the government.

4.8 Sampoorna Gramin Rojgaries yojna:

Sampoorna Gramin Rojgar Yojna is launched to provide additional wage employment in rural areas as also food security, alongside the creation of durable community, social and economic infrastructure in rural areas. It has been observed that more than 40 beneficiaries under Sampoorna Gramin Rojgar Yojna has been proposed in Asthaa, Bhivani, Bhadaura, Darchut, Puremanikanth, Amuwahi and Shankarpur villages of the block while lowest less than 20 beneficiaries under Sampoorna Gramin Rojgar yojna has been in proposed in Lakhipur, Atardand, Madaprpur, Chanduadin, Malak, Gahrauli, shahpur, Kandharpur villages of the Mangraura block to obtain wages in cash and food grains in kind through constructing various activities like Chackroad, nali, kharnaza, earth work, community development activities being planned, implemented by the concerned village panchayats.

4.9 India Mark II Hand Pumps

Water is an essential ingredient of our daily life. The importance of safe drinking water can not be under estimated because poor quality of water causes many diseases. India Mark II hand pumps are installed to obtain safe drinking water under various schemes viz., Member of Parliament Local Area Development programme, Member of Legislative Local Area Development programme, District Panchayats, block panchayats, village panchayats and other schemes launched by the government under the accelerated rural water supply programme (ARWSP). Under the Swajal dhara scheme 10% community contribution of the estimated capital cost of the scheme while 5% contribution is charged in case of predominantly scheduled caste habitations, while 90% funds towards the project excluding community contribution cost will be fully met by the government of India. Besides the about as per the requirement of the India Mark II hand pumps various village panchayats have proposed installation of more than 10 hand pumps in Konhdour, Ramapur, Dharauli Madapur, Shankarpur Madua, Raniganj, Atarsand, Sakara Koni, amuwahi, Dhousiya villages and some of the villages viz., Gajehati, aurangabad, Darchut and Bhivani villages have proposed installation of only one India Mark II hand pump while rest of the villages have proposed installation of 1 to 10 India Mark I hand pumps through different sources. Thus it can be s aid that most of the village panchayats and villages are seriously concerned to obtain safe drinking water to control the various diseases.

4.10 Pucca Road:

Construction of Pucca road through different sources have been proposed by the village panchayats in which more than 2 km long pucca road construction have been planned in Ramapur, Sharkarpur, Lakhipur, Chanduadit, Sakara, Salhipur, Kanjas, Katari, Padumpur, shahpur, Chaumuri, Varikala, sheshpur Adharganj, Sarouli, suryagarh, Jagannath, darchut, Saratikhan, Narayanur, Saray Jamuari and Utaras villages while less than one km. Puuca road construction have been proposed in SarayShankar, Hathsara, Narharpur, Madura Raniganj and Parasrampur villages of the Mangraura block

4.11 Kharanza Road:

Construction of kharanza road is being implemented under different schemes launched by the Government through Panchayati Raj, Institutions i.e. Village-Block-District Panchayats. Village Panchayat is autonomous independent body to plan the construction of kharanza road in their respective villages as per the local need of the village people. Most of the financial budget is being utilized by the village and Block panchayat for construction of kharanza road. It has been observed that more than one km kharanza road construction have been proposed in Lakhipur, Madaferpur, Malak, Parsanda, Chaumuri, Amuwahi, Dharauli, Muphrid, Sikari Kanupur, Kanhai Madhupur, Bojhi, Bhousia, Mandah, Varasaray, Gagehati, Aurangabad, Puremanikanth, Poorab Patti, Shivpur Khurd, Lauli Pukhta Khan, Mangraura, Sarasidih, Etawah, Bhadauna, Bhivani, Bhaidapur, Kansa Patti, Raigarh and Dehri

Digar villages while villages utaras, Sarai Zamuari, Sarasi Kham, Naranpur, Darchut, Suryagarh, Jagannath, Sarouli, Sheshur, Atharganj, Varikala, Chauri villages have propose more than 2 kms long construction of kharanza road while rest of the villages have proposed less than one km construction of kharanza road in their respective village panchayats.

4.12 Bridge:

Construction of bridge in the village panchayats are being implemented through village panchayats under various schemes financially supported by the government. More than two bridges construction are proposed in Madaferpur, Chanduadin, Sakara, Salhipur Kanjas, Katari, Sahpur, Barahapur, Bojhi, Sarouli, Pure Mandikanth, Poorabpatti Sarasikham, Sarasidin and Dehri Digar villages (Table-10).While 26 village panchayats have not proposed in the plan for construction of bridge and rest of the villages have proposed only one bridge construction in their respective village panchayat for smooth movement in their village.

4.13 Chackroad:

Chackroad is the basic link to connect the village from cultivated field to the main village link road. Construction of chackroad is being implemented by the village panchayat. Sampoorna Gramin Rojgar Yojna is the main scheme through which chackroad construction is being implemented to facilitate smooth movement from village to field. It has been observed that to facilitate field to field link connectivity more than 2 km chackroad construction is proposed in Shankarpur, Madura, Raniganj, Madaferpur, Sakara, Koni, Sarai Rajai, Sathipur, Kanjas, Malak, Gahrauli Khandharpur villages while less than one km chackroad construction is proposed in Shespur, Adharganj, Kanhai Madufpur, Suryagarh, Jagannath, Surangabad, Poorabpatti, Saraishankar, Lauli, Pukhtakhan, Darchut, Narayanpur, Sarai Zajuari, Etawah, Kensipatti and Dehri Digar villages of Mangraura block. Thus chackroad in the remote rural villages can be called as life link from village to field for village people, which has to be developed. 4.14 Health:

Health is one of the most important requirements of the downtrodden villages because due to socio-economic backwardness and ignorance most of the village people are facing various diseases. Thus medicine, health and family welfare programmes are basic requirements of the village people. It has been rewarded that village Bhawapur, Shankarpur, Madura Raniganj, Chanduadih, Sakara, Koni, Salhipur, Kanjas, Gahrauli, Chandauka, Barahupur, Sikari Kanapur, Bijli, Gagehati, Sarouli, Aurangabad, Puremanikanth, Poorabpatti, Lauli Pukhtakham, Narayanpur, Etawah, Bhaidapur and Dehri Digar village panchayats have proposed and planned to avail the facility of medical health & family welfare censer in their village panchayats because the rural health programmes is one of the important scheme of the government.

4.15 Electrification:

Rural electrification is also an important scheme of the Government under the various schemes of the government rural electrification programmes are being implemented. It has been observed that 50 houses electrification programmes have been planned in Kohndaus, Bhawapur, Madura aniganj, Sakara, Koni, Chandauka, Parsanda, Chaumuri, Varaha, Barakapur, Verikala, Asthara, Dharauli, Mufhrid, Sikari Kanupur, Sheshpur, Adharganj, Kanhai Madupur, Sarouli,Poorabpati, Shivpur Khurd, Saray Shankar, Hathara, Lauli Pukhtakhan, Darchut, Sarai Zamuari, utaras, Sarasidih, Etawah, Bhadauna, Bhivani, Raigarh Dehri Digar villages of the Mangrauna block while less than 20 house electrification has been proposed in the Lakhipur, Madaferpur, Chanduadih, Malak, gahrauli Sahpur, Kandharpur, Mangraura villages of the block Mangraura.

4.16 Animal:

It has been planned to complete the incomplete animal hospitals at Kohndaur village and construction of new animal service center at Augangabad village and availability of medicines and artificial insemination facilities in the respective villages have been planned through the concerned implementing agency including production of the cows and buffaloes

4.17 Welfare:

The scholarships for the scheduled caste, backward caste, minorities and below poverty line students have been proposed and pension, grants for marriage of downtrodden helpless persons and back up support has been proposed by the village panchayats to the respective line departments through village and block panchayats of Mangraura blocks. Pension and grants to poor, helpless widows are also proposed by the respective village panchayats. Besides there are different rural development programmes like integrated rural development programmes as per recommendation of the local Member of Legislative Assembly village Asthara, Dharouli Madhupur and Hathasara villages have been selected for complete saturation of link road, electrification, nail/kharanza, sanitation, free boring, swarn jayanti gram swarojgar yojna, Indira Awas, safe drinking water, establishment of primary schools and higher secondary schools old age pension allotment of surplus land for housing and pottery, verification of patta land, handicapped pension, support for equipments family welfare immunization and fisheries so that the complete integrated rural development may be ensured in the selected villages.

5. CONCLUSION:

Thus the planning is a means to achieve the development or planning is a organized process of which the people achieves its developmental goals. The planners have to provide developmental planning scientific-technical back up support to the grass root level village peoples representative and officials involved in village development and planning. The planning and development must be peoples participatory tapping the local talent and resources in order to make it sustainable. Efforts are being made to implement rural development programmes with a focuses on enhancing the livelihoods of weaker and vulnerable sections for sustainable development.

Village is a development unit in the new decentralization system of the government. Faster development is ensured assuming village as a center for development. In the decentralization scheme administrative and financial powers have been provided to village panchayats for formulation of their need base action plan, implementation of planned activities and maintenance of created assets for its sustainability. To ensure self-government of the panchayats need base action plan has been formulated.

District Pratapgarh has historical, cultural archaeological and religious importance. The planning and implementation of the programmes are ensured through planning committee of the district Pratapgarh with the participation of local bodies including rural panchayats and urban panchayats. Activities and planning process of the district planning committee is based on the participatory need base requirements of the local bodies because the development is through the people, for the people and by the people.

Agricultural activities have been promoted in Pratapgarh district, cultivation of oil seed and pulses have been promoted in which requisite seed, fertilizer, pest management and other technical back up support has been proposed. Promotion and propagation of Maiz cultivation has also been proposed in the district plan. National oil seed development programme has been implemented in the district which requisite supply of seed, fertilizers, pest management and extension programmes have been proposed in the district plan. Land development fertilizer and distribution field demonstrations, Kisan Mitra Yojna and other schemes have been proposed with view to increase the agricultural productivity of the district.

Financial support to 3070 small and marginal farmers have been proposed in which 442 farmers are proposed under special component plan scheme of the government.

Animal husbandry, animal health, medical treatment have been proposed in which completion of animal hospitals, construction of new animal hospitals and provision of medicines, animal health service centers etc. have been proposed. Support for inseminization of buffaloes and cows have been proposed. Besides above pigs, sheep and other animals development programmes have been proposed including grass land development for nutritious cattle feed production have been proposed in the district plan of Pratapgarh.

Reconstitution, strengthening and extension of dairy co-operative federations and dairy societies have been proposed in the district plan.

District fisheries development agency is engaged in promotion and development of fisheries activity in Pratapgarh district. It is proposed to train, educate technically demonstrate 100 fishermen and also proposed to develop 100 hectares ponds and to provide scientific-technical back up support and financial assistance including insurance schemes to the fishermen of the district Pratapgarh.

Social forestry programmes have been promoted in the district including rural and urban areas. It is proposed to implement 170 hect. Advance soil work, 170 hectare land plantation and another 200 hect. Land soil work and 75 hect. Land soil work under special component plan have been proposed in the district plan. It is also planned to raise 4.0 lakh nursery plants large scale propagation extension of social forestry and agro-forestry programmes have been proposed in the district plan.

Co-operative programmes are being implemented in the district and it is proposed o provide interest free loan to 10,000 scheduled caste farmers and below poverty line people for purchase of part item. Financial support for scheduled caste persons have been provided for self employment under the cooperative schemes of the government.

Various rural development programmes are being implemented in the district Pratapgarh. It is proposed to provide technical and financial back up support to 1964 beneficiaries and 354 scheduled caste beneficiaries under Swarn Jayanti gram Swarojgar yojna scheme of the government to generate employment and increase the income of swarojgaris.

Integrated wasteland development programme are launched under the drought prone area development scheme in Rs. 936 thousand has been allocated to achieve the goals to utilize available land resources to generate employment and increase the income of deprived rural beneficiaries.

Integrated rural energy programme is launched in which Rs. 105 thousand has been allocated in the district plan for installation of 130 light and 20 lights under special component scheme. Awareness, training programmes are proposed for appropriate utilization of additional sources of energy for which Rs. 33 thousand budget have been allocated.

To meet the shortage of housing in rural areas India Awas Yojna is being implemented . It is planned to construct 1290 low cost rural houses for poors and 774 low cost rural houses for scheduled caste beneficiaries under special component plan scheme.

Sampoorna Gramin Rojgar yojna is launched to provide wage employment in rural areas and also food security, under this scheme 15.93 lakh man days employment has been proposed.

It is planned to provide 25.89 km. Kharanza/nail construction for integrated development of the village for which Rs. 70.58 lakh has been allocated and Rs. 9.08 lakh for construction of multipurpose welfare center in 17 village panchayats of the districts.

Community development programmes are being implemented in the district for which Rs. 89.63 lakh have been allocated.

Rural small scale industry has been promoted in the district for which a sum of RS. 172 thousand has been earmarked in the district plan to facilitate selected 26 beneficiaries. Khadi & Village industries programme has been promoted for which Rs. 20.87 lakh has been allocated for support to the selected beneficiaries under this scheme.

Construction of road and bridges is the main priority for which Rs. 872.59 lakh has been allocated. It is planned to construct 36.02 km. Earth work, 45.07 km kharanza work and 54.07 km pucca road construction including 72 bridges in the district plan.

Private minor irrigation has been promoted in which 10 tube wells, 2 deep tube wells boring have been proposed. Ground water charging check dams construction of 34 ponds and 4 check dams have been proposed in the district plan. It is also planned to reinstall 6 unsuccessful tube wells and remaintenance of irrigation nail/gul etc.

Requisite machinery and equipment support has been also planned to strengthen the irrigation system and a sum of Rs. 40.99 lakh budget has been allocated under this scheme.

Environment awareness and other programmes have been planned in the district plan for which suitable financial budget have been allocated.

Financial allocations has been earmarked to attract tourism programmes in the district due to its archeological, historical, cultural and religious importance.

Development of educational and infrastructure and encouragement of students towards education has been the priority of the government. Shiksha Mitra Yojna is launched to promote primary education and 'Education of all' programmes are launched for which necessary budget have been allocated in the district plan. Similarly secondary education is also promoted to strengthen the educational infrastructure necessary financial budgetary provisions have been made in the district plan.

Pradeshik Vikas Dal scheme is launched to promote rural sports for which Rs. 4.86 lakh have been allocated and Rs. 14.31 lakh have been allocated to establish rural stadium to develop sports spirit among the rural youth.

Health and family welfare programmes are being implemented to provide best medical support in which allopathic, homeopathic, ayurvedic & unani hospitals infrastructural, medicines, equipments etc. as per the requirements financial budgets have been allocated in the district plan of Pratapgarh.

Supply of rural drinking water is being implemented by the Jal Nigam in which completion of 21 incomplete projects have been planned, repair and maintenance and installation of 340 new hand pumps, 600 rebore of failure hand pumps and replacement of G.I. pipes etc. have been proposed in the district plan. Urban drinking water programme has been promoted in which rebore of tube wells and installation of India Mark II hand pump have been proposed in the district plan. Construction of 1783 low cast latrines have also been proposed in the district plan.

Popularisation & implementation of programmes and strengthening the information system including exhibition, mela, publication, photography schemes have been incorporated in the district plan.

Various welfare programmes are launched in the district it is proposed to provide scholarships for scheduled caste, backward caste, minority and scholarships for poor general caste students have been incorporated in the district plan for which requisite financial budget have been allocated. Employment programmes and handicraft training programmes have been proposed in the District plan. Social welfare and handicapped welfare programmes are also incorporated in the district including women and child development programmes for which requisite necessary budgets have been allocated in the district plan of Pratapgarh.

Besides the district plan, need base action plan as perceived by the peoples of the district Pratapgarh has been also analysed in which land development wasteland reclamation agricultural development, horticultural development, gramodyog, Sampoorna Gramin Rojgar Yojna, Swarn Jayanti Gram Swarojgar yojna institution of Indira Mark II hand pumps, construction of road, bridges and chackroad, health and various programmes have been analysed for its implementation to met the common minimum requirement of the local people for integrated sustained rural development.

Panchayati Raj institutions have been strengthened and made more autonomous for the formulation of need base planning, execution and implementation of planned programmes, its maintenance for sustainability. Planchayats have been given more responsibilities for the implementation of rural development, medical health and family welfare programmes, animal hospitals, seed centers, marketing stores, village panchayats, education government tube wells, hand pumps and youth welfare programmes implementation at village and block level in the district.

Block planning for 62 village panchayats have been analysed in which major rural development programes implementation, based on the need base planning, monitoring and evaluation are the main responsibilities of the block panchayats. Financial support to the block panchayat is made available through 10th & 12th Finance Commission of the state which major grant is provide under the Sampoorna Gramin Rojgar yojna at the ration of 30% plan budget to the block panchayats for the planning and implementation of need base programmes. It is planned to provide 60% weightage for scheduled caste populated inhabitants and 40% to the other general caste population.

Block panchayats are independent and autonomous to plan their need base programmes and it implementation as per norms of the Sampoorna Gramin Rojgar Yojna. Block panchayats are engaged in the implementation of nail, kharanza, chackroad, earth works and repair and maintenance of the communities assets in the various villages of the Mangraura block Panchayats in wages are paid in cash and food grains in kind with the view to generate employment and increase the income of deprived rural multitudes and ensure food security to the downtrodden rural poors.

Village Planning for Mangraura block have been planned as per the need base recommendations of the 62 village panchayats. Most of the works which are being planned and implemented are the construction of nail/kharanza, chackroad, pulia, repair and maintenance of the village community assets located in the respective village panchayats.

Te main source of grants to village panchayats are the 10th Finance Commission and at the ratio of 50% grants under Sampoorna Gramin Rojgar yojna in which 50% wages are paid in cash and rest paid in kind as food grain to ensure food security by among the deprived rural poor. Need base action plan is formulated by the village panchayat, its execution, implementation monitoring and evaluation are also managed by the village panchayat.

Land development programmes in various villages have been proposed in which the reclamation of different wastelands have been proposed to meet the increasing demand of growing population for food grains, fuel wood, fodder, fiber, fruits and fisheries (F6) programmes. Most of the user land of the 28 villages are being for aonla plantation because Mangraura block has been declared as aonla belt for special package assistance to provide scientific, technical and financial support to the interest horticultural growers to increase the productivity of aonla and also the preservation and processing of aonla for value addition and to increase the income and generated employment for interested poor beneficiaries.

Most of the available waterlogged land have been proposed for developing ponds to promote fisheries culture with the view to utilize available land/water resources to generate employment and increase the income of the rural poor.

Agricultural and horticultural development have been proposed with the view to provide high yield variety of seeds and grafted fruit plants besides the other inputs including fertilizers, irrigation pest management etc. Establishment of agro-industries have also been proposed for optimum utilization of agro-base products for value addition.

Besides the agro-industries establishment of Gramodyog units have been proposed in the various panchayats.

Under the Sawaran Jayanti Gram Swarojgar yojna, Swarojgaries have been identified and proposed for the scientific technical back support and financial assistance as per the norms of the scheme.

Similarly under the Sampoorna Gramin Rojgar Yojna beneficiaries have been selected and construction of nail, kharnaza, chackroad, earth work have been proposed inn the village plan to provide wage employment and food security to the deprived rural multitudes. As per the need base requirement of India Mark II hand pumps to ensure safe drinking water installation of India Mark II hand pumps have been proposed under the accelerated rural water supply programme and swajal Dhara scheme of the government.

Construction of pucca road and kharanza road have been proposed by village panchayats s per the common minimum requirement of the village people, construction of small bridges, pulias on the constructed nail etc. have been incorporated in the village plan .

Chackroad is one of the basic lifeline link to connect village and farmer's field due to which special emphasis has been given to construct the chackroad in the village panchayats have been proposed.

Medical, health and family welfare programmes have been incorporated in the village plan to obtain minimum health services under the rural health scheme of the government.

Electrification of rural houses in the villages have been proposed under the rural electrification scheme of the government to ensure integrated rural development of the village located in the remote rural areas.

Animal welfare programmes and animal service center and animal disease control facility including medicines and inseminization of buffalo and cows etc. have been proposed by the village panchayats.

Welfare schemes including pension for old age persons, other grants to needy people, scholarships to scheduled caste, backward case, below poverty line general caste and minority student have been proposed as one of the need base action plan of the village panchayat.

Besides above various rural development programmes under integrated rural development programmes are also planned and implemented in the different village panchatyats of Mangraura block.

Thus the Panchayati Raj institutions are more effective, autonomous self government in the formulation of need base action plan, its' execution and implementation, monitoring and evaluation. The optimum utilization of available natural, social, economic and infrastructural resources to meet the increasing demand of growing population for integrated rural development has been ensured through Self Government of panchayati Raj-Lok Raj-Gram raj, in which scientific technical infrastructural facilities are procured to generated the employment, increase the income of deprived rural multitudes surviving in the remote rural villages, hence improving their socio-economic conditions, therefore such deprived section of the society are able move equally with the upper section of the society as per constitution rights.

Table -9 : Natural Resources Data Management System (NRDMS)
Pratapgarh district - Need Base Plan

Sl. No.	*Village*	*Land Dev.*	*Agriculture Dev. Quental Seed Distribution*	*Horti-culture Dev. No. of plant*	*Gramo-dyog unit to*	*SGSY Employ-ment*	*India Mark 2 Hand pump*	*Pacca Road*	*Kharanja Road*	*Bridge*	*Chakroad*	*Health Centre*	*Rural Dev. SGSY*
1	KalaKankar	19	927	1890	3	885	39	97	44	7	51	2	251
2	Babaganj	37	1074	1500	1	774	43	86	74	2	79	1	251
3	Kunda	16	1645	3360	7	713	52	79	34	10	39	3	251
4	Bihar	31	1329	7190	3	713	47	102	63	8	69	1	251
5	Sangipur	30	909	2993	2	788	29	39	33	7	99	1	191
6	Lalganj	28	1560	7903	4	660	34	45	71	4	106	2	166
7	Laxmanpur	41	964	2789	6	645	46	86	49	3	109	1	151
8	Sandwa Chandrika	35	1028	1609	3	728	47	97	61	5	66	2	176
9	Pratapgarh Sadar	71	1525	1503	13	603	50	58	63	9	68	3	181
10	Mandhata	59	1354	2601	2	749	34	83	90	3	95	1	194
11	Mangraura	39	1132	3407	11	732	39	63	91	2	78	1	141
12	Patti	69	1162	1000	7	608	36	74	69	1	72	1	150
13	Aspur Devsara	31	1192	956	3	759	38	79	79	1	97	2	181
14	Shivgarh	34	1329	1209	4	663	43	87	82	4	53	1	151
15	Gaura	17	995	1308	1	576	49	78	58	5	63	3	151
16	Sangramgarh	23	995	2100	9	680	48	93	67	2	72	1	171
17	Bababhel Kharnath	19	403	2300	6	696	35	84	83	3	78	2	110
	Total	599	19523	45618	85	11972	709	1330	1111	76	1294	28	3118

**Table -10 : Natural Resources Data Management System (NRDMS)
Mangraura Block, Pratapgarh district
Need Base Plan (Village Plan)**

Loc code	*Vill_name*	*Land Dev.*	*Water logged land Dev.*	*Agril. Dev. Seed Distribution*	*Horti-culture Dev.*	*Agro-industries*	*Gramo*	*SJGSY*	*India Mark II Hand pump*	*Pucca Road*
1	*2*	*3*	*4*	*5*	*6*	*7*	*8*	*9*	*10*	*11*
1	Konhdour	3.5	0	1.5	11	.3	1	14	15	1.50
2	Ramapur	12	4	2	5	1	1	30	12	2.00
3	Dharouli Madapur	28	0	3	0	3	0	42	10	1.50
4	Bhawapur	0	0	1	0	0	1	13	7	1.00
5	Shankarpur	12	0	2	0	2	0	10	13	2.00
6	Madura Raniganj	0	2	1	9	1	0	6	14	0.50
7	Parasrampur	0	0	3	3	1	1	16	3	0.80
8	Lakhipur	0	0	1	2	0	0	35	6	2.30
9	Atarsand	13	2	6	0	0	0	21	15	1.00
10	Madaferpur	9	0	2	9	1	1	27	9	1.75
11	Chanduadih	1	0	1	0	0	0	18	4	2.00
12	Sakara	10	0	5	0	2	0	30	12	3.50
13	Koni	0	3	3	0	2	2	5	14	1.50
14	Sarairajai	4	0	2	4	1	0	14	6	1.00
15	Salhipur Kanjas	0	0	3	0	0	0	19	9	2.00
16	Katari	0	4	1	0	1	1	30	6	3.00
17	Malak	0	0	1	0	2	0	15	3	1.00
18	Padumpur	1	0	3	5	1	0	16	2	2.30
19	Gahrauli	0	0	2	4	0	1	19	7	1.25
20	Sahpur	0	2	1	3	1	1	14	5	2.00
21	Kandharpur	0	0	1	6	1	0	13	2	1.50
22	Chandouka	5	7	2	0	0	1	12	5	1.25
23	Parasanda	6	0	2	7	1	0	16	7	1.50
24	Choumuri	3	2	1	0	0	0	16	7	2.50
25	Varaha	10	0	3	0	0	0	13	4	1.25
26	Barahupur	0	3	2	6	1	2	10	2	1.24
27	Varikala	0	0	1	3	0	0	12	7	2.75
28	Asthra	0	0	5	2	0	0	9	9	1.25
29	Amuwahi	0	0	3	4	0	0	7	13	1.45
30	Dharouli Muphrid	2	4	3	7	0	1	3	2	1.36
31	Sikri Kanupur	10	7	1	0	2	1	17	5	1.80
32	Sheshpur Adharganj	0	0	6	0	0	1	19	7	2.30
33	Kanhai Madupur	0	0	2	2	0	1	6	9	1.56
34	Bojhi	0	0	1	0	2	2	11	8	1.87
35	Bhousiya	0	0	3	0	1	0	3	11	1.24
36	Mandah	0	4	2	0	0	0	18	4	1.30
37	Varasaray	0	0	4	0	1	0	7	3	1.28
38	Gagehati	0	0	1	1	1	2	26	1	1.24
39	Sarouli	0	4	2	0	0	1	7	5	2.00
40	Suryagarh Jagannath	0	0	2	0	0	0	18	2	2.12
41	Aourangabad	9	0	1	1.5	1	1	9	1	1.75
42	Naraharpur	1	3	1	0	2	0	2	3	0.50
43	Pure Manikanth	7	5	4	0	1	1	11	3	1.50
44	Poorabpatti	2	4	3	3	0	0	10	3	1.25

Table -10 Contd...

Loc code	Vill_name	Land Dev.	Water logged land Dev.	Agril. Dev. Seed Distribution	Horti-culture Dev.	Agro-industries	Gramo	SJGSY	India Mark II Hand pump	Pucca Road
45	Shivpur Khurd	6	2	2	0	3	0	24	4	1.35
46	Saray Shankar	1	2	1	0	0	1	35	6	0.75
47	Hathasara	1	2	1	0	3	0	15	7	0.50
48	Louli Pukhtakham	2	0	2	5	0	0	10	3	1.25
49	Darchut	1	0	1	0	0	0	26	1	2.40
50	Narayanpur	5	2	3	0	2	1	21	5	3.25
51	Sarasi Kham	0	2	2	0	0	0	4	2	2.75
52	Mangroura	0	2	1	4	2	0	17	3	1.70
53	Saray Jamuari	5	4	5	0	0	0	2	7	2.40
54	Utaras	4	0	2	0	0	1	18	2	2.50
55	Sarasidih	1	0	4	3	0	1	22	8	1.50
56	Etawah	0	0	3	0	0	0	13	2	1.20
57	Bhadouna	0	5	1	2	2	1	33	4	1.40
58	Bhivani	2	0	3	0	0	0	24	1	1.24
59	Bhaidapur	1.5	0	2	1	1	0	16	3	1.30
60	Kansa Patti	3.5	0	3	2	0	0	19	5	1.25
61	Raigarh	1	7	1	4	0	0	7	2	1.80
62	Dehari Digar	4	3	2	5	3	0	18	3	1.25

Loc_ code	Vill_name	Kacha Road	Bridge	Chakroad	Health	Houses Electrification	Sampoorna Gram Rojgar Yojana
1	2	12	13	14	15	16	17
1	Konhdour	0.70	1	1.60	0	56	35
2	Ramapur	0.30	1	1.90	0	40	28
3	Dharouli Madapur	0.90	1	1.40	0	45	30
4	Bhawapur	0.15	0	1.90	1	56	32
5	Shankarpur	0.16	0	2.50	1	60	41
6	Madura Raniganj	0.40	0	2.10	1	71	28
7	Parasrampur	0.27	1	1.70	0	65	30
8	Lakhipur	1.15	0	1.20	0	30	15
9	Atarsand	0.27	0	1.50	0	48	38
10	Madaferpur	1.15	3	2.50	0	19	15
11	Chanduadih	0.50	2	1.50	1	26	19
12	Sakara	0.70	4	2.00	1	55	25
13	Koni	0.40	0	2.10	1	52	35
14	Sarairajai	0.35	0	2.70	0	15	28
15	Salhipur Kanjas	0.60	3	2.47	1	19	22
16	Katari	0.45	2	1.27	1	29	32
17	Malak	1.30	0	2.45	0	34	18
18	Padumpur	0.25	0	1.24	0	41	23
19	Gahrauli	0.30	0	2.47	1	23	14
20	Sahpur	0.15	3	1.50	0	16	18
21	Kandharpur	0.16	1	2.45	0	33	19
22	Chandouka	0.37	1	1.40	1	57	25
23	Parasanda	1.35	0	1.20	1	61	35

Loc_ code	*Vill_name*	*Kacha Road*	*Bridge*	*Chakroad*	*Health*	*Houses Electrification*	*Sampoorna Gram Rojgar Yojana*
24	Choumuri	1.65	0	1.60	0	53	31
25	Varaha	0.19	0	0.90	0	58	39
26	Barahupur	0.24	2	1.80	1	71	33
27	Varikala	0.36	0	1.50	0	75	28
28	Asthra	0.28	0	1.35	0	68	51
29	Amuwahi	1.50	1	1.26	0	38	42
30	Dharouli Muphrid	1.30	1	1.30	0	51	36
31	Sikri Kanupur	1.73	1	1.10	1	55	29
32	Sheshpur Adharganj	0.90	0	0.56	0	65	27
33	Kanhai Madupur	0.40	0	0.40	0	52	38
34	Bojhi	0.50	2	1.34	1	48	32
35	Bhousiya	0.78	1	1.47	0	35	39
36	Mandah	1.40	0	1.26	0	45	28
37	Varasaray	1.90	0	1.46	0	38	30
38	Gagehati	0.38	1	1.50	1	47	26
39	Sarouli	0.90	3	1.47	1	53	35
40	Suryagarh Jagannath	1.20	1	0.46	0	37	38
41	Aourangabad	1.50	0	0.38	1	31	23
42	Naraharpur	1.46	1	1.32	0	33	35
43	Pure Manikanth	0.70	2	1.30	1	28	42
44	Poorabpatti	0.30	2	0.40	1	55	28
45	Shivpur Khurd	0.93	1	1.60	0	70	39
46	Saray Shankar	0.15	0	0.90	0	50	32
47	Hathasara	0.16	0	1.20	0	65	28
48	Louli Pukhtakham	0.24	1	0.80	1	58	37
49	Darchut	0.25	1	0.56	0	52	46
50	Narayanpur	0.40	1	0.16	1	24	25
51	Sarasi Kham	0.27	2	1.17	0	44	33
52	Mangroura	0.30	0	1.23	0	17	28
53	Saray Jamuari	0.25	0	0.90	0	71	38
54	Utaras	0.40	1	1.20	0	63	33
55	Sarasidih	0.60	2	1.30	0	62	35
56	Etawah	0.19	1	0.65	1	68	36
57	Bhadouna	0.18	1	1.17	0	64	42
58	Bhivani	0.70	1	1.26	0	59	49
59	Bhaidapur	0.90	1	1.32	1	52	38
60	Kansa Patti	0.40	0	0.44	0	46	33
61	Raigarh	0.19	0	1.60	0	59	29
62	Dehari Digar	0.25	3	0.70	1	54	36

CHAPTER - VIII

CONCLUSION

1. INTRODUCTION:

Planning is a means to achieve development. Development is pursued with genuine concern for human values. Development means the evolution of the people in which the people acquires better perception and best control over its natural and human resources. There is a quest for evolving a model for planning development needs capapcity building at institutions of local self governance to prepare and implement-local sepific, integrated development schemes by assessing and utilizing available natural and human resources. Natural Resources Data Management System (NRDMS) has been adopted as a tool for collection and collation socio-economic data base including natural resources adopting Geographic Information System (GIS) for district-block-village level development planning. Geographically Pratapgarh district is endowed with natural and human resources. It has historical, cultural, archaeological and religious importance.

Socio economic data among the human resources and its various sub-indicators data have been collected, collated at block and village level. Similarly infrastructural data at village level for Mangraura block and at Block level for Pratapgarh district have been analysed for formulation of need base development planning.

Various rural development programmes being implemented at block level in Pratapgarh district and village level for Mangraura block have been collected for analysis need of the people and to formulate need base planning at village level in Mangraura block and block level in Pratapgarh district.

Need of the people and their requirement have been studied. As per requirement of the local people need base action development planning at village level in Mangraura block and at block level in Pratapgarh district have been formulated.

Development planning as per need of the people at village level will be a mile stone for integrated development of village-block-district Pratapgarh. No doubt the development planning adopting natural resources data management system (NRDMS) for collection and collation of data and its analysis at village level in Mangraura block and block level in Pratapgarh district will be model for integrated development of village planning, district Pratapgarh.

2. NATURAL RESOURCES:

District Pratapgarh is endowed with natural resources available natural resources have positive and negative impact in the overall development of Pratapgarh. Physiography of the Pratapgarh district is divided into mild and low land. The main river of the Pratapgarh district is soil river. Pratapgarh is covered by consolidated sedimentary rocks formulation and alluvium. Alluvium plain is formed by the ganges system.

Relief of the district is divided as mild and low land. General slope of the district is towards the east. Relief of the district is marked by a level plain which shows influence of rivers and streams. The flat terrain at some places shows entle undulations but in the vicinity of the river and streams the land is extremely dissected with the consequent development of ravines. Pratapgarh district is covered by unconsolidated sedimentary rock formation and alluvium and there is no exploitable mineral in the district. Kankar pan is available in the saline/alkaline land.

The largest among the rivers flowing through the district is Ganga river near the south-western border of the Pratapgarh district from Kalankar to Gotani, Sai river is the another river whose canals are in many places high and generally well defined. The banks of the Sai river are broken at certain places due to ravines and comprise of light texture soil, Naiya chamraura, Luni, Bakulati rivers are some of the important tributaries of the Sai river. The northern tributaries of soil river generally flow from north to south but those on the right bank are more meandering and generally flow eastward and finally join the Sai river in the north.

Climatic conditions of the Prataparh district are appropriate. Pratapgarh has maximum and minimum temperature of 48 c. and 6 c. respectively. Average annual rainfall of Pratapgarh district is 1000 m.m. of which Pratapgarh Sadar tehsil gets the minimum share followed patti and Kunda tehsils. Thus the overall rainfall of Pratapgarh district varies below 800 to 1000 m.m.

Salinity occurs in 52477 hectares area accounting for 82.55% of the total wastelands of the Pratapgarh district. The occurrence of salt affected wasteland is less extension to the north of Sai river than in the south. Saline land is conspicuously seen between Sai and Gaa river in Kunda and in the neighborhood patti and Pratapgarh Sadar tehsil.

Ravine land occurs in 3985 hectares area accounting for 6.27% of the total area under wastelands in Pratapgarh district. Ravine land is largely confined along banks of Sari, Dakulaki and Ganga river.

Pratapgarh district has about 1090 m.q.m. water out of which approximately 44% water is being utilized. Groundwater hydrology, water table contour varies from 110 m.a.msl. in north west part of the Pratapgarh to 90 m.a. msl. Water table contour in south east part of the district.

Pratapgarh district lacks forest and vegetation cover-Jhau, Dhak, Babool are the dominant trees in the plain land. Pipal, Bargad, Pakar, Ameltus and kachnar etc. are other common trees in district Praapgarh. Orchard groves specially mango, aonla, ber and other plants have been planted by the horticulture growers. Pratapgarh district has been declared as aonla belt. Aonla is being marketed within and out of the country.

Thus the available natural resources at village & block level in the district Prataparh contributes major role in the overall integrated development of the district. The natural resources are one of the major sectoral indicators, which will have an important role in the formulation of village-block-district plan of Pratapgarh. Need base action plan can be formulated considering the available natural resources of the village, block of district Pratapgarh. Thus it is observed that the natural resources will have an important role in the formulation and implementation of village development planning.

3. HUMAN RESOURCES:

Human resources play an important role in the planning process and also in the implementation of various developmental programmes. Human resources mainly consists of socio-economic and infrastructural sectors. An attempt has been made to analyze various indicators related to social sector responsible for the planning process and play an important role in the implementation and developmental programmes. The management of social sectors data is not properly geared to meet the information need of integrated development planning. There is traditional system of data collection which are not amenable for quick updation and holistic analysis and there is lack of information on quality of data.

Social indicators data at Block level has been collected from the secondary sources of information viz. District Statistical Hand Book of District Pratapgarh, while village level data has been collected through primary survey. It has been observed that data at village-block-district level are varying but there is no option left than to rely on such available data.

Since the main objective is to analyse the various social indicators with the view to planning process, therefore available data from various secondary sources of information have been analysed keeping the facts into consideration that these data are varying from one level to another, but the collected data through primary survey at village level is authentic because these data have been collected with the involvement of village level officials of Block Development Office of Mangrauna Block, Revenue officials, village Pradhan and other peoples representatives and the collected data have been duly verified by Block Development Officer, Mangrauna Block of District Pratapgarh.

Geographical area of Pratapgarh district is 3717 sq.km. Administratively district Pratapgarh comprises of 5 Tehsils, 17 blocks, 1105 village Panchayats. Previously there were only four Tehsils Raniganj was made new Tehsil and Babaghat Khar Nath dham was made new bock, few years back, therefore secondary data has been collected for only 16 blocks as per availability of data and rural developmental programmes and need based plan have been developed for 17 blocks including new Belkharnath Dham Block of Pratapgarh district. There are 62 village Panchayats in Mangrauna Block. Mangrauna block has been taken for village level analysis of village development planning.

Proportionate distribution of houses and households are recorded in Pratapgarh district as well as in Mangrauna block. Comparitavily number of households are more in numbers while houses are less than households because some of the families are divided and have formed separate households but still residing in one house, which has led an increase in the number of households.

Population of the district is 21,31,174 including male and female populations. It is clear from the collected information that Praapgarh district is density populated than the neighboring district. Scheduled case population of the district is also significant. It is observed that the scheduled caste population is found more in the remote rural areas. Proportionately Scheduled Caste population distribution is seen very low in the urban areas including city and marketing centers.

Educationally Pratapgarh district has not been developed because there are only 750950 educated persons in the district. As per the population distribution ratio numbers of Primary, Junior, Intermediate and Higher Educational institutions are very low, similarly the educated persons at different educational level are already nominal, which is evident from the available data and depicted in the map.

Thus it is observed that the significant distribution of farmers and farm labors, as per the total population makes it clear that agriculture is the dominant occupation in Pratapgarh district and in Mangrauna Block. Educationally, Pratapgrah district is not properly developed. The available data related to social indicators provide an indication that agriculture is the main economic activity which is labour intensive and low productive because of less application of high yielding variety of seeds, fertilizers, highly developed agricultural implements, insecticides-pesticides. Lack of awareness and knowledge for increasing productivity. Poor educational pattern has led to the social backwardness because the district has been ruled by kings, talukadars, zamindars which evident from the historical-cultural-religious-social importance of Pratapgarh district.

In view of the above the social, population, workforce, education pattern etc. and other major social factors are responsible for socio-economic backwardness of the Pratapgarh district because historically Pratapgarh district has been ruled and only certain section of the society could available on opportunity to development themselves while poor sections of the society i.e. scheduled caste, backward caste and minorities etc. were sufferers and working class and they were not given an opportunity develop themselves. Thus the down trotted deprived section of the society was bound to work as working class but recently the reservation in the district block and village panchayats have provided an opportunity to such socially backward people to involve themselves in the planning process and participate in the implementation of various developmental programmes. Therefore the process of planning and involvement of such socially backward people's representatives in the implementation of developmental programmes as well as a mile in the integrated development of village of Mangrauna Block and various blocks of Pratapgarh district.

4. ECONOMIC RESOURCES :

The agriculture is the main component of the economic activity in Pratapgarh. Most of the population of the district is dependent on agriculture. Planning process for economic development has been implemented crimping sustainable development of village with a focus on enhancing the livelihoods workers and vulnerable sections of the society. Attempt has been made to analyse the various agricultural activities at village level in Mangrauna block and at block level in Pratapgarh district because the agriculture plays an important role in economic development henceforth in the process of planning and implementation of developmental programmes for sustainable rural development.

Agricultural cultivation is the main occupation of the people because nearly 61% of the total area is under agricultural cultivation. It is also observed that approximately 76& of the population is analysed in agricultural activity at village level in Mangrauna block and also at block level in Pratapgarh district.

Land ownership pattern in Pratapgarh districts different and land concentration in the district is very high due to kingship, zamindari/talukedari traditions, few people are owning larger area of land while maximum number of people are owning less area of land which has led to small size of land holding. Thus it is observed that small size of land holding is found among maximum number of farmers while large size of land holding is with very less people causing land concentration. Land concentration has also affected the agricultural economy of the district because most of the people are working as farm labours and existing farmers are having small size of land holding which has badly affected the agricultural activity in the economic development of the district Pratapgarh.

Canal and private tube well is the main sources of irrigation. Most of the irrigated area is being covered under canal and private tube well irrigation, while other sources of irrigation and insignificant in Pratapgarh district.

Agriculture is the backbone of the economic activity of Pratapgarh district. Foodgrain production is the major cropping of the Pratapgarh district. Wheat and rice are the main crop of the food grain production, followed by Barley, Millet, Maize, Gram, Pea, Pigeon Pea. Cropping of the commercial crops are nominal in district Pratapgarh. Mustard, sugarcane, potato are the major commercial crops being cultivated in the village Mangaruna block and also in the district Pratapgarh. Food grains and commercial crops are being cultivated as per the individual requirements of the people but excess agricultural produce is also marketed, henceforth contributes an importance role in the economic development of the district Pratapgarh.

Agricultural implements are used in a traditional system. High tech agricultural implement applications is very significant in the Pratapgarh district. Use of traditional wood cultivator is dominant in the district while high-tech cultivator and tractor application in the cultivation is significant. Sprays as agricultural tool is applied in most of the villages of the district.

Fertilizer application is used without soil testing. Maximum application of NPK fertilizer is used with the view to increase fertility status of the soil. Balanced and scientific application of fertilizer in Pratapgarh district is very insignificant. Excess use of fertilizers has deteriorated fertility status of the soil. High yielding variety of seeds and application of insecticides and pesticides are not appropriate as per the requirement which has adversely affects the agricultural productivity.

Bio-gas has been promoted in the Pratapgarh district due to exceeds animals. Animal husbandry is an important occupation in Mangrauna block and Pratapgarh district. Cows and buff allows are an important animals in Pratapgarh district followed by sheep, goat, horse pig, hen/cock and other animals. Animal husbandry is being done to meet the individual requirement of the people and excess of it is being used for commercial purposes in Mangrauna block and Pratapgarh district.

Thus agriculture and animal husbandry are the main occupation in the Pratapgarh district and it plays an important role in the economic developments . Therefore agriculture and animal husbandry should be given due importance in the planning process and implementation of planned developmental programes as per the need and traditional occupations of the local people and for their continued participation in the planning and developmental schemes and sustenance of the implemented programes with the peoples involvement .

5. INFRASTRUCTURAL RESOURCES:

The infrastructural resources plays in important role in the economic development of any area. The available infrastructural play a key role in the process of planning. Therefore, available infrastructural resources must be given due importance in the formulation of planning because the existing infrastructural resources are the backbone of economic activity and a base for the formulation of need base action plan.

District Pratapgarh has the historical, archaeological religious and cultural importance which has potentialities to develop the tourism infrastructure of the district. The archaeological remains of Buddhist monastery available in the district can be developed a tourism infrastructure. The religious temples can also be developed for devotees and tourists as an infrastructure.

The transport and communication network of the Pratapgarh district is well developed. The roadways and railways network are connecting all the important places of the Pratapgarh district.

Drinking water programme is also being implemented at larger scale in Pratapgarh district. Some of the selected villages of the district has been saturated under drinking water mission programme while other selected villages are being saturated. It has been recorded that most of the villages have provided minimum drinking water facility but some of the villages are facing polluted underground water sources for which district administration has initiated suitable remedies to solve the polluted water.

The most of villages of the Pratapgarh district has been electrified and most of the households have been facilitated by the electricity and commercial electricity connection in the district is very nominal in rural areas excepting marketing centers and urbanized areas including urban areas as well. Therefore electricity infrastructure has to be promoted and developed to promote the economic growth and implementation of planned developmental programmes in the district Pratapgarh.

Medical health facilities are appropriate in the Pratapgarh district. As per the population ratio medical health facilities has to be promoted and developed. Animal hospitals are properly distributed in the Pratapgarh district.

Banking infrastructural, animal husbandry and educational infrastructure are properly distributed in the Pratapgarh district.

Small scale industries and agro-baked industries and Khadi & village industries and Gramodyog units are concentrated in the different parts of the district Pratapgarh. There are 1% industrial and 4% other workers. Temple of Belkharnath Dham stands in Yahiapur Dahicewan and Daudpur are noted for goodshed during the mutiny.

Thus Pratapgarh district has infrastructural potentialities to develop small scale and agro-based industries and tourism by utilizing the available local infrastructural resources. Therefore infrastructural resources needs a proper planning for the economic growth and development of the infrastructural resources of the Pratapgarh district. Thus infrastructural resources will be an asset in the planning process at village level in Mangrauna block and at block level in Pratapgarh district and it will be helpful in the implementation of planned developmental programmes with the continued participation of the people and sustenance of the successfully implemented planned village developmental programmes.

5. RURAL DEVELOPMENT PROGRAMMES:

Thus the rural development programmes have been given top priority in the district.

Integrated rural development programmes have been launched in 104 villages in which 16 programmes are being implemented besides this rural development, women development, social welfare and other schemes are being implemented in the priority basis to bridge the divide between rural to urban. It is argued that faster development is required to bridge this divide.

In view of the above it has been felt that the development should be participatory and it should be planned according to the local needs of the deprived rural multitudes. Development should be planned through tapping local talent and resources. Implementation of rural development programmes can be made more effective through peoples participation. \there fore self government programmes have been ensured with the view of the village as a development unit. Development should start from (bottom) village to block and district onward. The real meaning of democracy is the importance of the people and rural government in the main sole of rural development. Administrative, financial and programmes formulation and implementation rights and control are provided to village panchayats for self-government Different activities of related line departments are handed over to village-block and district panchayats and various committees have been formed to control the different rural development activities. The district rural development agency (DRDA) has been constituted i.e. Chairman-DRDA at present in the Chairman-District Panchayat forming 5 standing committees of the village-block-district panchayat to ensure successful implementation of the planned project.

Centrally sponsored several rural development programmes are launched in the district –

- Sampoorna gramin Rojgar Yojna
- Pradhan Mantri Gram Sudhar yojna
- Rural Housing
- Swarn Jayanti Gram Swarojgar yojna
- Watershed Development Programme
- Land Reforms
- Rural Wear Supply Programmes
- Central Rural Sanitation Programmes
- Pradhan Mantri Gramin Jal Samvardhan Yojna

Swarn Jayanti Gram Swarojgar Yojna is being implemented to generate self employment to have sustained income and to remove the poverty. Assistance is given to the poor families living under the below poverty line. Selected person under this scheme are callas 'Swarojgaris' There are 6804 swarojgaris selected in Pratapgarh district and 358 swarijgaries have been selected in Mangrauna block, suitable technical/financial back up supported are provided to the selected swarojgaris.

Sampoorna Gramin Rojgar Yojna (SGRY) has been launched in Pratapgarh district benefiting 4685 selected beneficiaries in the district out of which 149 beneficiaries have been supported in Mangrauna block.

Under the integrated rural development programme complete electrification of the selected villages are ensured. There are 156279 electrified houses in the district and 709 commercial electricity consumers in the district. Non conventional sources of energy in the form of solar light, solar water pump, bio-gas etc. are also promoted in Pratapgarh district.

There are 17 small scale industries of cotton, textiles, drugs, pharmaceuticals, light engineering and printing besides there are 4345 household-furniture, bamboo and cane work industries and agro-based industries, oil mill, rice mills are concentrated in the different parts of the district Pratapgarh. There are 5 Gramodyog units in Mangrauna block.

There are 973 food supply centers in Pratapgarh and 65 food supply centers in mangrauna block. It has been ensured that there are at least one food supply center in each village panchayat of the Mangrauna block of the district Pratapgarh.

Rural drinking water supply is ensured because water is an essential ingredient of our daily life. It is recorded that 24834 India Mark II Hand Pumps have been installed in district Pratapgarh. Local Hand Pumps alongwith India Mark II Hand Pumps are installed to meet the increasing demand of growing population.

Rural sanitation programme is launched in the district and 4375 rural latrines have been constructed. There are 199 low cost rural latrines constructed in Mangrauna block.

Rural Housing programmes is being implemented in the district with a holistic approach of "Housing for All". Indira Awas Yojna is launched to meet the housing shortage. Total 23355 houses are constructed in the district out of which 1694 number of rural houses are constructed in Mangrauna block.

Various welfare programmes are launched including scheduled caste, backward caste and minorities welfare programmes in which scholarships to needy interested students including other employment generation and welfare programmers are being implemented at village level in Mangrauna block and at block level in Pratapgarh district.

Construction of rural roads are ensured under various schemes in the district. There are 887 km. Rural kachha road constructed and 2428.36 km. Pucca road constructed in Pratapgarh district. Similarly 53 km. Long kachha road and 216 km long pucca road has been constructed in Mangrauna block.

Various women and child development programme have been launched in which 2013 beneficiaries have been supported under this programme- there are 140 women and child development beneficiaries in Mangrauna block of the district Pratapgarh district.

Several agricultural development programmes are being implemented to increase the agricultural productivity of district. Provision of high yielding variety of seeds, fertilizers, insecticides, pesticides. Kisan Credit Card including technical back up support and financial support are provided to the needy interested farmers under various schemes launched by the government.

Horticulture developments is also an important source of income in the district Pratapgarh sadar and Mangraura block has been declare as Aonla Belt while Patti, Kunda and Kalakankar blocks have been developed as Mango Belt in the district. Aonla cultivation is being implemented in the 20 villages of the Magraura block. There are several aonla fruits and vegetables preservation and processing units which has generated employment and increased the income of the deprived rural multitudes.

Fisheries Cultivations been promoted in the district and various schemes are launched to develop the fish culture in the district. Fisheries co-operatives have been formed to promote the fish culture with the view to utilize the available water and land resources to generate employment and increase the income of the downtrodden section of the society. Physical, financial and technical back up support including insurance policy support are provided to insure integrated development of fishermen of the district in Mangraura block 10 ponds are developed to promote fish culture in the waterlogged villages of the block.

Dairy development programme is being implemented in the district through formation of milk producers co-operatives in Pirupur, Makaipur, Raichandrapur and Poorabgaon through involving 40 beneficiaries integrated mini dairy schemes has been launched to improve the collection of milk and new milk producers co-operatives are formed on the Antu road and Pratapgarh to Patti road.

Integrated rural development programmes are being implemented in the district as per recommendation of the local people's representatives in which 104 villages have selected for complete implementation of 16 activities of rural development. Villages Asthera, Dharauli, Madhupur, Hathasura and Barahpur have been selected under the integrated rural development programme for saturation of earmarked 16 rural development activities.

The rural development programme are being implemented in the distinct in which peoples participation are not properly ensured and improper implementation of the sanctioned programmes and maintenance of the implemented programes has lead to the least sustainability of the implementation of the rural development programmes will lead to generate employment and increase income of deprived rural multitudes and improve the socio-economic conditions of the poor people living in the remote rural areas.

6. VILLAGE DEVELOPMENT PLANNING

The planning is a means to active the development or planning is a organised process by which the people achieves its developmental goals. The planners have to provide developmental planning scientific-technical back up support t the grass root level village peoples representatives and officials involved in village development and planning. The planning and development must be peoples participatory tapping the local talent and resources in order to make it sustainable. Efforts are being made to implement rural development programmes with a focus on enhancing the livelihoods of weaker and vulnerable sections for sustainable development.

Village is a development unit in the new decentralization system of the government. Faster development is ensured assuming village as a center for development. In the decentralization scheme administrative and financial powers have been provided to village panchayats for formulation of their need base action plan, implementation of planned activities and maintenance of created assets for its sustainability. To ensure self-government of the Panchayats need base action plan has been formulated.

District Pratapgarh has historical, cultural, archaeological and religious importance. The planning and implementation of the programmes are ensured through planning committee of the district Pratapgarh with the participation of local bodies including rural Panchayats and urban Panchayats. Activities and planning process of the district planning committee is based on the participatory need base requirements of the local bodies because the development is through the people, for the people and by the people .

Agricultural activities have been promoted in Pratapgarh district, cultivation of oil seeds and pulses have been promoted in which requisite seed, fertilizers, pest management and other technical back up support has been improved. Promotion and propagation of Maiz cultivation has also been proposed in the district plan. National oil seed development programme has been implemented in the district in which requisite supply of seed, fertilizer, pest management and extension programmes have been proposed in the district plan. Land development fertilizer, seed distribution, field demonstrations, kisan mitra yojna and other schemes have been proposed with view to increase the agricultural productivity of the district.

Horticulture development plan has been proposed in the district plan in which modernization of horticultural nurseries have been proposed. Production of upgraded fruit plants and availability of high yielding variety of seeds have been proposed in the district Plan. To promote horticultural activities in the district special package have been planned in which Kunda and Kalakankar blocks have been declared as Mango fruit belt and Pratapgarh Sadar block and Mangraura block have been declared as Aonla Belt. Intensification of horticultural fruit belts fruits and vegetables cultivation through technical back up support and field demonstrations have been proposed in the district plan of Pratapgarh.

Financial support to 3070 small marginal farmers have been proposed in which 442 farmers are proposed under special component plan scheme of the government.

Animal husbandry, animal health, medical treatment services have been proposed in which completion of animal hospitals, construction of new animal hospitals and provision of medicines, animal health service centers, etc. have been proposed. Support for inseminization of buffalos and cows have been proposed. Besides above pigs, sheep and other animals development programmes have been proposed including grass land development for nutritious cattle feed production have been proposed in the district plan of Pratapgarh.

Reconstitution, strengthening and extension of dairy co-operative federations and dairy societies have been proposed in the District Plan.

District Fisheries Development Agency is engaged in promotion and development of fisheries activity in Pratapgarh district. It is proposed to train, educate technically demonstrate 100 fishermen and also proposed to develop 100 hectares ponds and to provide scientific-technical back up support and financial assistance including insurance schemes to the fishermen of the district Pratapgarh.

Social forestry programmes have been promoted in the district including rural and urban areas. It is proposed to implement 170 hect advance soil work, 170 hectare land plantation and another 200 hect. Land soil work and 75 hect. Land soil work under special component plan have been proposed to raise 4.0 lakh nursery plants, large scale propagation extension of Social Forestry and agro forestry programmes have been proposed in the District Plan.

Cooperative programmes are being implemented in the district and it is proposed to provide interest free loan to 10,000 scheduled caste farmers and below poverty line people for purchase of part item. Financial support for scheduled caste persons have been provided for self-employment under the cooperative schemes for the government.

Various rural development programmes are being implemented in the district Pratapgarh. It is proposed to provide technical and financial back up support to 1964 beneficiaries and 354 scheduled caste beneficiaries under Swarnjayanti Gram Swarojgar Yojna scheme of the government to generate employment and increase the income of swarojgaris.

Integrated wastelands development programme are launched under the drought prone area development scheme in Rs. 936 thousand has been allocated to achieve the goals to utilize available land resources to generate employment and increase of deprived rural beneficiaries.

Integrated rural energy programme is launched in which Rs. 105 thousand has been allocated in the District Plan for installation of 130 lights and 20 lights under special component plan scheme, awareness training programmes are proposed for appropriate utilization of additional sources of energy for which Rs. 33 thousand budget have been allocated.

To meet the shortage of housing in rural areas Indira Awas yojna is being implemented. It is planned to construct 1290 low cost rural houses for poor and 774 low cost rural houses for scheduled caste beneficiaries under special component plan scheme.

Sampoorna Gramin Rojgar yojna is launched to provide wage employment in rural areas and also food security, under this scheme Rs. 15.93 lakh mandays employment has been proposed.

It is planned to provide 25.89 km. Kharanza/Nali construction for integrated development of the villages for which Rs. 70.58 lakh has been allocated and Rs. 9.08 lakh for construction of multipurpose welfare center in 17 village panchayats of the district.

Community development programmes are being implemented in the district for which Rs. 89.63 lakh have been allocated.

Rural small scale industry has been promoted in the District Plan to facilitate selected 26 beneficiaries. Hadi & Village industries programme has been promoted for which Rs. 20.87 lakh has been allocated for support to the selected beneficiaries under this programme.

Construction of road and bridges is the main priority for which Rs. 872.59 lakhs has been allocated. It is planned to construct 36.02 km. Earth work, 45.07 km. Kharanza work and 54.0 7 km pucca road construction including 72 bridges in the District Plan.

Private minor irrigation has been promoted in which 10 rube wells, 2 deep tube wells boring have been proposed. Ground water charging checkdams, constructions of 34 ponds and 4 checkdams have been proposed in the District Plan. It is also planned to reinstall 6 unsuccessful tube wells and remaintenance of irrigation nail/gul etc. Requisite machinery and equipment support has been planned to strengthen the irrigation system and sum of Rs. 40.99 lakh budget has been allocated under this scheme.

Environment awareness and other programmes have been planned in the District Plan for which suitable financial budgets have been allocated.

Financial allocations has been earmarked to attract tourism programmes in the district due to its archeological, historical, cultural and religious importance.

Development of educational infrastructure and encouragement of students towards education has been the priority of the government. Shiksha Mitra yojna is launched to promote primary education and necessary budgets have been allocated in the district plan. Similarly secondary education is also promoted to strengthen the educational information necessary financial budgetary provisions have been made in the District Plan.

Pradeshik Vikas Dal scheme is launched to promote rural support for which Rs. 4.86 lakh have been allocated and Rs. 14.31 lakh have been allocated to establish rural stadium to develop sports spirit among the rural youths.

Health and family welfare programmes are being implemented to provide best medical support in which allopathic, homeopathic, ayurvedic & unani hospitals infrastructural, medicines & equipments etc. as per the requirements financial budget have been allocated in the District Plan of Pratapgarh.

Supply of rural drinking water is being implemented by the Jal Nigam in which completion of 21 co complete projects have been planned repair and maintenance and installation of 340 new hand pump, 600 rebore of failure handpumps and replacement of G.I. pipes etc. have been proposed in the District Plan. Urban drinking water programmed has been promoted in which rebore of tube wells and installation of India Mark II hand pumps have been proposed in the District Plan. Construction of 1783 low cost latrines have also been proposed in the District Plan.

Popularization & implementation of various programmes and strengthening the information system including exhibition, mela, publication, photography schemes have been incorporated in the District Plan.

Various welfare programmes are launched in the district it is proposed to provide scholarships for scheduled caste, backward caste, minority and scholarships for poor general caste students have been incorporated in the District Plan for which requisite financial budget have been allocated. Employment programme and handicraft training programmes have been proposed in the District Plan. Social welfare and handicapped welfare programmes are also incorporated in the district including women and child development programmes for which requisite necessary budget have been allocated in the district Plan of Pratapgarh.

Besides the District Plan, need base action plan as perceived by the peoples of the district Pratapgarh has been also analysed in which land development wasteland reclamation agricultural development, horticultural development. Gramodyog, Sampoorna Gramin Rojgar Yojna, Swarn Jayanti Gram Swarojgar Yojna installation of India Mark II Hand Pumps, construction of road, bridges and chuck road, health and various programmes have been analysed for its implementation to meet the common minimum requirement of the local people for integrated sustained rural development.

Panchayati Raj institutions have been strengthened and made more autonomous for the formulation of need base planning, execution and implementation of planned programmes, its maintenance for sustainability. Panchayats have been given more responsibilities for the implementation of rural development, medical, health and family welfare programmes, animal hospitals, seed centers, marketing stores, village panchayats education government tube wells, hand pumps and youth welfare programmes implementation at village and block level in the district.

Block planning for 62 village Panchayats have been analysed in which major rural development programmes implementation, based on the need base planning, monitoring and evaluation are the main responsibilities of the Block Panchayats, Financial support to the Block Panchyats is made available through 10th 7 12th Financial Commission of the State which major grant is provide under the Sampoorna Gramin Rojgar yojna at the ratio of 30% plan budget to the Block Panchayat for planning and implementation of need base programmes. It is planned to provide 60% weightage for scheduled case populated inhabitants and 40% to the other general caste population.

Block Panchayats are independent and autonomous to plan their need base programmes and it implementation as per norms of the Sampoorna Gramin Rojgar yojna. Block Panchayats are engaged in the implementation of nail, kharanza, chock road, earth work and repair and maintenance of the communities assets in the various villages of the Mangrauna block Panchayat in wages are paid in cost and food grains in kind with the view to generate employment and increase in the income of deprived rural multitudes and ensure food security to the downtrodden rural poors.

Village Planning for Mangrauna Block have been planned as per the need base recommendations of the 62 villages Panchayats. Most of the works which are being planned and implemented are the construction of nail/kharanza, check road, pulia, repair and maintenance of the village community assets located in the respective village panchayats.

The main source of grants of village panchayats are the 10th Finance Commission and at the ratio of 50% grants under Sampoorna Gramin Rojgar yojna in which 50% wages are paid in cash and rest paid in kind s food grains ensue food security among the deprived rural poor. Need base action plan is formulated by the village Panchayat, its execution, implementation monitoring and evaluation are also managed by the village Panchayat.

Land development programmes in various villages have been proposed in which the reclamation of different wastelands have been proposed to meet the increasing demand of growing population for food grains, fuel wood, fodder, fiber, fruits and fisheries (F6) programmes. Most of the user land of the 28 villages are being for aonla plantation because Manrauna block has been declared as aonla belt for special package assistance to provide scientific, technical and financial support to the interest horticultural growers to increase the productivity of aonla and also the preservation and processing of aonla for value addition and to increase the income and generated employment for interested poor beneficiaries.

Most of the available waterlogged land have been proposed for developing ponds to promote fisheries culture with the view to utilize available land/water resources to generate employment and increase the income of the rural poor.

Agricultural and horticultural development have been proposed with the view to provide high yield variety of seeds and gaffed fruit plants besides the other inputs including fertilizers irrigation, pest management etc. Establishment of agro-industries have also been proposed for optimum utilization of agro-base products for value addition. Besides the agro-industries establishment of Gramodyog units have been proposed in the various village Panchayats.

Under the Swarn Jayanti Gram Swarojgar yojna, Swarojgaries have been identified and proposed for the scientific, technical back up support and financial assistance as per the norms of the scheme.

Similarly under the Sampoorna Gramin Rojgar yojna beneficiaries have been selected and construction of nail, kharnaza, check road, earth work have been proposed in the village plan to provide wage employment and food security to be deprived rural multitudes. As per the need base requirement of India Mark II hand pumps to ensure safe drinking water installation of India Mark II hand pumps have been proposed under the accelerated rural water supply programmes and swage Dhara Scheme of the government. Construction of pucca road and kharanza road have been proposed by the village Panchayats as per the common minimum requirement of the village people. Construction of small bridges/pulias on the constructed nail etc. have been incorporated in the village plan.

Chuck road is one of the basic lifeline link to connect village and farmer's field due to which special emphasis has been given to construct the check road in the village Panchayats have been proposed.

Medical, health, and family welfare programmes have been incorporated in the village plan to obtain minimum health services center the rural health scheme of the government.

Electrification of rural houses in the villages have been proposed under the rural electrification scheme of the government to ensure integrated rural development of the village located in the remote rural areas.

Animal welfare programmes and animal service center and animal disease control facility including medicines and inseminization of buff allow and cows etc. have been proposed by the village Panchayats.

Welfare schemes including Pension for old age persons, other grants to needy people, scholarships to schedule caste, backward caste, below poverty line general caste and minority student have been proposed as one of the need base action plan of the village panchayat.

Besides above various rural development programmes under integrated rural development programmes are also planned and implemented in the different village Panchayats of Mangrauna Block.

CONCLUSIONS

Thus the collection, collation and digitization of data through geographic information system being implemented under the Natural Resources Data Management System (NRDMS) is an asset to the village plannuers/panchayatiraj institutions/ peoples representatives because before formulation of their village plan they will have information on available, natural human, economic, infrastructural resources and progress of implement Ted rural development programmes and village planners can incorporate the local village people's requirement and ensuring peoples participation the village plan can be formulated because the village people have to formulate their village plan and accordingly with the continued peoples participation the planned programmes can be implemented, follow up action and appropriate monitoring and sustenance of the implemented programes can be ensure by the village Panchayat people. No doubt this study will be a mill stone for village planners, academicians, research scholars, village panchayat representatives, local administrative officials, peoples representatives and other interested persons engaged in village development planning.

The Panchayati Raj institution are more effective autonomous self-government in the formulation of need base action plan, its' execution and implementation monitoring and evaluation. The optimum utilization of available natural social economic and infrastructural resources to meet the increasing demand of growing population for integrated rural development has been ensured through Self Government - Panchayati Raj- Lok Raj- Gram Raj, in which scientific-technical-infrastructural facilities are procured to generate the employment, increase the income of deprived rural multitudes surviving in the remote rural villages, hence improving their socio-economic conditions, therefore such deprived sections of the society are able move equally with the upper caste section of the society as per constitution rights.

●●●

REFERENCES

- Misra, R.P. " Regional Planning" 1992, Concept publishing Company, New Delhi.
- St. Ouffer S.A. "Intervening opportunities : A. Theory relating Mobility and Distance American Sociological Review, Vol. 5, Dec. 1940 P.P. 845, 67 and W. Isard, Location and Space Economy, op. cit, P.P. 64-65, footnote 13.
- Mishra, R.P. (ed) "Changing Desceptions of Development problems" Singapore, Maruzem, Asia, 1983.
- Natural Resources Data Management System vision document published by Dept. of Science & Technology M/o Science & Technology, Govt. of India, Sept. 2003.
- Mapping of wastelands from satellite imagery Pratapgarh District, U.P., 1998, Published by RSAC-UP, Lucknow.
- Economic Register, Mangraura Block, District Pratapgarh.
- Revenue records of District Pratapgarh.
- District Statistical Hand book, Pratapgarh District.
- Primary Census , Handbook of Census Dept. 1991-2001.
- National Atlas & Thematic Mapping organisation, Dept. of Science & Technology, Govt. of India.
- Field visit / Primary survey for Data collection.

Annexure 1

Natural Resources Data Management System (NRDMS)
Pratapgarh District
A Social Information

Sl. No.	Block	Houses	Households	Population	Schedule Caste	Farmer	Farm Labour	Plantation & Husbandary	Non-Family workers
1	2	3	4	5	6	7	8	9	11

Sl. No.	Block	Construction Workers	Business Workers	Transportation& Communication	Other worker	Literacy	Primary	Junior	Inter
1	2	12	13	14	15	16	17	18	19

Annexure 2

Natural Resources Data Management System (NRDMS)
Mangraura Block, Pratapgarh district
Social Indicators

Loc_code	Vill_Name	Houses	House Hold	Population	Scheduled Caste	General Caste	Backward Caste	Others Castes	Farmers	Farm_Lab	Plantation and Husbandary
1	2	3	4	5	6	7	8	9	10	11	12

Loc_code	Vill_Name	Farm workers	Non-farm workers	Construction workers	Business workers	Transportation workers	Other workers	Literates	Primary
1	2	13	14	15	16	17	18	19	20

Annexure 3

Natural Resources Data Management System (NRDMS)
Pratapgarh district
A Economic Indicators

		Land Ownership										
Sl. No.	Block	Area in Hectare	0.5 to 1.00 hac.		1.00 to 2.00 hac.		2.00 to 4.00 hac.		4.00 to 10.00 hac.		Above of 10.00 hac.	
			No.	Area	No.	Area	No.	Area	No.	Area	No.	Area
1	2	3	4	5	6	7	8	9	10	11	12	13

		Source of Irrigation					Food Production (Area in ha.)					
Sl. No.	Block	Canal	Tubewell		Pond	Total	Rice	Wheat	Barley	Millet	Maize	Gram
			Govt.	Private								
1	2	14	15	16	17	18	19	20	21	22	23	24

				Commercial Crops (Area in ha.)					Agricultural Implements				
Sl. No.	Block	Pea	Pigeon Pea	Mustard	Suger-cane	Potato	Sanai	Chara	Cultivator		Hightech Cultivator	Agricultureal implements	Sprayer
									Wood	Iron			
1	2	25	26	27	28	29	30	31	32	33	34	35	36

Sl. No.	Block	Tractor	Seeds Depo		Rural Godam		Insecticides/ pesticides		Fertilize			
			No.	Capacity	No.	Capacity	Depo	Capacity	Nitrogen	P	K	Total
1	2	37	38	39	40	41	42	43	44	45	46	47

			Husbandary						
Sl. No.	Block	Bio-gas Centre	Cow	Buffallow	Sheep	Goat	Horse	Pig	Hen/ Cock
1	2	48	49	50	51	52	53	54	55

Annexure 4

Natural Resources Data Management System (NRDMS)
Mangraura Block, Pratapgarh district
A Economic Indicators

Loc_code	Vill_Name	Junior	Inter	Land_A_hec	Canal	Tube_Gov	T_Privat	Total	Rice	Wheat
1	2	3	4	5	6	7	8	9	10	11

Loc_code	Vill_Name	Barley	Maize	Gram	Pea	Pig_Pea	Mustard	S_cane	Potato	Sanai
1	2	12	13	14	15	16	17	18	19	20

Loc_code	Vill_Name	Chara	Cul_wood	Cul_iron	Ag_imple	Sprayer	N	P	K
1	2	21	22	23	24	25	26	27	28

Loc_code	Vill_Name	Total	Bio-gas	Cow	Buffalow	Sheep	Goat	Horse	Pig	Hen/cock
1	2	29	30	31	32	33	34	35	36	37

Annexure 5

Natural Resources Data Management System (NRDMS)
Pratapgarh district
Infrastructural Resources

Sl. No.	Block	Animal Hospital /Dev. Centre	Agro-Industries				Medical/Health	
			Small Industry		Khadi Gramodyog		Centre	Doctor
			Unit	Workers	Unit	Workers		
1	2	3	4	5	6	7	8	9

Annexure 6

Natural Resources Data Management System (NRDMS)
Mangraura Block
Infrastructural Resources (Village Plan)

Loc_code	Vill_Name	Elect_v	Low_c_h	Agro_ind	Gramo	Employ	P_Road	K_Road	Bridge	Chakroad	Health
1	2	10	11	12	13	14	15	16	17	18	19

Annexure 7

Natural Resources Data Management System (NRDMS)
Pratapgarh district
Rural Development Prograrmmes

Sl. No.	Blocks	Swarn Jayanti Swarojgar Yojana	PMRY	Energy		Cottage Industry	Gramo-dyog	Food Supply Centres	India Mark 2 Hand pump	Sanitation
				Electrified Houses	Commercial Electrification					
1	2	3	4	5	7	8	9	10	11	12

Sl. No.	Blocks	Rural Housing	SC Programme	BC Programme	Minority Programme	Women & Child Dev.	Pucca Road	Kaccha Road
1	2	13	14	15	16	17	18	19

Annexure 8

Natural Resources Data Management System (NRDMS)
Mangraura Block, Pratapgarh District
Rural Development Prograrmmes

Loc_Code	Vill_Name	SwarnJayanti Gram Swarojgar Yojana	Sampoorna Gramin Yojana	India Mark-II Hand pump	Sanitation
1	2	4	5	6	7

Annexure 9

Natural Resources Data Management System (NRDMS)
Pratapgarh district
Need Base Plan

Sl. No.	Village	Land Dev.	Agriculture Dev. Quental Seed Distribution	Horticulture Dev. No. of plant	Gramo-dyog unit to	SGSY Employ ment	India Mark 2 Hand pump	Pacca Road	Kharanja Road	Bridge	Chakroad	Health Centre	Rural Dev. SGSY
1	2	3	4	5	8	9	10	11	12	13	14	15	16

Annexure 10

Natural Resources Data Management System (NRDMS)
Mangraura Block, Pratapgarh district
Need Base Plan (Village Plan)

Loc_ code	Vill_name	Land Dev.	Waterlogged land Dev.	Agril. Dev. Seed Distribution	Horticulture Dev.	Agro-industries	Gramo	SJGSY	India Mark II Hand pump	Pucca Road
1	2	3	4	5	6	7	8	9	10	11

Loc_code	Vill_name	Kacha Road	Bridge	Chakroad	Health	Houses Electrification	Sampoorna Gram Rojgar Yojana
1	2	12	13	14	15	16	17